From School to College:
Articulation and Transfer

From School to College: Articulation and Transfer

Julius Menacker

American Council on Education • Washington, D. C.

To Mark, Terri, and Becky

Library of Congress Cataloging in Publication Data
Menacker, Julius.
  From school to college: articulation and transfer.
  Includes bibliographical references.
  1. Articulation (Education)   2. Universities and
colleges—United States—Admission.   I. Title.
LB2350.M43   378.1'05'8   74-11287
ISBN 0-8268-1295-9

Printed in the United States of America

Contents

60557

Illustrations

Table

Preface

This book is an attempt to examine the full range of school and college articulation considerations in the American educational system. It is frankly written from the perspective of a former university articulation officer who believes school and college relations to be one of the most sorely neglected aspects of the American educational system. The recent emergence of the community college as a dynamic new partner in this system has given articulation a new energy and impetus that must be assessed and directed to solidify current gains in the field and move professional practice to higher levels in the service of students passing from one educational level to another.

While numerous journal articles and speeches have been written on the subject of articulation, few have tried to deal comprehensively with the broad panorama of school and college articulation activities. It is my hope that this volume does that, at least to the extent that the major areas of articulation concern are uncovered and some of the more appropriate alternatives explored. In attempting to find the norm of current practice, as well as to define the background and origins of school and college relations, a number of practitioners have been consulted for information, new thoughts, and critical review of the manuscript.

Although it is not possible to mention all of the many persons who contributed to the work, I do want to call attention to those who were of exceptional help: Calvin L. Crawford, Middle States Association of Colleges and Secondary Schools; David Crockett, American College Testing Program; G. Robert Darnes, Illinois Junior College Board; Lee Noel, American College Testing Program; Donald Nugent, National Association of College Admissions Counselors; Paul Kadota, Chicago State University; E. Eugene Oliver, University of Illinois; Willis C. Jackman, William C. Price, and L. F. Robinson, all of the University of Illinois at Chicago Circle; and John Vacarro, College Entrance Examination Board.

A special note of thanks is due to Lowell B. Fisher, University of Illinois' coordinator of school and college relations and state chairman of the North Central Association until his retirement in August 1970. He was my mentor in articulation work and provided a model of professional skill and wisdom, as well as gentlemanly deportment, for which I am indeed grateful.

I also want to express special thanks to Douglas D. Dillenbeck of the College Entrance Examination Board, and to the College Board itself, for providing the initial encouragement and support to undertake this project. Janice Diehl, my secretary and friend of many years, was a constant source of encouragement and worked far beyond any reasonable level of expectation in typing manuscript drafts and correcting countless errors in it. Finally, I thank my wife, Nadine, and my children, Mark, Terri, and Rebecca.

While I must acknowledge the contributions of all these valuable helpers to whatever value this book has, I must bear sole responsibility for its deficiencies, as the final decisions were mine.

one

The Educational Concern

Only recently has "articulation" as a comprehensive term won educational acceptance, although "school and college relations," from which it was derived, has a long history. The main reasons for renewed interest in educational articulation are the recent pressures on college enrollments first from too many students and then from too few students. The rising aspirations of minority groups, and the addition to the tri-level American educational system of a relatively new fourth tier— the community junior college—further accentuated the need for sound planning for student transition. Still, many teachers, administrators, and specialists on students either are unacquainted with the terms or have only a fuzzy idea of their meaning. Further obscuring the concept of articulation is the multiplicity of definitions, each influenced by the writer's professional attitudes and interests. Such perspectives, taken together, however, assemble a broad definition of "school and college relations" or, more specifically, "educational articulation."

Defining Articulation

A college president defined articulation as "the linkage in progress along the learning continuum" that involves skills, insights, and wisdom, as well as subject matter.[1] Leland Medsker, a leading academic figure in junior-senior college articulation, finds the essence of articulation in joint efforts of individuals and institutions across a wide spectrum of activities; whether formal or informal, sponsored or voluntary, their endeavors facilitate the transfer of students from one

1. Harold C. Martin, "The Winds of Change and the Premises of Academic Continuity," *Colloquium on Academic Continuity,* ed. William E. Sullivan (Evanston, Ill.: Association of College Admissions Counselors, 1968), p. 9.

1

school to another.[2] Frederick C. Kintzer, another professor of higher education who has studied articulation, sees articulation ordering the continuous flow of students from one grade level or school to another. In its broadest sense, Kintzer calls it "the interrelationships between schools and colleges, quasi-educational institutions, and other community organizations—all activities that effect the movement of students."[3]

The broad views of the college president and professors of higher education accentuate the narrower, more specific interpretations of college admissions officers. One director of admissions confined articulation to a rather precise process—"the exchange of information between the high school and the university so as to make the lot of the student easier in effecting the transition from high school to 'higher education.'"[4] Another admissions director saw articulation as primarily a college public relations and recruiting activity which incorporates legitimate guidance. To him, conferences, literature, school visits, and similar activities are the vehicles of communication. For this former director of admissions at the Massachusetts Institute of Technology, "all of this activity . . . is a mixture of propagandist effort on behalf of individual colleges and guidance of a broader sort that has to do with categories of institutions and the realms of value inherent in the world of higher education."[5]

Interest in articulation has spread beyond the higher education community. As early as 1929, elementary and high school administrators expressed their concern for smooth academic transition by devoting the *Seventh Yearbook* of the National Education Association's Department of Superintendence to the subject. The *Yearbook* defined articulation as "that adequate relation of part to part of the educational system which makes for continuous forward movement [of students]."[6] More

2. Leland L. Medsker, "Problems of Articulation" (Paper delivered at the Illinois Conference on Higher Education, Allerton Park, Monticello, Ill., Nov. 5, 1964), p. 1.

3. Frederick C. Kintzer, *Nationwide Pilot Study on Articulation* (Los Angeles: University of California, Eric Clearinghouse for Junior Colleges), 1970, p. 1.

4. Harold E. Temmer, "Secondary School-College Articulation," mimeographed (New York: American Association of Collegiate Registrars and Admissions Officers, 1963), p. 1.

5. B. Alden Thresher, *College Admission and the Public Interest* (New York: College Entrance Examination Board, 1966), p. 38.

6. John D. Russell and Charles H. Judd, *The American Educational System* (Boston: Houghton Mifflin Co., 1940), p. 216.

recently, the Association for Supervision and Curriculum Development devoted its 1958 *Yearbook* to articulation, providing a comprehensive definition:

> The term "articulation" has usually been defined in the literature of professional education in terms of the relationships among various elements of the school program and in terms of the interdependence of the several parts of that program. . . . Successive units of the educational structure are said to be well-articulated when the parts are related to one another in a well-organized whole, when the various school levels are seen and are operated as interdependent parts of an ongoing and unified process of education.[7]

Reviewing various higher education perspectives on articulation, Warren W. Willingham found three common denominators: (1) the coordination of educational programs; (2) the processes and procedures whereby coordination is achieved; and (3) the coordination of a variety of programs, practices, and services.[8]

From experience as a university coordinator of school and college relations, the author offers the following overview of articulation:

> Formal education is most appropriately viewed as a continuous process beginning with the primary grades and extending through the highest level that a student's ability and resources can carry him. This is to say that one must not view the elementary school on the one hand and the university on the other as separate and distinct segments of the educative process. Instead, these organizational units must be viewed as administrative divisions that should in no way impede or interrupt the process of formal education, which has as its base a common body of knowledge that receives greater delineation as one progresses through successive stages of development.[9]

The various definitions of articulation are alike in many respects. Most descriptions emphasize communication among schools and colleges, institutional cooperation, and mutual understanding. A common

7. Association for Supervision and Curriculum Development, National Education Association, *A Look at Continuity in the School Program* (Washington: NEA, 1958), pp. 4-5.
8. Warren W. Willingham, *The No. 2 Access Problem: Transfer to the Upper Division* (Washington: American Association for Higher Education, 1972), p. 13.
9. Julius Menacker, "Subject Articulation between High School and College," *Clearing House,* December 1969, p. 220.

view conceives of education as a continuum that transcends organizational units. Integrating skills and attitudes as well as subject matter is important. The primary focus is on improving the transition of students through the units of the educational system, ancillary organizations, and activities. These few concepts, taken together, form the irreducible fabric of articulation, best characterized by the processes which promote continuous, efficient, forward progress of students through the educational system.

Articulation classifications

The elements of articulation can be subdivided in a number of conceptual ways. For example, one can divide articulation activities into formal and informal processes. Formal activities would include scholastic conferences for counselors, teachers, admissions officers, prospective students, or any combination of people convening in a sponsored program on articulation. Documents such as junior-senior college parallel programs or curriculum guides, admission information brochures, high school and college class profiles, and other written material published for counselor and student use belong to the formal category.

In contrast are the informal processes typified by an occasional telephone call from a community college counselor to an acquaintance working in a university admissions office. Although less noticeable, such practices can be more important to articulation than the formal processes. The effectiveness of day-to-day, low-keyed relationships is helped by professional respect based on mutual trust among the participants.

Articulation processes and activities can be viewed from the perspective of educational specialties, administrative articulation, subject or curricular articulation, and guidance centered articulation. Administrative articulation occurs when chief officers of schools or colleges commit their institutions to cooperative endeavors, the sharing of resources, or to certain policy changes for the good of students or the public at large. Curricular articulation emphasizes smooth academic transition in subjects spanning educational levels through communication and cooperation among all teacher specialists. Guidance centered articulation holds center stage in the theater of school and college relations. It is here that most articulation activity occurs, where the greatest amount of human and financial resources is allocated with the most concrete and beneficial results. The main concerns are program selection, course transferability, admission, academic and social adjustment, and the best choices of institutions by students and of students by institutions.

A distinction can be made between horizontal and vertical articulation. Horizontal articulation refers to problems of curricular integration and differences of instruction and general educational style that a student may experience in moving from one elementary school to another or from class to class in the same school or college. Information and attitudes in one curriculum area can be unrelated or even contradictory to the learnings in another area. Vertical articulation refers to the movement upward or downward through the elements of the educational system, as moving upward from elementary to high school or, as in a surprising number of recent cases, downward from the university to the junior college. To distinguish between horizontal and vertical articulation is important only when focusing on the *elements* of school organization, such as the curriculum or activities to be articulated. When one focuses on the articulation *process,* vertical and horizontal distinctions become less important, because school organization is articulated not by formal procedures but through the experiences of students. Good articulation requires a comprehensive view of the totality of student experiences in the educational system; then the parts or programs can be integrated into a meaningful whole.

Articulation is more than just an educational concern. According to Russell and Judd, it is important to the government for reasons both of economy and the promulgation of democratic ideals.

> The desirability of effective articulation between the units of the school system is evident for two reasons. The first is that economy in the educational process can be secured only in this way. If there are periods when continuous forward progress is not being made, the system cannot be said to be efficiently organized. The second and more basic reason is the need for effective articulation which arises from the fundamental concept of a democratically organized society. One of the ideals of social organization in the United States is that the way ahead for each individual must be kept open, so that he is allowed to progress to the extent of his capabilities. If there are points in the school organization or features of an educational program that block the continuous for-

ward progress of some pupils and do not permit them to
accomplish all that they are capable of accomplishing,
then the system fails to meet the ideals of democratically
organized society.[10]

Because educational progress can be helped or deterred by counselors, teachers, and administrators at every level, the main group of
educational professionals must be considered in the articulation process. It should be understood that there is no standard program of
school and college relations that is best for all schools, colleges, and
universities. As with most programs, the particular mission and phi-
losopy of the institution should determine the nature of articulation
activities.[11]

Problem Areas

One cannot easily evaluate "good" or "bad" articulation. By the same
token, it is not easy to conclude that articulation is completely absent
in one situation or operating at maximum capacity in another. School
and college relations are almost always evaluated in terms of the effectiveness of programs for institutional missions, student characteristics
and goals, and related matters. Yet, if a basic body of knowledge
about school and college relations is to develop and be refined, gen-
eralizations are necessary.

The reasons for poor articulation in the educational system are
threads in the historic fabric of American education. The system is at
once one of this nation's most remarkable achievements and one of its
most chaotic unwieldy apparatuses. It results from attempting what
no nation had tried before and what only a few have attempted since—
quality education for all that extends from elementary school to higher
education. Part of the idea of mass education, which was based on a
resolute faith in the ability and virtue of the common man, was the
premise that each person ought to be allowed to develop to his highest
potential.

The educational structure grew at a pace that matched both the
American faith in education as a vehicle for improving individuals and
society and the growing acceptance of education as an American birth-
right. Equally important was the deeply ingrained American attitude

10. Russell and Judd, *American Educational System,* p. 216.
11. Julius Menacker, "Articulation Services Appropriate to a Public Metropolitan Commuter Campus," *College and University,* Fall 1968, p. 61.

favoring governance close to the governed. Based on an inherent distrust of distant, centralized authority, American education became the responsibility of each state, which, in turn, delegated the major portion of authority for school control and operation to the local community. Each state developed its own peculiarities of finance, curriculum, and organization, and local communities developed emphases suited to their own needs and points of view.

The fragmented system of public education

Knowledge of the background of American education helps to explain the extent to which inarticulation exists in the American educational system today. France, Germany, Japan, the Soviet Union, and most other nations have no such problems, since curricula are planned at the national level. Procedures for transferring from one educational level to another are also worked out centrally and applied uniformly throughout the land. In contrast, the United States developed a pattern in which there are communities that have separate school districts and policy-making governing boards for public elementary schools, high school, junior colleges, four-year colleges, and universities. It is not uncommon to find towns with two or more different elementary school districts, a separate high school district, a separate junior college district, as well as other multiple statewide governing boards for college and university systems. In one instance, education for an Illinois town of about 20,000 is organized into three elementary districts, a high school district that also encompasses one neighboring town, and a junior college district that also serves several adjacent communities. The town is within the boundaries of four public statewide college and university systems; each college system has its own governing board responsible for two or more public institutions of higher education.

At the very least, a citizen of such a town always lives within seven educational governments. If he happens to move twice within the town, he could be within nine different educational jurisdictions, each with a different governing board. If he moves to certain neighboring towns within a ten-mile radius, he enters a new elementary district, a new high school district, and a new community college district.

Benefits roughly balance disadvantages in a system of highly localized common school districts and overlapping higher education governments. Local boards respond better to citizens and to local needs than would be the case for governing boards further removed. Innovation and flexibility are better encouraged, and a sense of community is more easily achieved among board, staff, and those served by the school. Also, the "system of systems" approach to higher education used in Illinois, where different boards control and make policy for different groups of colleges and universities, allows variety in higher education.

The most obvious disadvantage to local educational systems is the problem of coordinating curriculum, teaching, methodology, and general educational policies and goals. In the highly mobile American society, some coordination is necessary to ensure that students moving from one governmental district to another do not suffer from a loss of continuity in their educational progress. Certainly, the problem could be removed, but the cure would be worse than the disease: a constitutional amendment could give the national government control of public education. The Office of Education could then prescribe national curricula, teaching methods, and teacher certification requirements. Each community college transfer program would be well integrated with its senior college component, since the national educational authority would have established rigid specifications for both.

Such a development is not likely, nor would it be desirable. Local autonomy and the vigor and richness of learning experience emanating from the present diversity should be retained. A certain level of inarticulation should always be with us, because it is a healthy symptom of the rich diversity in American education. It is very important, however, to keep inarticulation within reasonable limits and to have the means of coping with it. The statement by James C. Stone is a good one to keep in mind regarding the need to combat negative effects of the American organizational pattern:

> Human learning is a continuous process, and the pattern of learning is seldom represented by the form of school organization. When the natural, continuous processes of learning are divided by the neat gridiron pattern of school structure so expedient in the management of large numbers of students, an artificial stratification of education develops and injects obstacles into the formal process of development.[12]

12. James C. Stone, "Articulation of Educational Units," *Encyclopedia of Educational Research,* ed. Robert L. Ebel, 4th ed. (New York: Macmillan Co., 1969), pp. 87-88.

Competition

Inarticulation stemming from localized, fragmented authority over public education is only half of the old obstacle to the continuous, efficient, forward progress of students. A fear exists among units of the educational system that another unit is intent on achieving dominance for its own narrow purposes. In the past, colleges were alarmed that multipurpose, comprehensive high schools would dilute the quality of higher education and force nonintellectual goals on collegiate education.[13] Currently, we see more of the opposite fear—that college admission requirements will dominate the school curriculum and foster narrow, pedantic education. A good illustration of such hostility and suspicion is found in an article titled "Is College Subverting Grade School?" Derek L. Burelson, the author, warns that "there are certain trends in our elementary schools that seem directly related to this drive to get children into college, and these trends are reasons for concern."[14] Burelson mentions specifically an overemphasis on all forms of standardized testing to determine track placements, neglect of pupils unlikely to attend college, and homework for the sake of promoting a "hard" scholarly environment. The most sinister trend uncovered in the article is the elementary school curriculum tampering by professors who overemphasize subjects that carry over to college.

Another broad cause for poor articulation is the tendency of teachers and administrators to concentrate on the curriculum of their level to such an extent that they ignore the learning goals of other levels. Such preoccupation would be present under the best conditions; however, the disconnected administrative nature of the American system encourages isolated curricula. Divisions compete, in one form or another, for funds and public approval. When a community is faced with tax increase referenda from the elementary district, voters decide the priorities for the high school and community college districts as well. As a result, each unit tends to stress the benefits of its own program instead of the broader needs of students throughout the educational system. Although combined elementary and high schools resolve district rivalries, separate school administrations experience competition among

13. R. Freeman Butts and Lawrence A. Cremin, *A History of Education in American Culture* (New York: Holt, Rinehart, and Winston, 1953), p. 388.
14. Derek L. Burelson, "Is College Subverting Grade School?" *PTA Magazine,* May 1967, p. 9.

teachers when teachers at one level feel superior to those at a lower level. At one time superior attitudes were reinforced by paying elementary teachers less than their high school colleagues with comparable education and experience. While such practices have been generally discarded, remnants of the attitudes that fostered them remain.

Institutional differences

Different educational goals at different levels exacerbate poor articulation. For example, selection is not an aim for common schools, but it is for many colleges. Democratic values receive much greater emphasis in the common schools than in higher education, while elementary schools place greater emphasis on socialization than do high schools and colleges.

The necessary specialization of the teaching staff contributes to poor articulation to the extent that most teachers fail to consider the total educational process. The teachers have little or no professional knowledge about problems of education at levels or in subjects other than those with which they are directly concerned. As a result, they have limited information about what instruction pupils have received previously, are receiving in other classes, or will receive from other teacher specialists during their educational careers.

That standards of promotion and advancement from one grade to the next are frequently vague and not well understood by teachers and pupils further obstructs student progress. The problem intensifies at the juncture of the highest level of one educational unit and the lowest level of the following unit, because it is difficult for teachers under separate administrative jurisdictions to arrive at a common understanding.

Even such mundane matters as the record system can influence the quality of articulation. Generally, records pass information only from teacher to teacher within a school, but in a few cases the complete record may accompany the student when he moves from one community to another or from one educational level to another.

Subject coordination

Poor articulation results frequently in poor curricular coordination. At one extreme, gaps in the curricular progress of the student are caused by a lack of communication between teachers of the same subject. Especially vulnerable are those subjects where the sequential development of skills is necessary for further learning, as in mathematics. It is not at all difficult to find students who, for one reason or another, never received instruction in performing arithmetic functions with fractions or with decimals. Such deficits often remain as an encumbrance throughout all the subsequent years of schooling.

The other extreme of bad coordination is unnecessary duplication in the curriculum due to poor communication. Both cases prevent the student from getting the most from his education. The student is either frustrated in trying to learn or bored to distraction by numerous reviews of the same material. How many times must a student hear about Columbus discovering America or the process of photosynthesis?

College entrance requirements further weaken articulation in a significant number of cases by adhering to a prescribed pattern of high school subjects. Basing their position on the "mind-is-a-muscle" theory, debunked over a half-century ago, advocates of subject requirements want to ensure that freshmen are prepared for the hard work of college with hard work in high school. Study after study, however, has shown the inconsequentiality of subjects studied in secondary school for college success.[15] At the same time, class rank or scholastic average in high school has proved to be the single best predictor of college success, especially when augmented with scholastic aptitude test scores. Specific subjects as factors of the predictive formula do not improve accuracy.

The transferability of credit from junior to senior colleges is one of the most urgent problems of articulation. Senior institutions confront community colleges with a bewildering variety of policy differences on credit acceptance. Courses accepted in transfer still might not count toward a degree. The clearest and least defensible example is the practice of some colleges to reject D grades in transfer, although D grades earned there apply toward graduation.

Articulation problems facing transfer students from community colleges are understood clearly when admission and orientation policies and programs for them are compared to similar policies for beginning freshmen. With a few notable exceptions (California and Florida for

---

15. Collins W. Burnette, *Studies Dealing with the Relationship between a Prescribed Pattern of High School Units for Entrance Requirements and Academic Success in College* (Columbus: Ohio State University, 1967).

example), the community college transfer student is generally treated as a second-class citizen at the senior institution.

The student coming to college through nontraditional routes presents special problems in transition that are fast achieving recognition. The four main categories of atypical students are the accelerated student, the disadvantaged student, the veteran, and the mature adult; less visible groups include foreign students and handicapped students.

Numerous less important problems will become more perplexing as articulation specialists resolve the matters at hand. In order to understand and cope better with the enumerated problems and their causes, one must first be aware of the historical development of school and college relations.

Historical Development

Deeply ingrained in the roots of American education is the multinational historical origin of each major unit of the educational system. The kindergarten, developed in Germany, was transplanted here well after elementary schools were solidly established. The elementary school, itself, was adapted to the American environment from a Prussian model. Our colleges were patterned after their English counterparts, and our prototype for graduate education was imported from Germany. Only the high school and the junior college are uniquely American creations. In an educational system built with such diverse components, it is not surprising that coordination problems exist, particularly when the factor of local control of public education is added. Further complexities have developed because the units did not materialize in serial progression. The precursor of the elementary school was followed by the college, then the high school, then the kindergarten, and, most recently, the community college.

In the early developmental stages, little or no attempt was made to coordinate sequential curricula or other elements of the school program. The chaotic and meteoric growth of the American system, compared to the centralized, orderly development of foreign education over a long period of time, may account for the oversight. Most western European nations now have a dual system with two parallel educational tracks, one academic and the other vocational. The American system, for the most part, differs from the European order by attempting to provide for the needs of all students within one educational system that supports many comprehensive institutions.

Americans were quick to appreciate the importance of a well-ordered, regularized system for progressing from one unit to another. The 1816 Constitution of Indiana states that, "It shall be the duty of the General Assembly, as soon as circumstances will permit, to provide by law for a general system of education, *ascending in a regular graduation from township schools to a State University*" (emphasis added).[16]

During the formative years of the educational system, mutual understanding and confidence were missing among colleges and secondary schools, as demonstrated by college admission requirements. Admission depended primarily on successful performance on a number of homemade subject examinations in such fields as Latin, Greek, mathematics, history, and so on. It did not matter if students had taken the subjects and performed well in them during their years at the secondary school or academy. In fact, it did not matter if applicants had never studied the material. The simple criterion for admission was successful performance on the tests.

Toward the end of the nineteenth century, the secondary schools, now more firmly established, convinced many colleges that both schools shared the common mission of preparing a small proportion of the nation's youth for the professions.

Emergence of voluntary accrediting associations

The secondary schools took the lead in developing shared policies and programs, since they had been, up to that time, the underdog in the relationship. During the closing years of the nineteenth century, the agitation and the growing recognition of the dependence of colleges on secondary schools for a constant supply of students resulted in the formation of regional accrediting associations, the memberships of which were composed of both secondary schools and colleges. The organizations aimed to establish uniform standards and regular relationships between the two levels. The New England Association of Colleges and Preparatory Schools was founded in 1885, and the North Central Asssociation of Colleges and Secondary Schools, ten years later. The first constitution of the North Central Association stated,

16. Russell and Judd, *American Educational System,* pp. 216-17.

"The object . . . shall be to establish closer relations between the colleges and secondary schools of the North Central States." [17]

By 1900 the two major accrediting associations, the North Central and the Middle States, had negotiated certain admission practices, agreed to reluctantly by the colleges. The North Central Association developed the plan, backed by a system of school accreditation, whereby principals certified students for college admission and universities inspected and accredited secondary schools. The University of Michigan was the first to use this system in 1871, and the arrangement was adopted quickly throughout the West.[18] The Middle States Association evolved a college admission procedure based on external entrance examinations which, in turn, led to the formation of the College Entrance Examination Board in 1900. The emerging secondary schools demonstrated vitality by participating fully in both admission procedures. As a result, the system of unilateral college-made examinations gave way to more cooperative methods of managing the flow of students from secondary to higher education. In the process, both levels adjusted to the other, improving service to their clients and to the nation in general, and bringing the educational system more in line with the practical issues of school and college relations. It was however, only the opening round in more than a quarter century of shifts and agitation in school and college relations.

National committees and commissions

Almost all of the important issues in school and college relations from 1900 to 1950 were deliberated by the various national committees and commissions established during that period to stabilize and integrate the high school into the educational system. The National Council of Education, founded in 1880 as a department of the National Education Association (NEA), was well established by the turn of this century. Significantly, the council included committees representing every educational level and group; it provided the impetus for convening the Committee on Secondary School Studies, more popularly known as the Committee of Ten, in 1892.

17. Calvin O. Davis, *A History of the North Central Association* (Ann Arbor, Mich.: North Central Association, 1945), p. 7.
18. Carnegie Commission on Higher Education, *Continuity and Discontinuity* (New York: McGraw-Hill Book Co., 1973), p. 15.

The Committee of Ten was dominated by college educators who considered secondary schools to be college preparatory feeder institutions that vigorously strengthened the muscle of the mind. It was not surprising, then, that the committee recommended studying Latin in 45-minute periods, five days a week for four years. Greek was prescribed for three years, five meetings per week the first year and four meetings a week for the last two years. The Committee of Ten also suggested that English be taught for four years, and that students study a modern foreign language, mathematics (algebra through trigonometry), and history for four years per subject with lesser time periods allocated to specific natural and physical sciences.[19] The most significant outcome for improved articulation was the committee's agreement to use the Carnegie unit as a standard academic measure, thereby giving colleges and high schools a common currency for supervising student transition. As with so many procedures designed to make articulation more orderly, the Carnegie unit also encouraged rigidities in admission and curriculum that are only now being remedied.

The curriculum developed by the committee included specific recommendations for elementary education, even though elementary schools were not represented among the Ten. The recommendations were a complete victory for the reactionary forces of higher education, who failed to recognize the emerging comprehensive and pragmatic nature of the high school.

The high schools did not take the defeat easily and agitated for a more liberal approach with greater emphasis on relevant subjects. The commotion encouraged changes in the admission policy fostered by the regional accrediting associations. It also helped bring about the formation of the Committee of Nine on the Articulation of High School and College, appointed by the National Education Association in 1910. The Nine called for a relaxation of rigid subject requirements for college admission and for a more flexible, pragmatic high school program that would better serve the needs of all youth. The Committee of Nine also made the first assertions that the college preparation of a minority of all students enrolled fulfilled only one aspect of a public high school's responsibility.

---

19. Frederick M. Raubinger et al., *The Development of Secondary Education* (Toronto: Collier-Macmillan Canada, 1969), pp. 54-55.

The report of the Nine was made in 1911, the same year that another NEA secondary school group, the Committee on College Entrance Requirements, issued this statement: "It has been our aim to make our plea general for the granting to preparatory schools [of] greater freedom in planning their courses of study to fit local needs and to develop interests, tastes and abilities of their students whom they serve."[20] The pressure led to the formation in 1918 of another school-college NEA commission called the Commission on the Reorganization of Secondary Education. Significantly, this group was chaired by a state high school superintendent. The commission issued cardinal principles for secondary education that suited the needs of America's ever more heterogeneous high school student body. The importance of articulation was recognized in four sections of the commission's report, which called for restructuring organization patterns. To better accommodate the transitional needs of students, the junior high school and junior college were recommended. The commission asked high schools to be more flexible in admitting and providing appropriate experiences for overaged elementary school students and insisted that "higher institutions of learning are not justified in maintaining entrance requirements and examinations of a character that handicap the secondary school in discharging its proper functions in a democracy."[21] The continuing democratization of American society, asserted the commission, demanded that both secondary and higher education serve the growing, disparate numbers of people wishing more liberal education. Even more striking was the call for secondary and higher education to accommodate demands for diverse vocational education.

Organization and policies were to be based on a broad interpretation of the relationships between units and students if educators followed the commission's recommendations. Such a trend would sweep away artificial barriers to smooth transition of students and lead educational units to serve students and the aims of American democracy with greater pragmatism. The commission's careful review in 1918 of educational articulation has had no parallel since.

The Eight-Year Study

Colleges resisted liberalizing tendencies, implementing the theories of mass education only as concessions were wrung grudgingly from

20. Ibid., p. 100.
21. Ibid., p. 116.

them by the schools and the public. It was the Progressive Education Association that finally challenged higher education's resistance to flexibility and change. In 1930, the association appointed the Commission on the Relation of School to College to determine if colleges needed an elaborate, rigidly prescribed set of subject requirements for admission.

The Eight-Year Study, as it is now known, examined 30 schools, 300 colleges, and nearly 3,000 students for the effect of the subject admission requirements on the success of college students. Participating schools were allowed to experiment with unorthodox curricula. Graduates of these schools were admitted to the participating colleges and compared to students similar in every respect other than secondary curriculum.

Altogether, 1,475 pairs of students were studied; those entering college in 1936 were studied for four years, the 1937 freshmen for three years, the 1938 group for two years, and those entering college in 1939 for one year. Among other significant findings, it was learned that students from deviant curricula:

- Earned a slightly higher total scholastic average.
- Earned higher grade averages in all subjects, except foreign languages.
- Received slightly more academic honors.
- Were more often judged to possess a high degree of intellectual curiosity and drive.
- Were more often precise, systematic, and objective in their thinking.
- More often developed clear or well formulated ideas concerning education, particularly in the first two years.
- More often demonstrated a high degree of resourcefulness in meeting new situations.
- Earned each year a higher percentage of nonacademic honors.
- Had a somewhat better orientation toward the choice of a vocation.
- Demonstrated a more active concern for what was going on in the world.[22]

Although the study's methodology was heavily criticized, it demonstrated that secondary schools were competent to develop their own

22. Ibid., pp. 199-200.

curricula for a diverse high school population that included the college-bound. Colleges did not have to direct the high schools as if secondary educators were less intelligent components of the educational system. The study had other important outcomes for school and college relations. Mutual respect increased between college professors and school teachers who had the then unique experience of meeting regularly. Teachers at both levels came to realize that neither approach to admissions fully resolved transitional problems and that the best solutions would be realized only through cooperative efforts. Recognition of the importance of communication and cooperation was as significant a conclusion for education as was the study's finding on curricula. The report of the Progressive Education Association marked a turning point in educational articulation, commemorated when many colleges abandoned subject requirements. Educational relations would still be far from congenial as long as traditionalism, vested interests, and snobbery perpetuated other problems and froze the atmosphere for heading off articulation problems yet to come.

Outside influences

During the 1930s, the high schools became well established and firmly committed to a diversity of roles. Colleges, however, still viewed articulation as the process of "finding ways and means of redirecting the schools' attention to college preparation and admission."[23] In 1941, the College Entrance Examination Board (CEEB) ceased external subject matter examinations in support of the Middle States Association's college admission procedure. The accrediting associations, which up to that time had examined schools only in terms of college preparation, extended their considerations to include the new comprehensive mission of the secondary school.

Striving for fair admissions practices, colleges adopted the achievement test in place of the defunct external examination. The Scholastic Aptitude Test (SAT) was first used in 1926. The colleges' reliance on any test indicated basic distrust of secondary schools, but the achievement test at least gave some flexibility to instruction within subject areas. The external examination had demanded rigid adherence to a narrowly prescribed course of study. The new tests, primarily managed

23. Richard Pearson, "The Changing School and College Relationship," *Journal of General Education,* April 1965, p. 2.

by the CEEB, liberated school and college relations from some of their restrictive fetters—college dependence on secondary schools known to offer the "right" kind of program. Such practices had excluded bright students who had not taken courses precisely convergent with the college's recommendations and the colleges' external examinations.

By the 1940s a number of interested bystanders were beginning to influence educational policies and practices. The general accrediting associations and the College Entrance Examination Board were increasingly vocal, although they still were basically controlled by the member schools and colleges that formed the organizations. Publishing firms with major shares of the textbook market exerted such influence on curricula that many pointed to them as being the most potent generators of a national curriculum, particularly at the common school levels. The American College Testing Program emerged in 1959 to compete with the CEEB, thereby breaking the latter organization's college testing monopoly and making the college aptitude test a far more common and accepted articulation tool. It would soon be the rare student who would not take one or the other test for admission to even a community college, which would use the results for counseling rather than admission.

A number of accrediting associations organized along professional interests. The narrower groups were concerned mainly with developing academic standards for professional studies. Among the professional accrediting associations, the American Association of Collegiate Schools of Business, the Enginering Council for Professional Development, and the National Council on Accreditation of Teacher Education have been leaders in vigorously working for quality education in their fields. At times the interests of the professional accrediting association conflicted with those of the broader general accrediting group, and both have obstructed institutional policy. However, tensions that existed and still exist among groups cannot be viewed entirely in a negative light because numerous successful efforts have advanced institutional articulation.

Social changes stimulated by World War II dramatically liberated school and college relations. Through the G.I. Bill of Rights, veterans were given a tremendous opportunity to resume their education and become qualified for new social and economic opportunities otherwise closed to many of them. While many returned to high school, most enrolled in institutions of higher education, forcing colleges to expand and liberalize academic and admission policies. A new external examination, the Tests of General Education Development (GED), gradually was accepted as an equivalent to the high school diploma for purposes of college admission. By the 1950s, the continuance of a general military draft led the United States Armed Forces Institute to offer a program of course credit applicable to both high school and college degrees.

The Advanced Placement Program, begun in 1955 by CEEB, greatly improved articulation by introducing college level courses in high schools for advanced students. Jointly planned by school and college subject specialists, the courses have been taught by high school teachers. College credit has been established by passing any of thirteen examinations and sending the results to the college of the student's choice. The tests were developed by high school and college experts and now cover American history, art, biology, chemistry, English, European history, French, German, Latin, mathematics, music, physics, and Spanish. Predictions for the future call for continued growth in the variety of offerings and number of participating schools and colleges. After a national review of high school programs, James B. Conant recommended that "every high school ought to strive for participation in the Advanced Placement Program."[24]

Advanced placement was developed, in part, as a response to criticism that exceptional student talent was being wasted and neglected in high schools. The program also attempted to remove procedural obstacles from the path of the academically talented or, as the jargon of the day expressed it, "gifted" students. Coming at a time of keen technical competition with the Soviet Union, advanced placement was widely acclaimed as a critical factor in the rapid production of trained brain power.

As important to interscholastic relations and talented students as was the Advanced Placement Program, it had an equal effect on teachers and administrators. College teachers began to have greater faith in the general competence of high school teachers, and high school teachers began to see college professionals as being just as earnestly concerned with the well-being and education of students. Communi-

24. James B. Conant, *Slums and Suburbs* (New York: McGraw-Hill Book Co., 1961), p. 145.

cation between individuals and institutions at the two levels increased by geometric proportions from pre-Advanced Placement Program levels, and a new era in school and college relations came into being. The program, however, did not have a truly national impact, because it generally affected only the brightest students and the "best" high schools. As knowledge and acceptance of the program becomes widespread, more students will benefit from advanced placement.

The next major articulation development resulted from a book that was not directed at articulation per se. Published in 1960, *The Process of Education* by Jerome Bruner explains how school curriculum practices can promote more efficient learning. The small volume sparked profound soul-searching and reconstruction in the schools and, to a lesser extent, the colleges. Bruner preaches that "any subject can be taught effectively in some intellectually honest form to any child at any stage of development." [25] The statement suggests the careful patterning of the spiral curriculum, whereby the basic knowledge of a subject is elaborated upon at successively more advanced grade levels. Another important notion presented by Bruner is the need to teach the inherent structure of basic subject areas instead of isolated facts and formulas that cannot be tied to a general pattern. Teaching the structure of subject fields allows students to increase their knowledge through insights generated on the basis of their own grasp of the subject's structure.

As Bruner's views gained acceptance, the implications for articulation became evident. If foreign language could be effectively taught in the elementary school, the high schools would have to build on the elementary school experience rather than commence traditional foreign language instruction. More to the point, the spiral curriculum would require close cooperation and communication among instructors at all grades and units of the educational system. Emphasizing the structure of a subject field meant that elementary and high school teachers would need the help of their colleagues in higher education who specialized in subject areas to develop curricula.

With a new sense of purpose and unprecedented financial support from the national government, schools and colleges began cooperative planning and programs in school curricula. While the emphasis was on

25. Jerome S. Bruner, *The Process of Education* (New York: Vintage Books, 1960), p. 33.

improving school curricula, the interaction of teachers and professors could not help but affect professional thinking and, in turn, college curriculum. Old professional associations were reorganized to include teachers of the same subject at all levels, and new ones were started for this purpose.

The community junior college

Education articulation had, by the early 1960s, become ingrained in the fabric of the American system of schools and colleges. It remained for a vigorous new unit of the system, the community college, to make articulation a prominent educational issue. Public junior colleges had existed since 1901 (Joliet Junior College of Illinois), but their growth was slow and their impact negligible until the late 1950s. Then community colleges began to have a greater impact on college attendance patterns than any other development in the past fifty years.

In 1921, the year in which the American Association of Junior Colleges was founded, there were 207 junior colleges (70 public and 137 private) with a combined enrollment of 16,000 students. Today, over 1,100 two-year colleges enroll about three million students.

The growth of community colleges has been so rapid that it is hard to sort out conflicting data. Frank G. Jennings claims that since 1969 more students have enrolled as freshmen in the community junior colleges than in the four-year colleges and universities.[26] Frederick C. Kintzer is more modest, claiming only 41 percent of all freshmen in 1970 to have enrolled in community colleges.[27] In either case, the growth of junior college enrollment has been dramatic.

For several years prior to 1969, a drive among community colleges had been gaining strength to demand that the senior institutions help to resolve a number of pressing articulation problems, especially in the area of admission and transfer of credits. Senior institutions, particularly public ones, have cooperated more frequently as they have come under growing pressure to admit transfers. In some cases, the senior level colleges have become dependent on transfer students for growth and even maintenance of enrollment levels.

26. Frank G. Jennings, "The Two-Year Stretch," *Change Magazine*, March-April 1970, p. 15.
27. Frederick C. Kintzer, *Middleman in Higher Education* (San Francisco: Jossey-Bass, 1973), p. xi.

Serious disagreements continue between two- and four-year colleges. However, colloquies now occur with a greater commitment of institutional resources and with a greater impact on institutional policies than can be found in other areas of interscholastic relations. For example, many colleges have established school relations departments entirely concerned with articulation. Although articulation still must cope with many critical issues, cooperation among educational levels may be entering a so-called golden age as school organization diversifies. Senior institutions have had to come to terms with the community college as the latter has emerged as a strong force in education, and the community college, on its part, has had to cooperate downward with the high school. All three units have thus been brought into closer harmony by the catalyst of the community college, and a higher level of articulation has been reached, even though some of the old problems persist. In the 1970s, there is more reason for optimism about the future of school and college relations than ever before. Still, the growing size, complexity, and importance of education, particularly higher education, makes efforts to cope with the continued need for improved articulation imperative.

two

High School and College Relations

Speaking at the twenty-fifth National Conference on Higher Education in March 1970, the late U.S. Senator Wayne Morse supported the high school college consultant:

> If America's multisystem or "systemless" apparatus for higher education is to work in the best interests of the individual, as well as society, high priority attention must be given to providing adequate counseling, guidance and evaluation, and appropriate data in the schools. Each student should have the opportunity and the necessary assistance to determine his own interests and talents and to assess the educational and career avenues open to him.[1]

Most high school counselors and college admission and articulation officers would agree with him and observe further that available evidence suggests a marked failure to achieve effective counseling. Information about what influences a student's choice of colleges came from a national sample of some eight thousand students taking the American College Test. According to the survey, advice from high school counselors or college consultants and talks with college admission counselors were rated as very low influences by both men and women.[2] Student impressions of the college faculty and scholastic reputation and, for men, even opinions of the college's athletic program ranked higher as influences. An institutional survey of nearly three thousand

1. Wayne Morse, "Commentary: Who Should Decide Who Goes to College?" mimeographed (Washington: American Association of Higher Education, 1970), p. 4.
2. James M. Richards and John L. Holland, *A Factor Analysis of Student Explanations of Their Choice of a College*, Research Report no. 8 (Iowa City: American College Testing Program, 1965), p. 4.

24

freshmen during their first quarter of attendance produced similar results. In response to the question of how student perceptions of the university were affected prior to enrollment, information provided by high school counselors was considered a hindrance by almost as many students as found it helpful (23.2 percent versus 27.4 percent).[3] Personal visits to the campus, talks with students already attending the school, and even college literature were far more favorably evaluated.

A five-year longitudinal study of 10,000 young adults from 37 high schools in 16 communities nationwide further confirms the need for improving advice and assistance to the college-bound. Almost without exception, those bright students who did not attend college had never been advised by their teachers and counselors of their ability level, let alone been helped and encouraged to find a college.[4]

A survey of academically strong Iowa high school seniors and their parents also challenges the effectiveness of high school counselors and college admissions officers. Parents ranked themselves as most influential, followed by brothers and sisters, high school counselor, friends in high school, friends already attending college, high school teachers, other relatives, and, in last place, college recruiters. Students agreed with their parents on the first two rankings but assigned less importance to the high school counselor, ranking him after friends both in high school and college. Students agreed with their parents on the least influential factor—the college recruiter.[5]

High school counselors and college admissions officers have difficulty communicating and cooperating, particularly when placing students in highly selective colleges. One survey of relations between admissions officers and counselors gathered so much negative information that the report was titled "Misunderstanding, Misinformation, and Mistrust."[6] The problems reported were less concerned with basic admission criteria than with inconsistent interpretations of specifics between high school counselors and college admissions officers.

3. Julius Menacker, "Improving the Admission Information Efforts of Institutions of Higher Education," *National ACAC Journal,* May 1972, p. 2.
4. James W. Trent, "A New Look at Recruitment Policies," *College Board Review,* Winter 1965-66, pp. 7-8.
5. R. F. Stahmann, G. R. Hanson, and R. R. Whittlesey, "Parent and Student Perceptions of Influence on College Choice," *National ACAC Journal,* July 1971, p. 22.
6. "Misunderstanding, Misinformation, and Mistrust," *College Management,* December 1966.

Counselors complained about the lack of information and authority on the part of traveling admission representatives, and admissions officers complained about the poor quality of recommendations sent by counselors for high school students. There were enough other problem areas to warrant the negative tone of the report's title.

Even so, the importance of high school counselor, college admissions officer, and articulation specialist to both prospective and new college students cannot be underestimated. Communicating effectively with each other and students, counselors, officers, and specialists facilitate the decision-making process for the student without appearing to influence his college decisions. The three specialists make a difference in patterns of college attendance by providing individuals with information helpful in making enrollment decisions, by participating in discussions that lead to policy and organizational changes at both levels, sensitizing faculty to the transitional needs of students, marshaling the support of parents and others in furtherance of the student's college plans, helping in obtaining financial aid, and in numerous other ways. The issue highlighted by the negative data is not the ineffectiveness of student personnel workers in the articulation process, but rather the need to improve their work and to reach more students.

The wider distribution of more information assists guidance functions that center around admission requirements at the same time that it fosters curricular continuity. James B. Conant, a respected observer of the educational scene, wrote, "One of the greatest weaknesses I have found in my visits to schools across the nation is the lack of coordination, or articulation, between what is taught in . . . schools." [7] Here the articulation specialist can become a catalyst. He should bring together teachers and administrators from all levels to develop academic practices and attitudes that facilitate smooth academic transition.

An old story illustrates some recurring problems in high school and college relations. A perturbed college president wrote to the principal of a nearby high school to complain about the inadequate preparation in English composition evident among freshmen received from that school. The president suggested that the principal concentrate on improving the performance of his English faculty. The prin-

7. James B. Conant, *Slums and Suburbs* (New York: McGraw-Hill Book Co., 1961), p. 70.

cipal responded that the majority of his English teachers had been educated at the president's college; perhaps the college should improve its training of English teachers. The principal further thanked the president for alerting him to the need to find alternate sources for new English teachers.

The story suggests the mutual dependence of high school and college programs, and makes plain the futility of efforts solely concerned with censuring one or another level for inadequacies in school and college relationships. More often than not, both levels share the blame, especially for making no effort to communicate and cooperate with the other agency. Attempting to fix blame for inarticulation is like trying to decide which came first—the chicken or the egg. Both exist. To improve articulation between high school and college, both agencies must attend primarily to the needs of students passing from one level to another, rather than to the protection of prerogatives or the fixing of blame. Even when both sets of professionals hold the most cooperative attitudes centered on students, as the following case study illustrates, insularity, outmoded tradition, and arbitrary barriers between high schools and colleges will still challenge those working to optimize relations between levels.

The following case study attempts to combine a number of articulation factors which affect any student. It is intended to demonstrate the extensiveness of articulation concerns, the importance of their resolution to a student's educational future, and the critical role of student personnel workers in this process.

Carl Jones: A Case Study

Carl Jones was in his final month of elementary school in the city public school system, when he had an appointment with a guidance counselor from the high school that he would attend the next fall. As he understood it, the purpose of the meeting was to plan his freshman program. He knew that his intention to pursue a college prep or vocational program would be discussed, and this presented a dilemma. He was not sure whether he wanted to attend college, nor did he know what school he might attend, or what subject he might study.

The counselor displayed considerable knowledge about Carl: Carl's reading score was above average for high school freshmen nationally as well as for the local school, but his mathematics score was barely average. Carl's grades showed excellent performance in the verbal areas, such as reading, English, and social studies; his work was less distinguished, but adequate, in the science and mathematics areas. The counselor understood that Carl was uncertain about college because of family finances and ignorance of college in all respects.

The counselor recommended the college preparatory program, because it would provide broader eventual options. Carl agreed to a program consisting of algebra, Spanish, world history, honors English, and the minor subjects of music and physical education. The counselor also gave Carl a pamphlet about the high school's organization, programs, and policies. Carl was invited to visit the high school on one of three days when the counselor would show him around the school, let him sit in on a class, introduce him to some of the students, and answer any additional questions that Carl might have then. Finally, Carl was given a card with the counselor's name and phone number on it.

At the freshman orientation program in the fall, Carl felt himself to be part of the student body with someone to whom he could relate— the counselor. Carl was surprised to find that he had been placed in sophomore Spanish, because his performance in elementary school Spanish had been judged equivalent to the first year of high school Spanish. The elementary and high school teaching staffs had arrived at that decision during summer meetings of the articulation committee, composed of representatives from the high school and all of its feeder elementary schools.

As Carl was about to begin his sophomore year, the same counselor asked him to make some important program decisions. Carl had done well during his first year and was beginning to feel that college was right for him. He had been thinking about architecture or English as possible majors. The institution that seemed most appealing was the state university, because it was comparatively inexpensive and had a high quality academic reputation. Carl's counselor told him that Carl needed to take four units of mathematics to qualify for the architecture program, plus two units each in Spanish, social studies, and science. Three units of English were also required. The subject pattern for entering the English program was more flexible in that only two years of mathematics were required. A consolidated five-unit requirement could be met with combinations of social studies, science, and a third year of mathematics or foreign language, instead of with two years each of social studies and science.

Carl decided to qualify himself for either subject pattern. He would have to drop his tentative plan of taking courses in art, music, and automotive shop, because high school graduation required four units of English and three of social studies; now, he had to take all the college requirements. Allowed only four major units per year, Carl needed a carefully planned academic program in order to qualify for high school graduation and admission to the university architecture program.

There would be room for only one course where Carl could pursue his interests. He expressed his disappointment to the counselor, who brought the matter up with the school's college consultant. The college consultant reviewed Carl's records and hit upon the thought that perhaps Carl would meet the two-year foreign language requirements as he had completed Spanish II in his freshman year. A search of the university's literature revealed no answer to the question. However, the college consultant had attended an admission information conference sponsored by the university in which the university's articulation officer had given the counselors a toll-free number to call when they had specific questions concerning college guidance.

The articulation officer, who when called did not know the answer, offered to raise the issue with the admissions office. The question proved new to both articulation and admissions, but after some discussion the director of admissions decided to accept Spanish II as the foreign language requirement if the high school would indicate credit for elementary school Spanish and Spanish I. The college consultant presented the issue to the high school principal, who would not make an immediate decision for lack of a precedent. He felt that the university should be satisfied with just the fact that Spanish II had been successfully completed. After all, he reasoned, quality rather than quantity should determine whether the foreign language requirement had been met.

The principal, a member of the University Committee on School and College Relations, promised the college consultant that he would raise the matter at the next meeting of high school administrators, university admissions, and articulation and college officers. The following week the committee discussion led to a compromise agreement, whereby the two-year foreign language requirement could be satisfied by the successful completion of Spanish II and a statement from the high school that Spanish I had been completed through elementary school study. As a result, Carl and others like him were granted an extra unit of elective study.

By the time Carl was ready to choose his senior year courses, he had received the results of both his American College Test (ACT) and his Scholastic Aptitude Test (SAT). Both scores were strong, with the ACT subtests in English and social studies reading and the SAT verbal section ranking highest. Discussing the results in terms of Carl's degree plans, the counselor pointed out that Carl seemed capable of achieving either the English or architecture degree, but his scores showed greater capability in English. Carl's lower middle-class background made the architecture degree appealing as a secure, practical, economic and social reward for college study, although he found English more attractive as a purely intellectually enjoyable experience. The counselor suggested that Carl weigh the two choices for a while and enroll in both an art major and the advanced placement English course. Perhaps such courses would give additional insight.

As the senior year began, Carl, as all other seniors, was scheduled for an interview with the school's college consultant. Upon hearing of Carl's indecision, the college consultant recommended what he called reality testing procedures. First, he arranged for Carl to visit the office of a local architect, talk with him, and observe him in his work. Next, Carl interviewed a university English professor and sat in on several introductory and advanced English courses at the university.

The college consultant suggested that Carl explore other colleges. He had Carl review the main college reference books in the guidance resources center, and convinced Carl to enroll with the College Admission Center of the National Association of College Admissions Counselors. As a result, Carl learned that a public commuter institution located in his city offered a program called History of Architecture and Art. Consulting reference materials and professors at the institution, he found that graduates of the program held jobs as architectural consultants or teachers; the program of studies seemed to offer the intrinsic aesthetic satisfactions that Carl had anticipated in an English program. Further, the newly identified public institution cost less because Carl could live at home instead of moving to the state university campus, 200 miles away.

Carl met the class rank, test score, and subject requirements for admission. He secured an application for admission, completed and returned it with his high school transcript, and mailed the forms instructing the American College Testing Program and the College Entrance Examination Board to forward his test scores to the commuter college's admissions office. Carl's only regret was that he would not live at a residential campus.

Carl successfully completed the first quarter at college, finding his studies enjoyable and satisfying. But he still felt that an important ingredient in his college career—residential college life—was missing. He had an opportunity to confide in his former high school college consultant at a college-high school articulation conference that included counselor visits with former students attending the college.

The college consultant offered to check into some transfer possibilities with a community college transfer counselor and report back to Carl. The high school consultant asked the counselor for information about transfer possibilities to an inexpensive residential college offering a degree in Art and Architecture History. After several days, the counselor called to say that something interesting had crossed his desk. A distant, private university had sent out flyers advertising openings and financial aid for community college architecture majors at the junior level.

The high school consultant told Carl, who was eager to find out if he could qualify and, if so, how much aid money he could get. Although the consultant knew Carl did not meet the requirement of junior standing, he wrote to the private university about Carl. Surprisingly, the institution had had difficulty fulfilling the terms of a national government grant that obligated the university to admit specified numbers of transfers to particular programs. Carl, offered admission and a favorable financial aid package, accepted the offer and achieved his desires to study one of his earliest program choices and to attend college at a residential campus.

Analysis

Most important among the good articulation practices illustrated was the facile use of the professional communications network among student personnel workers. The interaction of professionals, both formally in groups and on person-to-person bases, provided opportunities for overcoming transitional obstacles for helping the student through the organizational mazes of education.

The critical need for professional educators to keep in touch and to pay attention to transitional problems is highlighted by the student's uncertainty about future educational plans. Carl Jones, like many fellow college students, was not even sure of what major he wanted to pursue after attending college. Chance events determined his final college major. Clearly, student personnel workers exert great influence over the academic directions taken by students, not only through direct counseling interventions, but, as with Carl, by making known to students what options and opportunities are available before and after college enrollment.

That certain mechanisms can remove barriers to student progress at each level is another important aspect of school and college relations. Ad hoc administrative decisions, established procedures such as the Advanced Placement Program, orientation programs, and informational literature, however, are effective only when student personnel workers directly contact the student. Only then can problems be uncovered and referred to such agencies as a college and high school articulation committee or the College Admission Center. Personal contact is even necessary if students are to profit from such opportunities as the Advanced Placement Program, which, however well known, still is not used as often as possible. Counselors often must push students to take advantage of advanced placement. Adequate use of test scores and reality testing are also important.

Finally, many of the helpful articulation practices that assisted Carl through school would have been lost if the professionals involved had diverted their attention from the student to concerns of institutional prerogatives. The resolution of the foreign language problem exemplifies proper priorities.

Selection of Postsecondary Education

The process by which students move from secondary to higher education has been called the "great sorting" by B. Alden Thresher, former director of admission at M.I.T. He explains:

> This "great sorting" is a social process of great complexity, not fully understood by the students themselves, by their parents and advisers, or by the educators, in-

cluding admissions officers, who participate in it. . . . It is a product of an immense number of individual choices and decisions taken by millions of people, under the influence in part of calculations and estimates, projected a generation into the future and in part of beliefs, opinions, whims, ancient loyalties, and areas of ignorance scarcely amenable to rational estimate.[8]

Thresher is expressing a great truth here. As with Carl Jones, many students are unsure of their own academic interests and the proper college choice for academic, social, and financial reasons. At the same time, Thresher suggests, high school college consultants and their counterparts in college admissions and articulation are not sufficiently omniscient to make choices for students. Were college guidance practices highly developed, it would still be unwise for professionals to make important decisions for students. The appropriate role for student personnel workers on both levels is to provide prospective college students with the best possible information and selection strategies, well organized and rationally presented, so that the student and his family are in a position to make good decisions. Once decisions are made, student personnel workers can again play an important role by assisting in their implementation.

The professionals can perform adequately only if they are in contact with one another, exchanging information, reenforcing each other's efforts, and cooperatively planning improved techniques of assisting students and their parents. There are a number of ways in which these things can be done.

A variety of alternatives

The scope and diversity of postsecondary education in the United States is so great that it is almost impossible for a student to evaluate opportunities rationally without professional help. Of nearly three thousand colleges and universities, over seven hundred are two-year colleges, subdividing further into four main varieties—public comprehensive community colleges, private pretransfer junior colleges, and both public and private technical institutes. The technical institutes are concerned with preparing students for highly specific tech-

8. B. Alden Thresher, *College Admissions and the Public Interest* (New York: College Entrance Examination Board, 1966), p. 3.

nical vocations, such as drafting, refrigeration repair, or computer programming. Private junior colleges offer primarily the freshman and sophomore years of liberal arts college studies. The public community college, representing almost two-thirds of the two-year institutions, accommodates both vocational and liberal arts curricula plus remedial, adult and continuing education, and community services for their constituents.

Another important group of institutions is the private liberal arts colleges, many of which have traditions of academic excellence. Then there are the numerous state colleges which proliferated during the past two decades from public teachers colleges and normal schools. As a result, state colleges usually offer study in education as well as the liberal arts and sciences, but few can be considered to be truly comprehensive.

Due to the number of students served and resources for academic services, the public and private comprehensive universities loom over all other institutions of higher learning in their impact on school and college relations. The private universities include some of the most famous and influential educational institutions in America—Harvard, Yale, Columbia, Northwestern, New York University, Johns Hopkins, and so forth. Many of them rival the best of the private liberal arts colleges in the academic quality of their students and the excellence of their programs, while offering extensive and varied curricula to larger numbers of students.

The giant of higher education is the public university. As a group, these institutions serve the largest number of students and offer the most comprehensive curricula—agriculture, architecture, art, business, education, engineering, forestry, home economics, nursing, and many others, in addition to the traditional liberal arts and sciences.

Finally, the newest unit of higher education is the public "capstone" college or university. This type of institution, offering only the junior and senior years of undergraduate instruction, developed in response to the phenomenal growth of the community college. As would be expected, capstone colleges are located only in those states with developed community college systems. Such colleges mirror the four-year universities in the comprehensiveness of their offerings.

Other differences in orientation, scope or mission among American institutions of higher education can be identified by contrasting coeducational and single sex colleges, urban and rural settings, commuter campuses and residential ones, private colleges with a religious affiliation or orientation and secular institutions, special purpose colleges (those emphasizing a particular academic strength or focus, such as Massachusetts Institute of Technology) and those that are general in character.

Finally, there are the large number of postsecondary educational programs run by business, industry, and government. Annually enrolling several million persons, the programs range from simple classes on how to run a machine or make out a sales slip to advanced seminars for persons with doctoral degrees who must update their training. The courses span the academic gamut, including physics, chemistry and mathematics, and even the social sciences, foreign languages, and the humanities. In many private firms, several classifications of employees are expected to continue schooling for promotion, regardless of age.

Research is another aspect of education and training in American industry. As far back as 1964, approximately 500,000 people were working full-time in industrial research. Research and development programs had combined budgets of $11-12 billion, which more than doubled the total expenditure made by all universities for all purposes, including research.[9]

The educational program of the armed forces rivals commerce and industry in its scope and variety. Training programs and courses are required for many officers and enlisted men to perform duties as well as to gain promotions. An almost endless variety of self-enrichment programs are offered through such agencies as the United States Armed Forces Institute and off-campus university extension programs, as well as the college programs offered at the military academies. Other governmental agencies are as fully committed to educational programs as the military. Almost every national government executive department has extensive educational programs, ranging from agricultural experimental stations to the Fulbright international exchange program for scholars. The guidance worker who is not acquainted with the primarily noncollegiate postsecondary educational opportunities is not providing adequate service to his clients.

9. Harold E. Clark, "Noncollegiate Programs of Higher Education," *From High School to College: Readings for Counselors* (New York: College Entrance Examination Board, 1965), p. 35.

One strategy the high school counselor can use to help the prospective college student cope with multitudinous opportunity is the concept of "accessibility," developed by Willingham.[10] He assigns five levels of accessibility to the nation's institutions of higher education on the basis of either the cost of attendance or admission selectivity—whichever is higher.

I. Institutions in this level are purposefully open door. Tuition is free or quite low, and all high school graduates are accepted for admission. The majority of institutions are community colleges.

II. These institutions are almost open door. Selectivity is applied primarily in the lowest quarter of high school graduates, due more to space limitations than to arbitrary regulations on student quality. Tuition is not overly burdensome to those above the poverty level. The public community college dominates this category too, though a substantial number of public four-year colleges are also included.

There are practically no private colleges at either of the first two levels. The low tuition rates apply to state residents only, and in the case of many of the community colleges, one must also be a resident of the local community college district to qualify for low or free tuition.

III. This is the first level where many high school graduates have difficulty in entering college. If the usual requirement of the upper-half of class rank does not bar enrollment, then the higher tuition may effectively exclude the student. The most typical institution is the public four-year institution or one of its branches. A few public junior colleges are represented here, and this is the first level at which private colleges appear in noticeable quantity.

IV. Dominating this level are private colleges, many of which have a special purpose or religious affiliation. Although the group represents one-third of American colleges, the schools enroll only about 20 percent of all new students. Less than 11 percent of institutions at this level are public.

V. This group consists of the country's major public and private universities and the elite private liberal arts colleges. Roughly 80 percent are private and 20 percent are public institutions; however, the public institutions enroll nearly as many students as

10. Warren W. Willingham, *Free-Access Higher Education* (New York: College Entrance Examination Board, 1970), pp. 22-23.

the private schools. Most private and public schools are prestige institutions which practice selective admissions based on such variables as high school class rank or scholastic average, college aptitude test score, high school recommendation, high school subject pattern, personal interview, and extracurricular history. As a rule, the public institutions use only the objective criteria (such as high school rank or grades), pattern of high school subjects, and test scores. The private colleges and universities often augment data with more subjective variables.

Willingham's system is one example of how high school college consultants can organize known facts quickly to eliminate information extraneous to the selection of further education. Resource materials are available in a variety of forms. Presenting the data in some understandable and meaningful form is more important than the particular methodology.

Resources for improving selection

There is, of course, much in the way of psychological theory and counseling practice that is important in assisting secondary school students in making wise postsecondary educational or vocational plans. Certain major tenets of precollege counseling may be assumed as background.

1. Preadmission guidance should be a continuous process, beginning well before the student's senior year of high school.

2. The decision about whether to attend college, and then which college to attend, should be made by the student. The high school and college roles should be restricted to imparting intelligent strategies for making the decision and providing access to useful information related to the decision.[11]

3. Assistance to students making a college choice should involve not only purely academic considerations, but also cultural, social, and psychological factors.

4. High school consultants should give the student as much information and experience as the student finds helpful in choosing among alternatives.

11. Edwin Van Gorder and Frank R. Kemerer, "Helping Students Achieve Self-Actualization: A Case Study of Non-Directed College Counseling," *National ACAC Journal,* July 1971, p. 12.

5. College selection should be an introspective, self-evaluative process for the student in which he evaluates his strengths, weaknesses, and life goals to date.

6. The student should be encouraged to view college choices as revocable decisions. The American higher education system offers many opportunities for changes in curricula and institutions that need not jeopardize forward educational progress.

If principles of college guidance are to be successful, schools and colleges must cooperate. Only through an efficient communication system with colleges can high school college consultants proficiently organize information for high school students. Professional college guidance organizations, such as the National Association of College Admissions Counselors, the College Entrance Examination Board, and related associations like the American Personnel and Guidance Association, provide useful services and resources for students; the NACAC, through its College Admission Center, also assists counselors.

A number of new commercial guidance agencies have developed, some as adjuncts to large diversified corporations and others as companies specifically organized for providing college selection services. While many are quite reputable, others return little for the money. That inferior operations survive in spite of competition from inexpensive publicly organized services such as the College Admission Center indicates that professionals at both levels have not yet met the demand.

Both the American College Testing Program and the College Board provide additional information to students about college and to colleges about students. For example, the College Board's new Student Search Service supplies interested colleges with the names of large groups of applicants who meet any particular constellation of variables named, provided the student has participated in the CEEB Admissions Testing Program and completed the Student Descriptive Questionnaire, a part of the testing program. Another new CEEB service for colleges is the Expanded Summary Reporting System, a national profile of each year's college applicant group. Again, inclusion in the statistics depends on the student's participation in the College Board's testing program.

As for services to high school seniors, there is an expanded version of the College Board's *College Handbook* and a new, ambitious *Handbook of Member Colleges and Universities* produced by the NACAC. The two handbooks are the most prominent college references, but they are by no means the only ones. Many privately produced manuals and a growing number of computer-assisted college information systems sponsored by private corporations, public organizations, and institutional consortia are available but should be approached cautiously. Witness the rather fast demise of the Admission Search Kit, an elaborate package jointly sponsored by Minnesota Mining and Metallurgy and NACAC, that proved too unwieldy and expensive for practical purposes.

As previously noted, research indicates that the student's peers and parents are more influential in his college decision than either the high school counselor or college admission representative. Schools should therefore cooperate with colleges to involve people who influence the individual student. Research indicates that visits to college campuses have greater persuasive value than any of the printed material available to prospective students. All such factors must be considered in precollege guidance, and the use of teachers and administrators at both levels who have been identified as valuable guidance counselors should be weighed.

Both human and inanimate resources can be put to best use when precollege guidance includes as many different interest groups as possible in cooperative planning. Further, any planning or communication must be characterized by honesty and mutual respect. College representatives must be clear about their institution's goals and how the college's admission and academic policies support these goals. The high school people must know and be willing to discuss the school's strengths and weaknesses and similar information about students. Above all, the professional must concentrate on the student, not on institutional or personal concerns.

When high schools or colleges plan a college information program for high school students, they should begin by polling their own students, parents of high school students, teachers and administrators, and professional counterparts on the other level. The method—preplanning conference, correspondence, or telephone—is not as important as receiving and acting on the information. Other important sources of information are business associations, which themselves sponsor career conferences, agencies such as CEEB and ACT, professional associations which include financial aid officers, and similar resources. The collective viewpoints will not only make for a more relevant, effective program, but will also serve to improve communication and increase mutual respect.

The same is true for the development of high school or college literature to use when selecting colleges. Much of the literature only demonstrates the insularity in which it was produced. For example, many of the freshman profiles produced at universities better display the research and statistical virtuosity of the writer than help a busy college consultant guide each of 300 seniors through a pool of nearly 3,000 institutions to the right college.

The best profiles are relatively short and present only the most important data in the clearest terms possible. Data should include high school scholastic average or class rank and American College Test or Scholastic Aptitude Test scores for beginning freshmen; nonintellective characteristics such as family income, extracurricular activities, sex, age, and religious interests are quite useful.

It is in the area of attrition that profile writers reaffirm the adage "statistics don't lie, but statisticians do." The contortions engaged in to conceal the true rate of failure and withdrawal range from presenting data on classes long since graduated to confounding the data with advantageous categories, such as "eligible to return" and "not eligible to return"; many eligible to return may be on a serious probation while others never return. The colleges and universities that publish any attrition data are to be commended for at least recognizing the demand for information about student success rates. Most institutions simply ignore the matter.

Good profiles are those designed with the needs of the user in mind, but to produce this, the responsible university officials must involve high school persons in the basic content decisons. Honesty will serve the best interests of both high school and university in such matters as attrition data, even if there may be some temporary public relations disadvantages to the university.

Likewise, literature designed to attract students should be pretested on high school students for clarity, practicality, and motivational impact. The most important element in literature directed to students is a clear statement on admission requirements. Facts on the academic offerings of the institution, policies on advanced placement, institutional size, calendar, cost, financial aid opportunities, and similar useful information should be readily available. The material should be sent directly in response to mail, phone, and personal requests. However, the high school counselor, as a major channel for dissemination, should receive large quantities of such literature as soon as the college has revised it for the new admission period.

Because the production of college guidance literature is a joint responsibility, the high school should originate certain documents. One useful tool for students is a compilation of higher education institutions categorized in some rational way, as exemplified by the Willingham model. This document should also provide information to help the student do further analysis of possible college choices. Even more helpful is literature that stimulates students to compare their strengths and weaknesses to the strengths and weaknesses of the institutions they are considering. Obviously, involvement of college admission and articulation personnel would be helpful in producing the best possible college guidance literature.

Both high school and college should exchange useful data about the students moving between them. The college should provide reports on freshman performance and characteristics, comparing the entire freshman class to freshmen received from a particular feeder high school. It is important to get various school personnel involved in the feedback and planning process if the needs of the schools are to be met. For example, some high schools or their alumni in college may view performance reports on individuals as an unwarranted invasion of the student's privacy; other high schools may qualify for assistance in evaluating experimental courses if they obtain college performance information on former students who took that course.

For their part, high schools can report to colleges on the number and percent of graduating seniors who applied to the particular college; the relative quality of those applicants as opposed to all college applicants from that high school; and the performance differentials between the two groups as college freshmen. Follow-up surveys conducted by high schools on their graduates attending college have materially improved high school curricula and college guidance services. Colleges could profit from knowing these results, and this feedback device could contribute to the survey's validity by working with the high school to improve the survey design and procedures.

Good school and college relations procedures also ease parents, peers, and teachers in assisting students in finding an appropriate college. When a college representative visits a high school, he can take along one or two of the high school's alumni who are attending the college; or when prospective students visit the college, several of their alumni can be present for the program. College guidance persons at both levels can encourage teacher participation in either visitation program. High school personnel, with the consent of the college, can arrange parent-student programs and parents-only programs at which college representatives are present. College personnel can initiate supplemental visits by soliciting invitations to speak to parent-teacher associations and parent groups about college admissions and related topics. A particularly good topic to interest parents is financial aid. The college financial aid officer can be enlisted to speak, or high school and college can cooperate by presenting financial aid information to parents from the viewpoints of professionals working in this area at both levels.

The section would not be complete without paying some attention to the role of the college admissions representative. He should not be solely a recruiter for his employing institution. Rather, he must become a college resource person who can assist counselors and students with general information and selection strategies. The function requires a professional person committed to a career in the field of college guidance. All too often the admission representative position is staffed by young persons with undergraduate degrees in the liberal arts who accept the job as a way station while formulating definite career plans. The representative's role becomes limited to reciting catalog descriptions and the specifics of written admission policy. Such an individual does not generally have the expertise or will to provide students and counselors with adequate assistance in the college selection process.

The career oriented person, preferably holding a graduate degree in guidance and counseling, higher education, or a related field, usually proves more valuable to the employing institution because his service to students and school personnel wins their confidence; that respect frequently generalizes to the institution itself. Additional benefits accrue from a student applicant pool that is more compatible with the college's goals and the presence of a professional who can act as a liaison between school and the college. He or she maintains continuous two-way communication between colleges and schools. Building on his strategic position in the information network, the counselor can catalyze policy changes in the areas of admission, orientation, application procedures, high school college guidance practices, and even high school and college curricula.

Admission Policy

The single greatest influence on school and college relations is college admission policy, with which not even professional collaboration and excellent college guidance procedures can compare in importance. In the final analysis it is admission policies and procedures that dictate who gets to go to which college. It is vital, then, that admission policy be congruent with institutional goals, a requirement that demands institutional introspection about strengths and weaknesses, faculty aspirations, roles designated by the board of trustees, alumni, or the general public. All too often, freshman admission policy at four-year institutions rests on only two considerations—enrolling the proper number of new freshmen, and seeing to it that they are of the highest possible quality.[12] Usually, both standards are otherwise unrelated to institutional goals. At some colleges institutional goals may be so poorly defined that admission policy can do little more than help maintain solvency through freshman quotas and the tradition that academically better input builds an academically better college. At other institutions, the two items are the only policy elements, because no one has attempted to relate broad institutional policies to admission policy.

The consequences of admission policy determine the college's impact on schools and society to such an extent that a college must closely examine a selective admission policy before judging the school's effectiveness as a social institution. For example, many standard admission practices unintentionally influence the composition of a class in terms of sex, minority group enrollments, economic background of enrollees, and other student characteristics that may not exist in a freshman class.[13] Similarly, selective admission practice may inadvertently alter school-college articulation to the detriment of the college itself and the schools and students involved.

12. Emery R. Walker, Jr., "Admission Requirements in Action," *College Admissions: The Interaction of School and College* (Princeton, N.J.: College Entrance Examination Board, 1956), p. 56.
13. Julius Menacker, "Admission Practice as an Instrument of Public Policy," *National ACAC Journal,* November 1968, pp. 18-20.

Even community colleges committed to open door admissions have generated unmeant counterdevelopments. Too often, indiscriminate admission policy, divorced from orientation and counseling, turns open door into revolving door admissions. Many community colleges, as a result, have modified the open door policy to admit any high school graduate yet retained selective admission requirements for particular college programs. For example, enrollment in the college transfer program may require a particular SAT or ACT score or the removal of academic deficiencies. Admission to the dental technology program may depend on satisfactory performance on manual dexterity tests and so forth for other programs. Even at the open door community colleges, then, admission policy has important ramifications.

Abundant research evidence corroborates the validity of the most common college admission requirements, especially that of the most widely used variable, the high school record. Class rank, or high school grades, is the single best predictor of college performance. When the score earned on a test of scholastic aptitude (ACT, SAT) is added as another variable, prediction is improved.[14] Notably absent is hard evidence to support the validity of other popularly trusted variables, such as high school subject patterns, high school counselor recommendations, and personal interviews.

Articulation between high school and college, then, will be improved by establishing those admission policies most conducive to the steady, efficient forward progress of students. While colleges formulate and administer the policies, high schools can and do have an effect on them. Schools can serve as critics and interpreters of the effects of college admissions policies. Also, since the first law of college admissions is to produce a group of new students, colleges must necessarily be concerned with the attitudes of high school professionals and students.

One instance of excellent cooperation to improve university admissions policy happened at the University of Washington in 1970. At the annual Principals-Counselors Conference, the university's guests were asked to suggest survey questions that could be used to query all of the state's high school counselors about their views on current admission policy and possible changes in policy. Questionnaires were sent to all

---

14. Alexander W. Astin, *Predicting Success in College* (New York: Free Press, 1970); S. A. Kendrick and C. L. Thomas, "Transition from School to College," *Review of Educational Research*, February 1970, p. 167.

counselors, the responses summarized and then sent to all participants. The institution's philosophy was expressed on the summary's cover page: "The university recognizes its responsibility in coming up with the final decision as to what should be done with its admission policies, but at the same time it realizes the value to be gained by receiving viewpoints from secondary school personnel." [15] This attitude and procedure epitomize good articulation.

High school subject requirements

Colleges setting curricular requirements on admissions contribute to an interesting articulation syndrome. Certain high school teachers staunchly support the practice as a means to force students to take unpopular, but presumably necessary, courses that are not required for high school graduation; they find allies among university faculty representing the same disciplines. At the same time, most admissions and articulation officers recognize that high school subject patterns do not effectively predict college performance. A college that requires curricula excludes automatically many students whose academic characteristics promise greater achievement than is predicted for conventionally admitted students with minimum class rank and test score qualifications. Subject patterns can create unnecessary problems of articulation and often thwart the announced objectives of institutional admission policy.

Subject requirements persist from tradition. For the first three centuries of American education, tests on particular subjects or satisfactory completions of certain subjects at accredited high schools were the main admission criteria. General high school performance as a reliable predictor of college performance and scholastic aptitude tests were introduced and proved valid comparatively recently. By the early 1940s, the newer criteria had replaced the examination of particular high school subjects as an absolute admission requirement at most colleges and universities, although many schools still considered the high school subject pattern or at least recommended a preferred pattern. While research on performance predictions was a major reason for the shift in criteria, the new comprehensive nature of secondary

15. J. Robert Long, "Summary of Admissions Questionnaire," mimeographed (Seattle: University of Washington, Office of High School Relations, 1971).

schools gave vocational-technical career fields and the general education concept equal standing with the college preparatory program.

A growing secondary school system coupled with broader research on the usefulness of high school performance and aptitude tests still did not change those institutions where powerful faculty interests supported subject requirements. In many cases, faculty from different disciplines competed for power and recognition, resulting in an actual increase in the number of subject requirements. Faculty authority without involvement in articulation leads to a myopia that can be very damaging to school and college relations. B. Alden Thresher captured the essence of the problem:

> Because the faculty thinks in terms of particular disciplines and bodies of subject matter, its natural impulse is to lay down rather minute specifications about prerequisites for admission. . . . The definition of what is "decent" or "reasonable" may, of course, include anything one wishes—from spelling to an acquaintance with *Hamlet;* from arithmetic to the second law of thermodynamics. The phrase "college preparation" embodies the quite unconscious arrogance—indeed, the innocent arrogance—of generations of college teachers immersed in this thinking.[16]

As a result, one particular subject supersedes another in a college's admission requirements, depending on the relative influence of academic departments rather than academic wisdom.

All the while, common sense and readily available research evidence suggest no relationship between high school subject patterns and college performance. Numerous high quality colleges and universities are shown to ignore high school subjects yet produce well-educated graduates; they have no greater attrition rates than colleges adhering to subject requirements. Collins W. Burnette reviewed over a score of studies, conducted from 1923 to 1964, on the relationship between specified high school patterns and college performance. He concluded that "the preponderance of research . . . indicates that there is little or no relationship between specific patterns of high school units and academic success in college."[17] Burnette then speculated that

16. Thresher, *College Admissions,* p. 18.
17. Collins W. Burnette, *Studies Dealing with the Relationship between a Prescribed Pattern of High School Units for Entrance Requirements and Academic Success in College* (Columbus: Ohio State University, 1967), p. 3.

"academic success in college may be a function of individual intelligence, motivation, value pattern, and work skills, rather than completion of a certain number of units in subject fields." [18]

How subject requirements affect the quality of the student body was investigated by the Special Committee on College Admission Policy of Harvard University's arts and sciences faculty in 1960. The committee was formed to obtain "greater precision in specifying formal demonstrations of achievement in key subjects" as an admission requirement. The committee decided against adopting subject patterns as an admission requirement, reporting in part that Harvard should respect the autonomy of feeder high schools. Of greater importance than specified units, in the committee's opinion, was the general quality of the applicant. In other words, the committee considered quality more important than quantity:

> A four-year mathematics requirement would have kept out of Harvard no fewer than 126 of the 344 students who graduated *summa cum laude* in the classes of 1957 and 1958. The three-year secondary school language requirement would have excluded 127 of the same select group.[19]

Here, at an institution committed to the highest educational standards, distrust of high school program decisions and misplaced faith in outmoded admission requirements almost produced a policy that could have diminished student quality and antagonized feeder schools without producing any benefits.

How much more productive to good school and college relations it would be if colleges relied on the good judgment of high schools to adequately prepare applicants; colleges then could concentrate admission requirements on qualitative measures of ability, such as class rank or test scores, instead of imposing the rigid straightjacket of subject patterns on high schools.

Changing academic policy

High schools, freed from college admission requirements, have developed many of the best current educational innovations. Even so, both levels must cooperate to ensure the availability of policies and

18. Ibid., p. 5.
19. Special Committee on College Admission Policy, *Admission to Harvard College* (Cambridge: Harvard University, 1960), p. 2.

procedures designed to promote a smooth transition from the secondary to the collegiate level. At present, the situation is one of the secondary level acting and the college level reacting.

There is a trend among secondary schools to move away from traditional ways of organizing courses and evaluating students. Increasingly, the teacher's role is changing from that of an educational broadcaster to an educational decision-maker who helps students learn how to learn. The teacher diagnoses individual needs, interests, and abilities and then tailors a unique learning program and a set of objectives for the student. The student's activities are organized by such frameworks as modular scheduling or contract plans, which place the emphasis on meeting specified learning objectives rather than clock hours in class. Some of the more radical schools in the new wave of individually prescribed instruction techniques are even abandoning grades, or at least eschewing failing grades, and are showing resistance to college demands for class rankings.

The new mode of thinking has led to the development of interdisciplinary courses when such classes seem required to meet student needs. For example, an ecology course may combine science and social studies, or a literature course may put together English, a foreign language, and history. Such developments have fostered the notion that student achievement should be measured in terms of the student's individual ability rather than against some arbitrary absolute standard chosen by either faculty or individual teachers.

Diversity among high school curricula and differences in grading practices and in ranking policies have long caused frustration among college admissions and articulation officers, general administrators, and faculty. Some areas of continuing concern are documented by research findings. Surveying a national sample of secondary schools, James S. Terwilliger found widely diverging opinions among teachers and administrators on practices used to assign grades.[20] The data suggest that the only reliable way to determine what a grade really means is to ask the teacher who assigned it. According to the survey, 75 percent of the responding schools use ability groupings, but only 25 percent formalize grading differentiations among tracks. A related issue is the weighting of grades in tracked subjects for computing class

20. James S. Terwilliger, "Self-Reported Marking Practices and Policies in Public Secondary Schools," *NASSP Bulletin,* March 1966, pp. 5-37.

rank: only 9 percent of the schools give special weight to honors or advanced placement courses. Some schools give only *A*'s and *B*'s in accelerated courses, assigning additional weight to those classes when determining rank in class; other schools do neither.

Terwilliger found that schools use different methods to rank graduating students. Some calculations are based on the last two years as opposed to all four years. Other schools count all courses while yet others, using various definitions, count only "academic" courses. To further complicate matters, some schools provide two class ranks, one "academic" and the other all-inclusive.

Several months after Terwilliger's study was published the NASSP Joint Committee on School-College Relations surveyed college admissions officers on their views of class ranking.[21] Nearly half, or 49 percent, of the respondents require class rankings; 43 percent request it but will consider applicants without it; and only 8 percent do not ask about rank in class. Size or type of institution does not correspond to institutional policy, however, colleges can be grouped into three categories according to the use they make of class rank information. One group considers class rank initially to screen applicants from further consideration. Another group uses rank in class as one of many variables in a predictive equation to determine admissibility, while the third group refers to the statistic as only one measure of admissibility.

Most respondents (66 percent) prefer rankings that use only academic courses, and 67 percent want the whole class ranked, not just the college-bound. The practice of weighting honors and special college preparatory courses when calculating rank in class is favored by 60 percent.

The Terwilliger and NASSP studies show the high school record to be an imprecise gauge of students that is variously constructed by high school personnel and diversely utilized by college personnel. Additionally ambiguous are the differences in class sizes, instructional quality and resources, and student quality among high schools.

Changes in secondary school curriculum, grading, and ranking do not present college admissions officers with greater problems of selection because the officers have never had the advantage of an exacting selection instrument. The problem now is to retain predictive benefits

21. National Association of Secondary School Principals Joint Committee on School-College Relations, "Rank in Class," *NASSP Bulletin,* November 1966.

inherent in class ranking and grades—indications of student interest, motivation, and ability—through better methods.. College student personnel officers, faculty advisors, and teachers must also recognize the need to cope with the new, wider variety of courses and programs that high school graduates will be presenting.

Consider the ramifications of specially tailored secondary programs for bright students who enter college as viewed by Otto F. Kraushaar:

> Suppose that within the next two decades good college matriculants were to arrive equipped with ten years of foreign language, with training in mathematics at least through calculus, proficient in written and spoken English, with a solid foundation in biological and physical sciences, and a good general education in the arts. What would the colleges make of this millenium? [22]

Kraushaar answers his question by pointing out that "because of the inertia and conservatism of the colleges and universities, the gap between the possible and actual in college education seems to be widening. As matters stand, the colleges . . . have really only one answer [that is] more intensive and deeper specialization." [23]

Kraushaar's pessimistic assessment, written several years ago, may be wrong. The traditionally revered grading, credit, and curriculum systems of the university seem to be responding to leadership and challenge from the secondary level. Stanford University, for example, discontinued *D* and *F* grades in 1970; the sole penalty for not satisfactorily completing an undergraduate course is loss of credit toward graduation. The use of pass-fail systems has become widespread among a majority of colleges and universities. Colleges now offer more interdisciplinary courses and more experimental degree programs tailored to student demands.

The basic answer to both problems of evaluating the preparation of high school graduates for college and integrating secondary educational experience with college education lies in improved articulation between school and college. "As gross disparities in articulation between its [high school] subject matter and that of higher education

---

22. Otto F. Kraushaar, "How the Changes in the School Curriculum Affect Colleges," *The Changing College Preparatory Curriculum* (New York: College Entrance Examination Board, 1962), p. 78.
23. Ibid., p. 79.

become fewer," writes Thresher, "such academic devices as 'entrance requirements' play a diminishing role." [24]

It is first necessary to retire the seemingly easy solution of more testing. Tests are already available for college aptitude (SAT and ACT), high school subject mastery (TGED, SAT Subject Examinations), and college subject mastery (CLEP); however, these are only behavior samples of limited usefulness. Such tests tell little about academic motivation, interest, and expectations—matters that are as relevant as the level of academic proficiency. Furthermore, available tests do not evaluate much of the cross-disciplinary, problematic experiences that many of the better high schools and colleges now provide for their students. Students are already heavily tested, and to increase the amount of testing—either standardized instruments or school-made comprehensive examinations—would overemphasize the contributions of these relatively short, tense experiences to college placement.

For the college applicant who has spent most of his high school career under an individually prescribed contract plan, the first admission hurdle is professional communication across educational levels. Ideally, the high school would explain its curriculum and evaluation system to the college and appraise the student. A relatively minor problem for the small, selective liberal arts college, the open door community college, and some large private universities, personalized admissions data prove totally insufficient for large public universities with objective, regularized criteria for determining admission.

Typical comprehensive state universities process thousands of applications each year, utilizing only data that can be fed to a computer. The essential items are a social security number, a class rank number, and a test score number. Often, massive organizational inertia results in only token consideration of atypical credentials. In practical terms, public funds are insufficient to finance the staff necessary to evaluate variant credentials and to justify highly individualized admissions decisions to the tax paying public.

If a university would develop reports on freshman performance, comparing each high school's products with all freshmen, interlevel professional communication would have a fruitful beginning. If the

24. Thresher, *College Admissions*, p. 5.

high school would pay attention to the reports and supplement them with its own analyses, the opportunities for solving selection problems would be so much better. Much of the new data being supplied by CEEB and ACT is also helpful. Teachers, counselors, and administrators could compare the general preparation of unranked applicants and of those taught under individually prescribed programs with that of applicants who have had traditional preparation and credentials. Careful study and analysis of students who succeed will produce better performance predictions of more lasting importance.

High school recommendations will have to become more significant. Research indicates that high school counselors are not sure of the value of their own recommendations and that college admissions officers do not consider such recommendations to be reliable. The situation can be remedied by moving communication from speech-and-reaction to dialogue.

The best admissions decisions might well come as the result of direct interaction of school counselor and admissions officer. Selection would reward readiness and preparation for college rather than past achievement. A wealth of divergent information and experience would be brought to bear on the selection problem, and decisions would have to stand the test of logical expectations for success and service to the student.

The shared admissions process would stimulate teachers and counselors to pay more attention to students in order to discuss intelligently with other professionals the admissibility of each student. Such practices would certainly lead to better general guidance and education for high school students. Applicants would assume more personal significance for admissions officers who had debated the merits of each case. Admissions officers probably would continue their interest in successful applicants, thereby stimulating better advising and counseling for enrolled students.

The logistics of such a process present a problem that can be solved. The professionally trained college admission representative should do more than make known the college's advantages; when he visits a school, he should make admission decisions based on conferences with students, school professionals, and credentials analysts. Doubtlessly, the atmosphere and importance of the representative's visit to the high school would be improved, making the distribution of information to students and counselors much more efficient. The admission representative would be seen as an emissary. Similarly, the admission conference hosted by colleges for high school counselors would offer more meaningful information and better service to students if deliberations on admission decisions became a major part of the conference. Certainly, more administrators, counselors, and teachers would attend the meetings.

Other convenient opportunities for interaction occur when school counselors and admissions officers gather at local, state, and national conventions. The annual convention of the National Association of College Admissions Counselors, for example, features a school-college information exchange where participating college representatives set up tables and answer questions posed by school counselors. The site could easily accommodate meetings between counselors and admissions officers to make admission decisions. The annual national meeting of the Chicago Entrance Examination Board in New York also affords an occasion for new, meaningful school and college interaction, and the same is true for the many regional College Board meetings.

Were such forms of interaction accepted nationwide, participation by the College Entrance Examination Board and the American College Testing Program would be stimulated. Both organizations already report many useful findings to schools, and both have data systems with the flexibility to incorporate new material.

Many examples could be presented to make the point that innovation in academic practices at the secondary level does not injure articulation. A few traditionalists at high schools and colleges view changes at the other level as destructive to good transition because any change upsets the status quo, which has been achieved with difficulty. Such a negative attitude offers little hope for dynamic homeostasis in school and college relations. Educational policies and practices must continually adjust to changing student needs regardless of administrative inconveniences.

Important for articulation is the pliancy built into the school and college relationship that allows for changing policies and practices. Receptiveness to change and a belief in the importance of articulation generally lead to academically sounder and more efficient procedures, as should be the case for college responses to individually prescribed high school programs, variable unit credit, and the selective or even wholesale discontinuance of scholastic rankings by high schools. While high school performance and tests in general retain their predictive validity, new approaches to the current needs of admissions policy are now being encouraged. The clearest call for reevaluation of criteria is heard in the Carnegie Commission's report on higher education and the schools, *Continuity and Discontinuity*. The report questions the appropriateness of traditional tests for women and minorities and points to the decreasing significance of class rankings because of changing grading practices and increasingly diverse secondary and higher educational curricula. The commission does not presume to have the solution, but its recommendation expresses the belief that answers can be found:

> Experimentation with college admission practices should be encouraged, In particular, more experimentation is needed to determine the quality of testing as a basis for admission and placement, the importance of student motivation and life experience as indicators of promise. . . .[25]

The recommendation suggests that colleges should not be rigidly wedded to the best criteria of past and stabler times. The report goes on to challenge the notion that predicting success should be the major goal of admission policy. The answers appropriate to such questions are just beginning to be debated. If there is one fruitful avenue for developing admission policies that keep pace with current changes on the secondary level, it surely lies in the articulation process.

Orientation

Examining admission procedures at public urban colleges, a doctoral study recently found that admissions staffs do little to promote good orientation and extracurricular adjustment to college in contrast to the time and effort spent on academic areas.[26] In another study, students ranked the ten major obstacles in moving from school to college. Three of the ten were not scholastic concerns: participating in social affairs, overcoming the fear of college instilled by parents and teachers, and

25. Carnegie Commission on Higher Education, *Continuity and Discontinuity* (New York: McGraw-Hill Book Co., 1973), p. 52.
26. David E. Hooten to Julius Menacker, October 1970, summary of data collected by questionnaire for "The Admissions Function in Public, Urban Colleges and Universities" (Ph.D. diss., Rochester Institute of Technology, 1970).

understanding the organization of a university (course numbering, departmentalization, and so forth). Another four, while academically related, touched upon general orientation to freshman behavior: developing good study habits, studying for understanding instead of memorization, adjusting to accelerated classes and greater competition, and learning how to take notes on lectures.[27] In a third study, college freshmen commented on their major adjustment problems. The three most frequently cited problems—handling the work load, understanding new teaching methods, and assuming greater independence—reveal a need for better orientation. The freshmen attributed low grades to poor self-discipline, poor time budgeting, and extracurricular distractions.[28]

The research suggests a need for articulation designed to help high school students cope with college life. Student personnel officers charged with college counseling and orientation bear most of the responsibility for such a program, but much can be accomplished through articulation channels, depending on the demographic characteristics of the prospective students. For example, all colleges, whether they enroll students from just the local area or from across the nation, can correspond with new entrants before they arrive on campus. Besides explaining policies and procedures related to freshman academic and social life, letters should help students and parents to identify with the college in order to dispel any unfounded fears. Brochures might familiarize prospective students with the services and even the atmosphere on campus.

At the University of Illinois at Chicago Circle, the need for giving prospective students more information and a feel for college life led to the development of a series of informal letters from a variety of faculty and staff persons. The following letter was designed to give future students an idea of how professors view them and their new college milieu:

Dear 348-46-2938:
 When—and if—computers take over our lives completely, when—and if—Orwell's *1984* becomes a reality,

27. Raymond B. Fox, "Improving Relations between High Schools and Colleges," *Clearing House,* February 1962, p. 326.
28. Julius Menacker, "Chicago Circle Students Evaluation of Their Transition from High School to College," mimeographed (Chicago: University of Illinois at Chicago Circle, Office of Admissions and Records, 1968), p. 17.

this is the way you might be addressed. And then our human relationships with the young people on our campus might become—as someone has already said of one of the nation's leading multiversities—"remote, fugitive, and vaguely sullen."

Not yet, though. And not for you. Nonetheless, our best intentions will not prevent you from feeling somewhat alone, like a visitor to a vaguely alien land, during your first few days at Chicago Circle—alone in the presence of fourteen thousand young people more or less your own age and from a background similar to yours.

Actually, you won't be alone in your newness on this campus. A good one-third of your fellow students will likewise be "new" here—getting acquainted with the school, its programs, its teachers, and its students, just as you are.

Nearly half of them will be from Chicago public high schools, about a quarter from parochial schools, another quarter from the suburbs. But nearly four hundred will be "foreign" students—from Iran and Iraq, from Hong Kong and Seoul, from Canada and Turkey, Greece and other nations.

After surviving the grind of advisement and registration, six thousand students just like you will be worrying about their new courses. They'll be looking for their lockers, for the bookstore, for the library. They will be wondering where they will eat, where their teachers have their offices, where their next classes are, whether they will *ever* feel at home here.

Six thousand "new" students like yourself will be riding the escalator at Chicago Circle Center to the Pier Room on the second floor. They will look for—and not always find—a familiar face at one of the tables. Like you, they may feel uncomfortable alone in a crowd where everyone seems to know everyone else. Everyone, that is, except you.

So what do you do to break through, to know your fellow students and to be known by them?

Informal ways are perhaps the best. How about saying "Hello" to the one next to you in French on Tuesday? Or asking what high school or college he came from, or what's his next class? If he or she has transferred from a junior college, you may be talking with another Arthur Goldberg or a future Gwendolyn Brooks, both of whom were junior college products. Pick out someone who is sitting alone in the Pier Room and ask if you can share a table. And then gripe about the noise, the food, the courses you're taking, or the teachers. You're sure to find a common complaint in one of these.

Talk to the person at the locker next to yours, to the girl waiting outside class for the bell to ring, to the one who sits next to you in the library. It's one chance in three they will all be new students, too, and just as anxious as you are to break the ice and get acquainted.

In another of these letters you'll learn about the opportunities to join a club, go to a mixer, attend a lecture, sign up for a committee, get a job on the newspaper, sing in the choir, play on a team, or become active in student government affairs. There will be opportunities for you to bowl, swim, or just sit in the Excedra until someone comes along.

Don't be pushy, but don't be too reserved, either. And in two or three weeks you'll be eating with one bunch, riding to and from school with another, doing laboratory experiments with a third.

One thing more. You'll probably find the work different here—perhaps a little harder, more demanding. But your first quarter will be the hardest—and it's over in eleven short weeks, including final examinations.

Keep your work up to date, do your assignments on time, and before you know it, it will be early December. You'll know fifty fellow students by name, recognize the faces of at least a hundred more. You'll be able to walk blindfolded from Taft to Grant, to Jefferson, to LC A6. And you'll wonder how you ever could have felt strange here. Honest.[29]

The letter for new freshmen focuses on experiencing college life, while other letters concern student services, academic policy, and other formalized topics. In all cases, letters are drafted from the recommendations of the college staff, high school counselors, prospective freshmen, and enrolled students. The college staff, lacking omniscience, could not hope to discern all of the general freshman concerns without the help of those people closest to the new enrollees.

In our multimedia environment, preenrollment orientation for colleges with localized population can be promoted by closed-circuit television. A typical program might film a college classroom in action, the activity of a study skills development group, or any number of endeavors or services. Similar orientation programs could also be

29. Sent to entering freshmen in Spring 1969 by the Office of Admissions and Records, ed. Willis C. Jackman, Acting Associate Dean, College of Liberal Arts, University of Illinois at Chicago Circle. Used by permission.

presented on local radio stations. New forms of film packaging and projection make it feasible for distant colleges to mail high quality audio-visual messages. For the less affluent college, the cassette is an excellent supplement to personal visits. Mailed alone, the cassette can augment printed matter or a classroom discussion or a pertinent advising session. Even a recording of a semi-structured student rap session would be a stimulating supplement for college representatives and high school counselors.

The college drawing from a limited local area ought to arrange for students to visit their former high schools to meet those seniors who will attend the college; a reverse visit can then be arranged to bring high school students onto the college grounds. The meetings should be informal, unstructured conversations without any prepared agenda. Colleges drawing from distant areas can develop material for discussions about the college led by high school counselors; an even better approach is the utilization of recent college alumni living in areas that have future students. Local alumni of distant schools can visit with neighborhood students in much the same way as enrolled students from local colleges meet future college classmates at the high school.

While the college with a nationwide student body cannot hope to have many applicants observe its classes, college and high school representatives can point to local institutions with similar student bodies and atmospheres for students to visit. Students can better imagine the college environment and can experience limited reality testing. In all cases, colleges can provide future students with sample course outlines, reading lists, descriptions of student services, and the like which will give students a better feel for the nature of college life.

As with so many other areas of articulation, good school and college interaction concerning orientation will improve policies and procedures at both levels. The interaction of personnel on the two levels, students, parents, and teachers will help identify and solve nonscholastic articulation problems which few could verify and none could solve independently.

three

From Two- to Four-Year Colleges

The higher proportion of freshmen now enrolled in two-year colleges attests to the success of the world's most dramatic and successful experiment in higher education. The community college has provided access to a variety of postsecondary educational programs for hundreds of thousands of students who would not have otherwise had the opportunity for advanced education. Many would have been excluded from the traditional four-year institutions because of inadequate high school records or test scores, financial limitations, the need to stay near home, and a plethora of other reasons. The vast pool of new college students—far more heterogeneous in ability and interests than any previous group—has added a whole new dimension to educational articulation in the past two decades.

Transfer among colleges became popular during the 1960s. Senior institutions then began to give serious attention to junior-senior college articulation. In general, the senior college admissions officers saw five recurrent problem areas. First, few data were available to determine the proper grade point average for transfer admission. Second, the rapid emergence of new community colleges that had not been accredited presented a problem of how much of which credit should transfer under what conditions. Third, variations in university departmental requirements complicated the establishment of uniform credits for studies involving skills and specific knowledge. Transfer raised a fourth issue concerning how much credit a university should honor from a two-year college: Should there be an arbitrary limit, or should any number of credit hours be accepted? What role, if any, should the associate degree play? Fifth, community college experimentation in programs and courses, while commendable, caused difficulties for senior institutions in establishing equivalencies and course placement. Also, few guidance data accompanied the community college transfer as compared to the beginning freshman, and many transfer students lacked defined educational goals even after two years at the community college.[1]

Leland Medsker, speaking about the nineteenth annual conference of the American Association for Higher Education, put the problems involved in the junior-senior articulation into four categories: the student: his academic goals in relation to the academic and economic resources available to him; the curriculum: guidelines for accepting transfer credit and degree requirements and coordination of teaching methods, materials, and examinations; student personnel services: development of financial aid and transfer orientation programs and exchange of information to improve counseling at both levels; facilities and resources: establishment of enrollment quotas and priorities, methods for diverting students to junior colleges, differentiation in specialized programs offered by two- and four-year colleges, shared use of facilities, and coordination of calendars.[2]

As the decade of the 1970s opened, Kintzer claimed that the heart of the articulation process lay in three major activities: admissions evaluation of transfer courses and grades; curriculum planning, advising, counseling, and other student services; articulation programs that include types of representation, machinery, procedures, and communication between institutions.[3]

Some issues have been ameliorated considerably during the past few years. The remaining issues, with varying levels of severity, still concern the states with significant community college programs. One pervasive problem of junior-senior college articulation is the attitude of professionals at both levels. As Edmund J. Gleazer stated, "Articulation is both a process and an attitude, and . . . attitude is the more important of the two, for without it there can be no workable

1. Charles W. Sanford, "The Transfer Student," mimeographed (Urbana: University of Illinois, Office of Admissions and Records, 1961), pp. 1-8.

2. Leland L. Medsker, "Problems of Articulation" (Paper delivered at the Illinois Conference on Higher Education, Allerton Park, Monticello, Ill., Nov. 5, 1964), pp. 3-4.

3. Frederick C. Kintzer, *Nationwide Pilot Study on Articulation* (Los Angeles: University of California, ERIC Clearinghouse for Junior Colleges, 1970), p. 2.

process." [4] While criticism has been primarily directed to senior college personnel, community college professionals must increasingly share the blame for counterproductive attitudes. In the early years of the junior college movement, the senior institutions richly deserved the one-sided criticism for resisting policy change in accordance with the needs of transfer students. Community college students and faculty were greeted with suspicion and derision.

Now that community colleges have become firmly established in higher education, the two-year institutions are as prone to narrow, selfish attitudes as were their senior college counterparts. The literature has not yet caught up with this fact except in a few rare instances. Raymond E. Schultz, writing in the *Virginia Journal of Education,* criticized junior college articulation practices for lacking the sensitivity to channel students with lower abilities into technical-vocational programs better suited to their potential than college transfer programs, for maintaining a double standard—one for transfer students and one for terminal students—and for ignoring the policies and programs of senior institutions. [5]

Part of the problem with interpersonal relationships stems from the ambiguous role of junior college faculty. Only a very few of the newest faculty members specifically planned careers as junior college teachers or administrators. Most came to their jobs from high school career positions, and others came because they could not teach in a four-year college without completing the doctoral degree. Still others had found reduced openings in senior institutions for teachers with their doctorates. The mixture of the two groups produces an unusual combination of contradictory feelings that militate against positive attitudes toward four-year college personnel. The university professor is viewed by some junior college faculty members as remote and unconcerned with students and by others with feelings of inferiority or envy. While community college personnel who conform to such generalized attitudes are a distinct minority, there are enough of them to make articulation more difficult. Exacerbating the problem are some senior

4. Edmund J. Gleazer, Jr., "Recognizing the Expanding Role of Junior Colleges in Higher Education," *College Admission Policies for the 1970s* (New York: College Entrance Examination Board, 1968), p. 80.
5. Raymond E. Schultz, "Articulation in Undergraduate Higher Education," *Virginia Journal of Education,* September 1969, pp. 16-17.

college professors who see junior college teachers as imposters demeaning the title of professor.

Both groups contain persons who fear that their counterparts are intent on wresting influence and control from them. Such fears materialize as threats by community colleges and as attempts by senior college personnel to restrict transfer credit or subject it to degrading forms of scrutiny. Senior college restrictions invite junior college reprisals whereby students are directed away from the offending university to other institutions (usually unnamed) which are said to be more accommodating. In such machinations students become pawns in the struggle. The approach cannot help the community college or their students and further divorces college personnel from the community college's point of view. Bulldozer tactics should be anathema to articulation personnel and administrators: They only work when the facts are so clear that a gentler approach would have produced the same results and brought more wholesome future relations.

The critical need for collaboration between junior and senior colleges has often led state agencies to take a hand in compelling cooperation and orderly transition processes. Good articulation, however, results from mutual concern for students making the transition rather than institutional prerogatives. To illustrate the manner in which several of the identified issues of junior-senior college articulation affect the student, the case study of Betty Jones presents many of the complexities of the process.

Betty Jones: A Case Study

When Betty met with her counselor at the end of her junior year in high school, she knew that she ranked in the lower half of the junior class and that her board scores were lower than those of most of her friends. She hoped that she would be eligible for the state university or one of the popular liberal arts colleges in neighboring states, although she would need financial aid to attend the private liberal arts college she preferred. Her worst fears were realized when the counselor informed her that she was ineligible for either institution because of her low class rank and test scores.

The counselor suggested that Betty start at the local community college, an inexpensive institution which would accept her. Apparently considering the prospect humiliating, she refused to consider the community college, insisting instead that the counselor tell her about several private colleges and distant public institutions which might accept her. She also asked for and received advice on making a special appeal for admission to the state university.

By the second month of her senior year, Betty was convinced that she could not afford the private, out-of-state college to which she was admissible. She called on the person at the state university to whom she had been directed by her counselor and discussed exceptions to the institution's admissions policy. During her interview, the university admission counselor told her that she had little chance for special admission. He, too, encouraged her to enroll at the community college. Her counselor had recently shown her the performance records of previous graduates of her high school, many of whom had lower ranks and test scores than she; they had gone from high school to the community college and were now successfully enrolled at the state university. Betty was now more receptive to the idea of entering the two-year institution, but she was still hesitant.

Learning that her field of interest was sociology, the counselor showed Betty a curriculum guide that had been jointly prepared and approved by community college and university officials. The guide clearly indicated how she could parallel the progress of a university student in the lower division who was pursuing a sociology degree. According to the document, she would have the same protection against changes in degree requirements that the native university student enjoyed, that is, both students would have the option of electing the old or new requirements. Once she completed at least one year's work at the junior college, her admission to the state university would be based solely on her college record, not on high school grades or test scores. If she had a cumulative C average on enough junior college hours, she would be admissible. The counselor, however, recommended that she complete two full years before transfer and that she closely follow the courses recommended in the curriculum guide.

Betty enrolled at the community college after graduation and carefully followed her curriculum guide in planning her first term courses. Chance acquaintances in her social science survey course, however, interested her in the police science program. She talked to her community college counselor about police science and decided that this two-year career program offered more excitement and direction for her than the four-year sociology plan, especially since the police science program included some sociology courses and led into a specific professional field.

By the time Betty enrolled for her final semester, a new goal had emerged for her. The college transfer counselor had spoken to one of her police science classes about a new state university program, discussed at a recent articulation conference at the university. Administration of Criminal Justice was now a four-year degree program with the same basic objectives on a higher level as the community college police science program. Betty had the opportunity to combine her original desire for a liberal arts degree with her career choice and, in fact, to have better career preparation than the community college program could offer.

The new plan raised a serious concern for Betty. Not having planned her program for transfer, would she lose course credit when she entered the university? She asked the transfer counselor who offered to use her as a test case to establish guidelines of transfer credit and program integration for the new area.

The counselor arranged an informal conference through his university articulation contact on the matter. Participants were the university's director of community college articulation, the head of its criminal justice department, an associate dean of the liberal arts and sciences college (since criminal justice was attached to that college), the head of the community college police science program, the community college transfer counselor, and the community college dean of transfer programs. It soon became clear that the main point of contention would be the application of community college police science courses toward the major requirements in criminal justice. The two department chairmen were diametrically opposed on this issue. The community college head insisted that all his courses count as degree credit for the major, while the university head considered none of the courses applicable as major credit. The dean suggested a general compromise, such as giving elective credit for the community college police science courses, but the community college transfer dean and counselor and the university articulation director pushed for closer review of each junior college course so that at least some would count for degree credit. The three finally proposed a second meeting at which course outlines, instructors' qualifications, and other matters would be discussed.

At the next meeting, the community college people showed that another four-year college with a similar program in police science had already agreed to accept six of the eight police science courses for credit toward the major. Spokesmen verified that the community college instructors, while less qualified academically than their university counterparts, were far more experienced as professionals in their teaching field. The university department head countered by saying that his program emphasized broad theory rather than personal experiences. The transfer dean and articulation director moved the discussion to a comparison of the professional courses. Three of the community college courses were soon approved as equivalent, but a problem developed on the fourth course. Although similar topics and texts were taught at both institutions, the university course required senior standing and two specific upper level sociology courses as prerequisites. The university head insisted that the products of the courses could not be comparable regardless of the material in the two syllabi.

A compromise was reached whereby transfer students would receive credit only if they could pass a university examination on the course material. If the student failed the proficiency examination, the course would transfer as elective credit. Two other courses were also judged appropriate for elective credit, and the remaining two were considered too biased toward technical procedures for the more theoretical base of the university program.

It was at this point that the associate dean dropped a bombshell. He claimed that none of the community college courses should transfer because they were part of a technical-vocational career program that was independent of the college transfer program. The community college itself had made the distinction, and it should not now distort the intent of its own institutional program with improper use; to do so would make the program neither fish nor fowl and dilute its quality and usefulness for students. To the associate dean, the issue was clear: The university would accept college transfer courses but not "career" courses, which were based on an entirely different set of presumptions.

The university department head was quick to accept the dean's line of reasoning, but the articulation director and community college personnel raised strong objections. They argued that the courses should be used for whatever benefits students could derive, regardless of the program type. The university representatives countered by asking why, then, did the community college bother to distinguish between transfer program and "terminal" career programs? The response was that distinctions were necessary for guidance purposes and state regulations that required a balance between college transfer and career programs. However, areas could overlap, and a student with appropriate college transfer experiences should not be penalized because of a program label.

The liberal arts dean asked the articulation director if university policy did not forbid accepting credits from terminal programs. The director said it did, but he argued that students with courses of an ambiguous classification should not suffer from an arbitrary either-or policy. The case of Betty Jones, he pointed out, was exactly the instance for which the university's discretionary policy was designed. The college dean backed down, and a curriculum guide was drawn up and signed by university and community college representatives, formalizing the credit transfer agreement and providing guidelines for police science students who might wish to transfer to the Administration of Criminal Justice program.

Betty was advised of the transferability of her courses, and she applied to the university with a scholastic average that was well above C. She anxiously awaited a positive response, but transfer applications were considered after all freshman cases, and Betty did not receive her admission confirmation until early August.

Betty was introduced to university life at an orientation program that she considered unsatisfactory, dominated as it was by freshmen interests. Discussions of college scholastic regulations, the meaning of "credit hours," a lesson on taking lecture notes, and the like were not very valuable; she was more interested in information about major requirements, elective options in the upper division, and job placement services.

Betty's experiences with advisors and registration were similarly disappointing. Whereas freshmen were given literature and knowledgeable faculty advisors to guide them in program selection, she had neither. She finally completed her program request form only to find that two of her courses were already closed. Spaces were available in the freshman courses, but she needed upper level courses. She ended up with a reduced program load.

During Betty's first week of classes, she went to the liberal arts and sciences college office to plan the balance of her degree program and learned that she had not been allowed general education credit for her physical science survey course. The university's general education requirement in physical sciences required specific courses in chemistry, physics, geology, astronomy, or mathematics. Betty contacted the transfer counselor at the community college who, in turn, contacted the articulation director. The articulation director said that credit for the science survey course should have been allowed, since the more restrictive policy cited by the college office had been abandoned to accommodate the numerous community college transfers now enrolling at the university. The director checked with the liberal arts office and found that one of the credentials analysts had lapsed into the old policy by error. The mistake was corrected.

Betty next saw her community college counselor when she was a senior about to graduate. The occasion was an articulation conference sponsored by the university for the purpose of bringing together community college counselors and their former clients who were then attending the university. She was pleased by the counselor's interest when he inquired about any transfer problems that his former students were having at the university, and she was glad to report that she had none.

Case study analysis

Betty's case is similar to that of many students without clear goals who choose the community college as a second choice. She coped well with the intra- and interorganizational college structures because adequate guidance and articulation systems were available to help her. Although she did have problems, she was able to find reasonably satisfactory transitional service because both the community college and the state university were cognizant of the need for articulation and were staffed to offer it. The case illustrates how the explosive growth of community colleges has left both two-year and four-year colleges without the fully developed policies and programs needed for masses of transfer students. The deficiency in this case was balanced by the cooperation of articulators at the two levels.

Fortunately for Betty, an information feedback system was operational when she made her college plans. Knowledge that many scholastically able high school graduates chose the community college helped reduce Betty's prejudice against the school and encouraged her to view the community college as a step along the road to a university degree. Equally important, her first opinion of community colleges was corrected with solid evidence and guidance from the curriculum guide and reports of transfer performance.

When she changed programs at the community college, Betty was in step with many of her peers. Indeed, one of the traditional purposes of the community college has been to allow students to experiment in subjects and programs. At this point Betty ran afoul of one of the major impediments to smooth junior-senior college transition—the distinction between the self-contained career program and the college transfer program. While the distinction serves the diverse needs of student and community college goals, it creates transfer problems for students moving from one program to the other. Only the timely intervention of articulation personnel and other professions at both levels enabled Betty's changes in program and plans to culminate successfully. However, students who change goals as well as programs encounter more serious problems that lead to an almost inevitable loss of credit.

After transfer to the university, Betty met with some of the typical problems that assail students transferring to large universities where student personnel and academic programs are geared to the more sizeable and traditional freshman class. Her problems show the slowness with which four-year colleges have adapted to the needs of the community college transfer and highlight the need for continuing contact between junior and senior college personnel even after the transfer of students.

The rapid growth of community college programs makes collaboration between the two levels essential. There is a need not only for long-range procedures but also for ad hoc decisions as unanticipated articulation problems appear. The commitment of the community college to maintain an administrative and programmatic flexibility that will allow for continual adaptation to student needs, regardless of precedent, demands an unusual amount of attention to coordination. When such a stance is contrasted with the typically very conservative, slow-moving character of the university, the problem of integrating policies, programs, and procedures between the two becomes apparent.

Currently three of the major categories of articulation concerns existing between junior and senior colleges are problems related to admission, curriculum integration, and student orientation.

Admission

When broad samples of community college freshmen are compared to freshmen at four-year colleges, the four-year students score higher on measures of scholastic ability. One study that used a large national sample found four-year freshmen earning American College Test composite scores that averaged two-and-a-half standard scores higher than those earned by junior college freshmen (20.5–18.0). The high school grade averages of four-year freshmen also exceeded their community college counterparts by .33 of a grade point (2.65–2.32).[6] However, the differences are not nearly as great as they once were. In Illinois, for example, only 6 percent of community college freshmen had graduated in the top quarter of their high school class in 1968; by 1970, the percentage of community college students coming from the upper quarter of high school classes had risen to 17.4 percent.[7] The quality gap continues to close as state higher education master plans restrict the number of freshmen entering public four-year institutions and expand the junior college systems.

Although the gap is narrowing, old prejudices remain among some faculty and administrators at senior colleges who remember the great qualitative differences that once existed. Such thinking is presently reinforced by transfer students from the lower range of the total community college ability group, which is and will remain quite broad. Some universities exhibit their distrust of the community college product by insisting that applicants either meet certain minimum high school admission criteria or present a higher scholastic transfer average than is necessary for native students in good standing. Other institutions simply require the higher average as standard policy. For

6. *The Two-Year College and Its Students* (Iowa City: American College Testing Program, 1969), pp. 111-12.

7. Illinois Junior College Board, *Report of Selected Data and Characteristics of Illinois Public Junior Colleges, 1970-71* (Springfield: Illinois Junior College Board, 1971), table 14.

example, a survey of northeastern colleges and universities revealed that about 20 percent still require a higher average for transfer students than for students in good standing in their institutions.[8] Yet the overwhelming majority of institutions participating in the survey acknowledged the good potential and performance of their junior college transfers. Many even reported "a high rate of persistence toward a degree, a low attrition rate, confidence of a probability of success equal to the native student, and a low incidence of academic failure."[9]

The well-known Knoell and Medsker study found similarly encouraging indications of successful performance among junior college transfers in ten states during the 1960s.[10] According to the study, transfers experienced a grade average drop in the first term after transfer but recovered in successive terms, and the majority eventually approached their pretransfer averages. Yet—the Knoell-Medsker finding having been repeatedly corroborated [11]—some four-year institutions still require more than a minimum scholastic average or still use high school records and tests, even though all the evidence points to the conclusion that college performance is the best predictor of future college performance.

A related problem is admission policy for students whose records contain a preponderance of terminal credit as opposed to transfer credit. Some institutions count all college work in determining the transfer average regardless of the transferability of particular courses, while others do not consider terminal courses for any purpose, including the admission average. If the purpose of admission requirements is to predict the potential performance of applicants, then a previous example from high school articulation is instructive. The Eight Year Study proved that the quality of performance in any high school subject was a better predictor of performance than the par-

8. Victor P. Meskill, "Transfer Student Performance and Admissions Policies and Practices for Transfers," *National ACAC Journal,* July 1971, p. 24.

9. Ibid.

10. Dorothy M. Knoell and Leland L. Medsker, *From Junior to Senior College: A National Study of the Transfer Student* (Washington: American Council on Education, 1965).

11. John R. Hills, "Transfer Shock: The Academic Performance of the Junior College Transfer," *Journal of Experimental Education,* March 1965; Earl S. Elliot, "The Academic Achievement of Transfer Students and the College Comprehensive Tests," *Journal of College Student Personnel,* May 1972.

ticular courses taken. The same principle applies to junior college students moving to the senior institution.

Far more common is the problem of four-year institutions attaching less importance to the recruitment and admission of transfers than to the enrollment of beginning freshmen. Inferior status is expressed by the paucity of catalog information for transfers and the absence of literature about specialized policies and procedures. The situation has been documented by Willingham, who found that five out of six of the 146 colleges and universities he studied had no special literature for transfers.[12] Furthermore, freshmen commonly were accepted for admission, advised, and registered before transfer students as a matter of policy. Willingham has reported that only about 25 percent of colleges encourage transfers in publications or visit junior colleges to talk with prospective transfers.[13]

Data on financial aid are similarly distressing. Almost half of Willingham's sample of colleges and universities reported that aid requests from transfer applicants exceeded institutional resources, and less than 20 percent of the institutions had set aside any aid specifically for transfers. The colleges' priorities were strikingly revealed by Willingham's finding that 33 percent of all new freshmen received aid, compared to only 14 percent of transfers.[14]

It seems clear that many senior institutions still harbor a general prejudice against the community college transfer regardless of the data on transfer performance. With all the problems of admission policy, a policy is now emerging at many community colleges to exclude failing grades from their evaluation systems. Community colleges have adopted the philosophy that their primary mission is to help students progress in higher education and that dismissing them for academic failure hampers this objective. Consequently, the institutions have developed a policy which provides for a student to receive an X grade or an *incomplete* in courses which otherwise would have been failed. Students are asked to finish the requirements of the course according to a number of options, at which time the X is replaced by a standard

12. Warren W. Willingham and Norhan Findikyan, *Patterns of Admission for Transfer Students* (New York: College Entrance Examination Board, 1969), p. 25.
13. Ibid., p. 9.
14. Ibid., p. 26.

grade symbol of A, B, C, or D. There is generally no time limit imposed, and receipt of an X does not prejudice opportunities to earn an eventual A. Wary of the attitudes of senior college admissions officers, some junior colleges will not even show the X on a transcript sent to a senior institution; when course requirements are satisfactorily completed, a supplementary transcript is sent. Some community colleges even maintain two transcripts, one for export, the other for internal use.

Here is an example of the need for good communication and understanding between the two levels. Each holds to an academic philosophy that contrasts sharply with the other. The senior institution believes in the necessity of evaluative criteria to separate the wheat from the chaff, thereby assuring that their degree will vouch for a relatively uniform quality of student performance. Junior colleges, on the other hand, are more concerned with serving the needs of the individual student, and they completely reject the function of arbiter in the survival of the fittest.

There are certainly elements of wisdom and merit in both positions. The question is how do officials at the two levels resolve the conflicts in the best interest of students moving from one level to the other? In 1966, a joint committee on junior and senior colleges, comprised of members from the Association of American Colleges, the American Association of Junior Colleges, and the American Association of Collegiate Registrars and Admissions Officers, published a set of guidelines for junior-senior college relations that offered the following recommendations for improving articulation through admission practices:

> 1. Public four-year colleges and universities should adopt an over-all C average as the standard for admission from junior college, provided they can accommodate all applicants who are thus qualified. At the same time:
>
>> (a) Efforts should be greatly intensified to counsel students, who qualify but who have a relatively poor chance for success in some institutions or in some programs, toward appropriate institutional and career choices.
>>
>> (b) If facilities are limited and if quotas for new transfer students are established, priority should be given to the applicants who have the highest proba-

bility of academic success after transfer. Except for a few specialized programs, junior college students should be strongly encouraged to complete all of their lower division work before transfer since their probability of subsequent success is thereby improved.

2. Performance in a junior college transfer program is the best single predictor of success in a four-year institution and therefore should count most heavily in the admission decision.

(a) Junior college students who were ineligible to enter a four-year institution at the freshman level because of poor high school records should not be denied admission as transfer students on these grounds. However, as a condition for transfer, they may be expected to make up deficiencies, earn a grade point average in junior college which is above the minimum required for graduation, or both.

(b) Aptitude and achievement tests scores may be useful to counselors as supplementary information in assisting junior college students to make wise decisions about transfer. However, applicants who qualify for transfer on the basis of their grades in junior college should not be denied admission because of test scores.

3. Admission standards should be stated in such a way that junior college students may know at any time whether they will be eligible to transfer when they complete their lower division program, i.e., standards should be clear and objective.

(a) A specific minimum grade point average for transfer should be stated by the receiving institution, as well as any subject matter and unit requirements which must be met in order to transfer with upper division standing.

(b) Junior college students should be strongly encouraged to complete their lower division programs before transfer. However, the requirements of an associate degree as a condition for transfer appears to unduly restrict the mobility of good students between the two types of colleges.

4. (a) Grade point differentials for pairs of junior and senior colleges, and for native and transfer students at various levels, may serve a useful information function. However, they should not be used as a basis for raising grading or admission standards, unless there is other evidence to show that standards are inappropriate, e.g., a very high rate of attrition after transfer.

(b) Recommendations from junior college deans or counselors should be determinative only in non-routine cases, e.g., applicants who barely meet minimum admission standards for transfer. However, more effective means should be found for transmitting information about transfer students who are capable of honors work, independent study, or leadership roles.

(c) In order to receive equitable treatment in competing for housing, financial assistance, and the like, transfer students should be tentatively admitted no later than the beginning of their last term prior to transfer.

5. Transfer applicants from *new* junior colleges should be admitted on the same basis as applicants from regionally accredited colleges, until such time as regular accreditation is appropriate. If accreditation is then denied, or granted and later withdrawn, admission should be on the basis of the particular merits of individual applicants.[15]

The guidelines do not give easy answers to all problems of junior-senior college admission, however, they do provide an excellent framework on which additional policies and procedures can be developed. Four-year colleges must examine admission policies and practices in light of their support for institutional goals and clientele. Two-year colleges must examine their academic policies in light of the suitability for the various needs of their students. Difficult conflicts arise because of the clash between the goals of two-year colleges and those of the senior institutions to which many students aspire. The best resolutions will come from the freest, most open dialogue between people at the two levels.

Curricular Integration

The most serious current impediment to the efficient, forward progress of junior college transfers is the integration of two-year programs with the four-year counterpart and, specifically, the transferability of credit from one level to another. As in many other areas of articulation, the controversy is fraught with inconsistency and even hypocrisy as may

15. Joint Committee on Junior and Senior Colleges of the Association of American Colleges, American Association of Junior Colleges, and American Association of Collegiate Registrars and Admissions Officers, *Guidelines for Improving Articulation between Junior and Senior Colleges* (Washington: American Council on Education, 1966), p. 64.

be seen in the transfer policy on D grades. Many four-year colleges will not accept D grades for transfer even though the D's earned by native students count toward graduation. The policy is permitted even though the two-year college has been approved by the same accrediting body as the senior college.

What sort of logic can support the practice? If junior college D's equate to senior college F's, then junior college C's should be counted as D's at the receiving institution, and so forth. Grade values are not exchanged like currency because of the virtual impossibility of controlling grading practices within institutions. The policy converts the junior college instructor's lowest passing grade to a failing grade for the transfer student in terms of future usefulness of the course credit. Such a discriminatory my-course-is-better-than-your-course practice should be stopped. Grades earned at one accredited institution should serve as valid currency at another. Interestingly, senior institutions are not the only ones who subscribe to the pattern. At least one public community college known to the author requires a sufficiently high grade point average before transfer grades of D will be accepted toward the associate degree. Yet, the institution complains as loudly as any when their D's are rejected by the minority of colleges subscribing to the practice.

States where some colleges and universities are reported to have policies that either reject D grades or qualify their acceptance are Alabama, Alaska, Arizona, Delaware, Georgia, Maine, Maryland, Massachusetts, Missouri, Nebraska, New Hampshire, New Jersey, North Carolina, Pennsylvania, Rhode Island, South Carolina, Utah, Vermont, and West Virginia.[16] Only Georgia, Missouri, North Carolina, and Pennsylvania, among nineteen states, can be considered to have important junior college movements; the inclusion of such states points out the negativism that is present in the area of course transferability.

A more important source of curricular inarticulation is simply a lack of coordinated information and effective student counseling on the part of responsible persons at both levels. This is one of the reasons why Knoell and Medsker found that over half of a large national sample of junior college students lost credit in transfer, and 8 percent

16. Kintzer, *Nationwide Pilot Study,* p. 2.

lost the equivalent of a full semester of college credit.[17] The causes for credit loss were, in order of importance, credit exceeding the maximum allowed to community college transfers, poor grades, and courses considered below the collegiate level.[18] Willingham and Findikyan studied the same problem five years after Knoell and Medsker and found that 10 percent of two-year college transfers lost at least one semester of credit.[19] The latter study suggests that the problem had not improved during the five years from 1964 to 1969—a time of unprecedented expansion of community colleges. Willingham and Findikyan did not analyze the reasons for credit loss. They concluded that "transfer students are still losing a significant amount of credit" and speculated that "some colleges may use credit as a hedge in the case of marginal admission cases; thus, a doubtful case is admitted with some number of credits disallowed."[20]

One common general policy that affects credit transfer is the limitation of transfer credit to one-half of the total college credits needed for graduation. If the four-year college, for example, requires 120 semester hours for graduation, 60 hours will be accepted from the community college: Either the first 60 hours earned or the most useful 60 hours are counted. Clearly, the latter selection is the preferable policy, because it is based on a good concept of articulation—that policies regulating the transition of students from one level to another should be of maximum benefit to the student yet preserve institutional integrity and goals. It may seem reasonable that, by definition, students at a two-year college can obtain only two years of degree credit. However, if a student, by spending more than two years at college or by taking extra courses, transfers with more than 60 hours, he should not be penalized by arbitrarily limiting transfer courses to the first 60 hours taken.

It could even be argued that a student who had earned seventy or eighty useful hours should be able to apply all hours toward a baccalaureate degree. Why should credit be discarded if it has an equivalent in the four-year curriculum? Does such restrictiveness really

17. Dorothy M. Knoell and Leland L. Medsker, *Factors Affecting Performance of Transfer Students from Two- and Four-year Colleges* (Berkeley: University of California, Center for Study of Higher Education, 1964), p. 64.
18. Ibid., pp. 64.65.
19. Willingham and Findikyan, *Patterns*, p. 30.
20. Ibid., p. 17.

protect the integrity of the senior institution? There seems to be no limitation on the degree other than residency requirements for students graduating from one senior institution who have transferred from another. The main test for accepting credit should always be to provide the student with the most useful options. The American Council on Education *Guidelines for Improving Articulation between Junior and Senior Colleges* suggests:

> Ideally, no maximum should be placed on the amount of credit which may be transferred from junior college. Four-year institutions may protect the integrity of their degree by adopting an upper division residence requirement which the junior college student must meet after transfer. If some maximum is set:
> a) Junior college credit equal to approximately half the baccalaureate degree program should ordinarily be accepted in fulfillment of unit requirements for the degree. The amount of credit normally earned by native students in the various major fields during the first two years may serve as a guide in allowing transfer credit.
> b) Subject credit should be given for all junior college courses which satisfy baccalaureate degree requirements, irrespective of any restrictions on the amount of credit which may be transferred. However, students may be required to take additional electives or advanced courses in the upper division to satisfy unit requirements for the degree.[21]

Problems arise not only in implementing the recommendations literally but even in following their spirit. Many of the problems occur because of an unfortunate tendency to forget that the student is a complex being with diverse, changing, multiple goals, interests, strengths, and weaknesses. The more introspective and serious the potential transfer student, ironically, the more likely he is to encounter credit transfer problems. At issue frequently is the distinction between transfer and terminal courses. Most community colleges divide into the transfer program, designed for students who intend to transfer to a senior institution, and the career program, designed to prepare persons for direct entry into occupations. If all students were simple, robot-like persons, programmed at high school graduation to pursue one career path or another, and if guidance and counseling for higher education were much more expert, the dichotomy of transfer and terminal

21. Joint Committee on Junior and Senior Colleges, *Guidelines,* p. 9.

courses would not be a problem, for students would not change their minds or exhibit new abilities or enthusiasms. They do, however, and the problem exists.

As with many articulation problems, both levels share the responsibility for inarticulation. Some senior institutions tend to rely on neat, easily administered formulas for credit that approve transfer courses and reject terminal ones. Courses in a terminal police science program, the example used in this chapter's case study, illustrate the possible complications when individuals and academic usefulness of courses are considered. Another example can be found in engineering curricula. Many terminal programs include courses in drawing, physics, chemistry, and other areas that may be slanted differently from the usual university engineering course. Before disallowing such credit, a senior institution should examine the courses carefully to determine if the content will be of value to the student in further study. If so, the credit should be applied to the degree. Programs may be labeled as terminal, but courses never should be.

While the university is wrong to attempt to impose unrealistic dichotomies on junior college courses, the two-year college is wrong arbitrarily to label courses as terminal in order to disguise a skimpy supply of offerings in a particular field. Two-year colleges also often fail to guide students adequately toward the best type of program or the most advantageous changes. Finally, senior institutions often accuse junior colleges of lacking academic responsibility in specifying and advertising course prerequisites that are necessary for a "legitimate" transfer course. Indeed, it is on the basis of prerequisite specifications that many of the decisions to accept or reject ambiguous transfer courses are made.

A related problem is the lower division versus upper division label. Particular university departments are loath to equate a course from a junior college, defined by the university as lower division, with a course that the university has designed for the last two years or upper division. The four-year college takes the position that the university course is placed in the upper division because the course assumes certain experiences and prior information for maximum benefit. The community college retorts that their students have mastered the material without the preliminary experiences and should therefore receive the credit. A case in point would be education programs in which the educational psychology course is offered in the junior year after an introductory psychology course and an introductory education course. As with any course, the senior college faculty can bemoan the junior college teacher's lack of a doctorate and the sparse background of the student, both of which diminish the meaningfulness of the course and applicability of the learning. Yet, the hard fact is that the student has mastered the course material. Therefore, it should be considered as equivalent to the senior college's course. No system as yet exists for consistently and logically distinguishing between upper division and lower division courses. Some analysts contend that a certain maturity is necessary to profit from upper division courses, yet the average community college student is several years older than his university counterpart.

Certainly, if a course purports to be the same but is merely a shallow imitation of the four-year one, it should not be treated as equivalent. One way to determine correspondence is to look at the course prerequisites. For example, if a calculus course is taught without a mathematical prerequisite, one could reasonably question the authenticity of such a course's claim to baccalaureate credit. Similar tests could be applied to numerous science and mathematics courses beyond the introductory level.

While the method works reasonably well for the hard sciences, it loses value when applied to many courses in the social sciences, humanities, business, education, and many other areas less dependent on the mastery of sequential skills. As a result, senior people in such fields develop "obstacle courses" to preserve their specialties from the encroachments of the junior college. Contrived regulations of professional accrediting associations or institutions are developed for the purpose of arbitrarily excluding transfer credit.

This is not to say that all of the arguments for using community college courses to replace upper division courses are invalid except on the basis of course prerequisites. Higher education must shift the burden of proof from the community college to demonstrate the legitimacy for transfer of courses to the senior institution to deny the transfer of credit. Decisions should always be based on the merits of course usefulness for moving the transfer student toward his degree in the most educationally sound, expeditious way. One true story illustrates the point. A university was criticized for not accepting the introductory mathematics courses from its largest feeder community college, which had seven semiautonomous campuses. In fact, the courses in question were accepted from one of the branches but not from the other six. The executive secretary of the university mathematics' department explained that the courses were accepted from the one campus because the university people had confidence in the mathematics department head at that campus. He was surprised to learn that the subject of his trust had transferred to another community college campus two years ago and was presently heading a department whose courses were not transferable. The present mathematics chairman at the campus where credit was allowed was completely unknown to the university mathematics professors.

Another cause of curricular inarticulation is the propensity of academic personnel on both levels frequently to change course design, degree requirements, and similar aspects of the academic program. The changes are generally healthy in that student needs are continuously examined, and flexibility and innovation are encouraged. At the same time, curriculum adjustments cause great confusion for the community college student and his counselor who are concerned with fitting programs for transfer, and for the senior institution when analyzing the status of transfer courses and programs. An obvious remedy is proposed by *Guidelines:*

> Transfer students should be given the option of satisfying graduation requirements which were in effect in senior colleges at the time they enrolled as freshmen, subject to conditions or qualifications which apply to native students. The option should be stated explicity in the catalogue of the senior institution.
>
> Senior institutions should notify the junior colleges as early as possible of impending curriculum changes which may affect transfer students. Junior colleges should also advise the senior institutions of proposed changes in their transfer courses and programs. When a change made by the senior institution necessitates some type of change in the junior college, the latter institution should be given sufficient lead time to effect the change with a minimum of disruption.[22]

The guideline can be criticized for not going far enough in specifying the obligation of the community college. *Guidelines,* however,

22. Ibid., pp. 11-12.

was developed in the mid-1960s, when junior colleges were not yet at their present stage of power and influence. Since there are now ample signs that the two-year colleges have developed some of the same conservatism and rigidity as many senior colleges, the guideline should be extended to show the mutuality of responsibility and effort that must exist.

The best approach to problems of credit transfer is the critical path strategy, similar to that concept's use in physics and systems analysis. Programs and courses are designed by the community college for maximum utility, regradless of the eventual direction taken by the student. Thus, a student in a business career program, such as retailing or "mid-management," would have great flexibility in his marketing or management courses; through special projects and other course options, his experience might parallel the university course's specifications. Individualized symbols for academic bookkeeping could be easily devised to indicate the unique accomplishments of each student. Similarly, the four-year institution could make the best use of transfer credit by accepting first the most useful credit and then, moving down, the most favorable credits. Maximum use of transfer credit can be realized only if those responsible for granting credit make a conscious effort to ask the question, "How can this transfer course best help the student move forward to graduation?"

A long-standing issue in maximum use is the application of transfer courses to meet graduation requirements for a well-rounded education. Some senior institutions take the position that particular courses for general education cannot transfer for any number of narrow reasons. For example, the social science requirement might specify a choice of a three-course sequence in any one of the social science areas of psychology, history, or sociology; so a student with a two-course sequence in a social science survey and a third course in a specific social science finds himself lacking the requirement. Or the student presenting lecture courses in the natural sciences is told that only laboratory courses will satisfy that general education requirement.

Those refusing to use a broad definition of general education assume that their institution's general education requirements were established with specific purposes in mind that would be violated by loose applications of transfer credit. People convinced by such arguments are always quick to note that the course can be used as elective credit. But the critical path of the transfer credit has been obstructed with little reason. As was stated in the Harvard report on *General Education in a Free Society* general education must be defined "in the broad sense of completeness as a human being, rather than in the narrow sense of competence in a particular lot." [23] The committee identified three wide areas of learning that accomplished the goal—the humanities, the social sciences, and natural science and mathematics; it remains hard to delineate further the "right" specific experiences within each area. The Harvard committee noted even then that "many specialists . . . are ready to testify eloquently to the fact that their specialty . . . is, in and by itself, a liberal education." [24] The committee exhibited its own confusion by troubling over whether general education survey courses or special courses were best: "A general survey is apt to be a dreary and a sterile affair, leaving little residue in the minds of students. But we also wish to reiterate the principle that narrowly specialized courses which may be far more thorough do not provide the answer to the evident need for some approach . . . to the problems of a general education." [25]

If a distinguished committee composed of such people as Arthur M. Schlesinger, Paul H. Buck, Robert Ulich, and George Wald had trouble deciding how best to structure general education, it seems reasonable to urge senior institutions to take the broadest view and allow much leeway in applying transfer credit in humanities, social science, and natural science (including mathematics). Liberalized general education graduation requirements should adhere to the critical path concept of allowing transfer credit to find the best fit in the transfer student's degree requirements.

Problems of transfer credit are becoming more important as more students transfer, more community colleges are formed, and as a new type of public institution—the capstone university—develops to serve transfers exclusively. Public universities and state higher education coordinating agencies are responding with broader general rules for transfer credit degree applicability. The most common result is the regulation for public institutions that lower division general education

23. *General Education in a Free Society: Report of the Harvard Committee* (Cambridge: Harvard University Press, 1945), p. 4.
24. Ibid., p. ix.
25. Ibid., p. 215.

requirements are automatically satisfied for the transfer student holding an associate degree. Kintzer's recent research led him to conclude that "the associate degree is rapidly becoming the basic transfer instrument. Even this plan, however, is not problem free." [26] The approach retains the inherent weakness of exacting specifications that are fundamental to the general regulations designed to restrict transfer credit. While such edicts may be necessary in these frenetic times in higher education, they risk being substituted for individual evaluation of each student's unique complex learning experience.

If students are to progress in the most beneficial and academically sound manner, departmental chairmen and faculty who have the ultimate decision-making power will have to support broad application of transfer credit at both levels. In the last analysis, it is the professor who determines the content of community college courses and programs and the guidelines for acceptance of transfer credit at senior institutions. Deans, admission directors, and articulation officials can help to stimulate coordination and understanding, but the critical decisions must be referred to the academicians. The most useful role that articulation personnel can play is the bringing together of professors to discuss the problems of student transition.

Orientation

Long recognized as an important instrument of articulation, orientation does much to help students resolve adjustment problems stemming from a fear of the unknown and social and academic naivety. It is a rare college that does not support some form of organized orientation, especially for college beginning freshmen, ranging from elaborate week-long affairs to simple programs measured in hours. Unfortunately, such an important articulation service rarely is extended to transfers in a manner that serves their unique needs. A general lack of awareness of transfer orientation needs and institutional inertia account for the myopic view that junior college transfers, having had previous college experience, do not need to be oriented to college.

Donald H. Buckley confirmed the finding in a study that compared freshman and transfer expectations at a senior institution; his study concludes:

26. Frederick C. Kintzer, *Middleman in Higher Education* (San Francisco: Jossey-Bass, 1973), p. 30.

Both transfer and freshman students seem to participate in a collective belief that is constructed in response to the wishes of the group and held uncritically. This leads to an imaginary or fictitious anticipation of the college experience. . . . Transfer students' expectations have the same mythological character as freshman expectations. . . .

We cannot assume that transfer students, even with previous college experience, begin with different expectations than freshmen. Both tend to exaggerate their expectations. . . .

This lack of sophistication and idealization of college life has implications for our orientation programs. The necessity of freshman enculturation has been recognized for some time. New students, other than freshmen, have been neglected or at best only superficially considered. This study points out the need to expand our process of orientation and assimilation to include transfer students.[27]

Other evidence supports criticism of orientation services for transfers. A study of 635 senior institutions by the National Association of Student Personnel Administrators found that less than 20 percent of the institutions provide any kind of special student personnel program for transfer students. Even more revealing, 37 respondents made it a point to assert that they did not favor "separating" transfers from native students in any special programming way.[28] Willingham's survey of transfer admission practices found that only 29 percent of the institutions he studied offered special orientation services to transfers.[29] Finally, a survey of community college transfers recently admitted to a university produced the response from 60 percent of them that their transition could have been eased by an orientation program specifically designed for transfer students.[30]

Community college students need their own orientation program not only to acclimatize them to a new social-academic system, but also to support their self-esteem and proper role-definition. It is

27. Donald H. Buckley, "A Comparison of Freshman and Transfer Expectations," *Journal of College Student Personnel*, May 1971, p. 188.

28. "Transfer Student Study," mimeographed (Washington: National Association of Student Personnel Administrators, Division of Research and Program Development, 1971), p. 5.

29. Willingham and Findikyan, *Patterns*, p. 25.

30. Julius Menacker, "Junior College Transition Survey," mimeographed (Chicago: University of Illinois at Chicago Circle, Office of Admissions and Records, 1970), p. 3.

analogous to the plight of the one boy with three sisters who finds that all the entertainment activities planned by his parents are geared to female interests.

The best way to begin planning a program is to ask currently enrolled and prospective transfers what they see their orientation needs to be. It is also important to involve community college student personnel specialists in a cooperative way in which ideas and responsibilities can be shared forthrightly. Agenda for transfers should not be limited by traditional freshman programs. For example, some orientation activities could take place at the community college, taking advantage of the tendency for community college transfers to select senior colleges close to home. The change in location also suggests the use of community college personnel in senior college orientation activities.

Many of the usual freshman orientation activities are valuable to transfers and should not be rejected simply because the programs were designed for freshmen. There are any number of activities that seem particularly useful for transfer students, such as:

- An introduction to the demands and requirements of upper division courses, and the differences between them and introductory or survey courses taught during the first two years of college study.
- An intensive exploration of potential major fields of study for new transfers, who soon must make a definite curriculum commitment.
- Opportunities to become personally acquainted with professors and upper classmen in the department of their major.
- An introduction to graduate school and employment opportunities and requirements in the various fields.[31]

As for most other areas of articulation, the main requirements for an effective transfer student orientation program are sensitivity to student needs and the will to meet those needs. Research clearly proves that there is "transfer shock" for the community college transfer. Administrative policies and procedures can do much to mitigate the shock, but the face-to-face human contact found in a good orientation program seems indispensable for integrating transfers quickly and smoothly into senior institutions.

31. Julius Menacker, "Are Junior College Transfers Second-Class Citizens?" *National ACAC Journal,* January 1970, p. 5.

four

Needs of Atypical Students

Most articulation policies, programs, and procedures are designed for two major, traditional classes of students—middle-class beginning freshmen in their late teens and slightly older transfer students. This is as it should be, for the two groups form the overwhelming majority of students in American higher education. However, schools and colleges are now emphasizing the educational needs of atypical students who are out of the mainstream of college preparation, ability, socio-economic level, and age. Attention has been drawn to the admission and articulation needs of atypical students by the dramatic shift within the last decade from a scholastic philosophy of college admission to the present societal view.[1] The former position implies close attention to restrictive entrance and exit standards and traditional curricula, while the latter, contrasting view sees a college education as an instrument of social change, functioning to expand opportunities for those who, for one reason or another, are not part of the mainstream college-going population.

The trend toward social consciousness has as its main philosophical supports the historical American faith in the power of education to remedy social ills and to contribute to the democratization process, and the more recent civil rights movement, demanding that society expand opportunities for those unable to succeed by traditional routes. The major beneficiaries of the societal view of higher education have been the poorer minority groups—Negroes, Mexican Americans, Puerto Ricans and, most recently, American Indians. As an important social movement, social consciousness has had a number of unexpected

1. Warren W. Willingham, *Free-Access Higher Education* (New York: College Entrance Examination Board, 1970), p. 9.

ramifications. The attitude stimulated by the civil rights movement grew to include such diverse groups as adults who had not had an earlier opportunity for a college education, the physically handicapped students, Vietnam veterans, and foreign students.

Attention to the general needs of the economically and educationally disadvantaged brought forth the realization that every person who aspired to a college education could profit from special attention to their unique needs. Colleges could respond if they were willing to accept a more student-centered viewpoint. Many colleges and universities launched experimental programs in the 1960s to recruit and assist the disadvantaged. Almost every special academic regulation proposed for disadvantaged groups had surprising relevance for improving the academic program for all students. For example, when it was agreed that the disadvantaged would not be dismissed for poor scholarship before completion of a full year, faculty and administrators began questioning the wisdom of dropping any freshman on the basis of one term's evidence of ability. Often, a general regulation was adopted to prevent the academic dismissal of a freshman before he had attempted a full academic year of study. The next logical step—applying the principle to transfers—would not be far off.

The case of the City University of New York (CUNY) is instructive. In the early 1960s, pressure was generated to force CUNY, a public institution serving mostly middle-class citizens, to extend educational opportunities to the disadvantaged. As a result, two comparatively large-scale special programs were established—Search for Education, Elevation and Knowledge (SEEK) and Project Discovery. Both were judged successful and highlighted the need to radically overhaul general admission policy and academic programs. CUNY decided to change from traditional elective admission to open admission. The latter policy was designed to admit all high school graduates and to provide supportive services and academic policies that would assist the many atypical who would enroll. In this way, CUNY would be able to play a much more important role in societal integration and democratization than ever before.

The philosophical essence of CUNY's change in admission policy was dramatic. Academic and entrance standards became of less concern than exit standards. The CUNY vice-chancellor for academic affairs stated the point neatly: "Standards ought to refer to what a

university does for its students, rather than to their opening handicap.
. . . Standards must clearly be tied to the kinds of degrees a university
awards, not to the batting average of its dean of admission."[2] This
idea is gaining momentum, as illustrated by the Carnegie Commission
on Higher Education's 1973 admonition that colleges adopt the "value
added" concept whereby quality is determined more by what a college
does for the students it enrolls and less by the characteristics of
entering students.[3]

Once such a philosophical position is accepted, responsibilities for
articulation become much more complex, particularly for colleges and
university authorities. Articulation must adapt and be as flexible as the
admission requirements and academic regulations that meet the needs
of each student, no matter how atypical. Just as all methods of
admission, instruction, curriculum, or academic regulations are not
equally suitable for the increasingly heterogeneous students entering
higher education, so, too, all methods of articulation are not equally
appropriate to the various subgroups of students. At CUNY, the main
motivation to change to open admission was to increase the percentages of black and Puerto Rican enrollment. Instead, most of the newly
created free-access spaces were taken by the children of working-class
white families. Certainly, here is a lesson for articulation.

The Disadvantaged Student

While there is some question about the reliability of data on the
enrollment of minority students in higher education, some reasonably
good comparative estimates have been made about college populations
in 1970 (see table 1).

These data take on more meaning when it is noted that 4.3 percent
of the population of all identifiable American subgroups attend college,
as opposed to the following percentages for the four minority groups:
black Americans, 2.0; Mexican Americans, 1.0; Puerto Ricans, 1.3;
American Indians, 0.6; and total minority, 1.84.[4] More recently, the
following percentage breakdown was reported for the 1973 college

2. Timothy S. Healy, "Will Everyman Destroy the University?" *Saturday
Review of Literature,* Dec. 20, 1969, p. 55.
3. Carnegie Commission on Higher Education, *Continuity and Discontinuity*
(New York: McGraw-Hill Book Co., 1973), p. 3.
4. Ibid., p. 15.

TABLE 1

Minority Enrollment in Colleges, 1970

Minority Group	Population	Percent of U.S. Population	College Enrollment	Percent of College Enrollment
Black Americans	23,550,000	11.5	470,000	5.8
Mexican Americans	5,000,000	2.4	50,000	0.6
Puerto Ricans	1,500,000	0.7	20,000	0.3
American Indians	700,000	0.4	4,000	0.1

Source: Fred E. Crossland, *Minority Access to Colleges* (New York: Schocken Books, 1971), pp. 10, 13.

freshman class: white/Caucasian, 88.5; black/Negro/Afro-American, 7.8; American Indian, 0.9; Oriental, 1.1; Mexican American/Chicano, 1.3; Puerto Rican-American, 0.4; other, 1.55.[5]

Regardless of which analysis one chooses, it is clear that minority group members are not fully represented in American higher education, both in terms of the percent of total college population or the percent of all other groups in college. In order for the four minority groups to reach the general population's college-going percentage of 4.3, black enrollment would have to increase by 543,000 (116 percent), Mexican Americans by 165,000 (330 percent), Puerto Ricans by 45,000 (225 percent), and American Indians by 26,000 (650 percent).[6]

The only encouraging sign is the steady growth in the last several years of minority group enrollment, both in total numbers and in percentage of the total college population. The percentage of black enrollment in colleges as compared to total college enrollment was 2 percent (700-800) in 1900.[7] In 1970 it was nearly 6 percent, and in 1973 almost 8 percent.

While the increase in black enrollment can be attributed mostly to an increasing sense of social justice that pervades the American conscience, improved techniques of recruiting disadvantaged students and communicating with their parents and counselors also have played

5. *Chronicle of Higher Education,* Feb. 11, 1974, p. 8.
6. Fred E. Crossland, *Minority Access to Colleges* (New York: Schocken Books, 1971), p. 16.
7. Ibid., p. 30.

a role. Much more needs to be done (witness the CUNY situation), and, fortunately, a good deal is now known about how to do it. First, one must know the client in order to be of service to him.

Not all members of the four minority groups are disadvantaged in any of the various senses in which the term is used. Also, members of majority groups often qualify for inclusion—particularly Appalachian whites and other people from most ethnic, racial, and religious groups in the nation. Further, it is as true for the disadvantaged population as for any other that there are more differences within a group than between groups. The disadvantaged have been described as having in common such characteristics as:

> low economic status, low social status, low educational achievement, tenuous or no employment, limited participation in community organizations, and limited ready potential for upward mobility. . . . These are people who are handicapped by ethnic and cultural *caste* status. . . . More and more of these people are concentrated in the decaying hearts of our great metropolitan centers.[8]

The schools that serve the disadvantaged are generally inadequate to the socio-cultural and educational needs of the students, partly because the budget, staffing, and curriculum for the schools are determined by middle-class norms and attitudes. High school guidance and counseling are as affected as any other area. Counselors are inundated with paper work and students whose severe problems demand a great deal of individual attention. Truancy, discipline, and other negative aspects of student behavior and adjustment preoccupy the counselor, leaving him little time for college counseling and assimilation of quantities of information about different college requirements, programs, financial aid opportunities.

Even with enough time and staff, the standard methods of college guidance and articulation that are satisfactory for the middle class do not prove as effective for poor and minority students. College guidance for the disadvantaged must use more direct methods that involve concrete motivations, immediate gratification, the liberal and strategic use of secondary reinforcers, and a variety of informational vehicles and motivational methods. Articulation methods designed to meet

8. Edmund W. Gordon and Doxey A. Wilkerson, *Compensatory Education for the Disadvantaged* (New York: College Entrance Examination Board, 1966), pp. 1-2.

such criteria and compensate for counselor work patterns that impede good college guidance for the disadvantaged can do much to improve the college transitions of disadvantaged students.

The colleges must take the lead, for their resources and capabilities are superior to those of the typical ghetto high school. In one excellent articulation program, colleges invite local high school students to the campus for college information sessions, typically held at the high school. Disadvantaged students are thereby given the opportunity to experience the concrete reality of a college campus at the same time that counselors are relieved of the time-consuming tedium of arranging a college day or night program. The high school counselor would still have to inform students of the college programs and encourage the selective attendance of all those who could conceivably benefit from one program or another. Colleges could initiate cooperative programs involving a number of similar institutions from a wide geographic area. Even here, college sponsorship is superior to a program held at the high school, because in either the single or multiple institution program, prospective students can talk with not only admissions representatives, but with deans, professors, and, most important, minority group students attending the host institution.

College students provide excellent role models for the hesitant college aspirant, who may have no friends or relatives with direct college experience. With the cooperation of high school counselor and college representative, some minority group college students could be scheduled to go to the high school to speak to groups of possible college applicants. The college students could become excellent liaison personnel carrying information between high school and college counselors and providing both with truths about the problems of minority group college placement that may have escaped the professionals.

The high school counselor remains in the critical position for facilitating college attendance by the nonprivileged. He is at the center of the communication network and has the most direct and easy access to the student. In order to be effective, the high school counselor must utilize available resources, the most important of which is the community.[9] The counselor must recognize the need to articulate with the

9. Paul Kadota and Julius Menacker, "Community-Based College Guidance for the Disadvantaged," *Personnel and Guidance Journal,* November 1971; Julius Menacker, *Vitalizing Guidance in Urban Schools* (New York: Dodd, Mead & Co., 1974).

community on a basis that is as professional and effective as articulation with colleges. Any number of persons in any disadvantaged community can be identified as key communicators—shopkeepers, clergymen, gang leaders—and asked to serve as elements in an effective college information communications net. From an administrative standpoint, school authorities will have to redefine the counselor's job description to permit appointments away from the school grounds and evening and weekend hours on an irregular basis. The counselor can often be more effective with students on the playground, in the pool hall, or standing on the street corner than he can be behind his desk.

The procedure, in the final analysis, rests on equally effective relations with colleges. The counselor must be able to trust the college representative and be in easy, ready communication with him. The best case-in-point involves financial aid, an area that frequently is misunderstood by the disadvantaged. Since the counselor is closer to the student, he should serve as liaison between student and college admissions officer, making the student's financial requirements clear to the college and interpreting the financial aid offer to the student and his family.

The counselor must insist that the financial aid offer be stated in simple terms, and that it be adequate. In particular, aid involving loan commitments must be made clear, and the counselor should attempt to negotiate such items in the student's favor. When college representatives prove unreliable or evasive about such matters, or when the college representative is not empowered to make such commitments, the school counselor should intervene to protect and help the student in the negotiations. Financial aid is an example of a concrete, tangible benefit for the student and his family, and it must be properly utilized. High school counselors may have to educate college administrators to the ramifications of aid to the disadvantaged, but the two professionals can form an effective partnership to increase college attendance among the disadvantaged.

The cooperative relationship between high school and college should not end upon the student's enrollment. The nonprivileged student will need a good deal of support as a new college student, particularly if he enrolls at one of the majority of American colleges and universities that have very few minority group members. Stable communication between student and counselor and between counselor and college personnel will usefully supplement the other supportive services offered by colleges to the disadvantaged. The counselor could interpret test scores, provide the content of high school courses, and cope with many personal matters that could well spell the difference between success or failure for a disadvantaged student during the critical first months in college.

The student's former high school counselor also can serve as a very useful liaison between the college and the student's family. He can interpret to parents the nature of their child's problems and assist the parents in providing the most appropriate support for the student. The counselor can report back to the student about family conditions, helping to smooth out communication problems and misunderstandings insofar as he is capable of doing.

Specialized recruitment conferences for minority group members can be a useful device for recruitment and general orientation. While such procedures risk separating the disadvantaged from the mainstream of college life, the limited and intelligent use of the restricted group procedure can be very beneficial. Conferences should be cooperatively planned and implemented. The high school should select students for attendance, recommend elements of the program, and participate in the program. One of the main segments in such conferences should feature role models. Adult minority group members who are professors, college administrators, elected or appointed government officers, or holders of similar positions can serve as excellent keynote speakers. Minority college students can be most usefully employed as leaders of small group discussions or rap sessions.

Whatever else is discussed or presented, it is critical that part of the program address the direct, concrete benefits of college enrollment and graduation and the contributions of financial aid. Then college education must be related to the personal benefits that can accrue to the student and his family. Areas of employment where minority representation is small and being actively sought should be presented. Finally, such standard information as comparative earnings of college graduates and high school graduates should not be neglected.

The use of minority college students should extend beyond conference participation to take advantage of the students' particular ability to encourage prospective minority college students. Miami-Dade Community College experimented successfully with articulation programs using minority students as counselors.[10] The students were trained as articulation aides and sent back to the high school from which they graduated or to the neighborhood in which they lived to identify potential enrollees and provide them with pertinent information. Peer relations contributed greatly to the success of articulation for disadvantaged students, and the program at Miami-Dade will be expanded in the future. Another obvious advantage of such a program is that it creates employment, an additional source of financial aid, for the disadvantaged college enrollee. The main caveat to observe in developing a program of student counselors is that the aides must be well trained, given accurate, current information, and trained not to exaggerate admission or financial possibilities. It may well be worse to build false hopes and expectations in a student than never to have recruited him.

Outside the strict confines of the school and college relationship lies another important articulation resource that can improve the educational transition of disadvantaged students. Various private and voluntary associations are dedicated to helping minority students enroll in and successfully complete college; chief among these are the National Scholarship Service and Fund for Negro Students (NSSFNS) and the National Achievement Scholarship Program (NASP) of the National Merit Scholarship Corporation. Both agencies identify promising black college students and find financial aid for them. Recently, NSSFNS has taken a more vigorous role in articulation by expanding its services from the dissemination of lists of potential black college students to the sponsoring of regional admission information conferences for students in New York City, Chicago, Atlanta, and elsewhere. Partially funded by contributions from participating colleges, the conferences involve high school and college personnel in cooperative planning. The conference features lunch and a cafeteria-style information program where representatives of colleges, ancillary organizations (such as the College Board and American College Testing Program), private educational foundations, and state scholarship agencies host a table or booth. It is difficult precisely to assess the real value to the disadvantaged of such programs, but certainly they make a positive contribution and should be continued.

10. Albert K. Smith, "Bridging the Gap—High School to Community College," *Junior College Journal,* February 1970.

High school and college articulation personnel should be aware of many other organizations that operate locally or regionally, as well as those associations serving the national level. The Ford, Carnegie, and Rockefeller foundations, the Southern Education Foundation, the College Board's Project Access, the Urban League, Office of Education programs (such as Talent Search and Upward Bound), and the Office of Economic Opportunity's community action agencies are among the major sponsors of national programs. State efforts are exemplified by the programs of the New York College Bound Corporation and efforts of such statewide agencies as the California Coordinating Council for Higher Education and the Indiana State Scholarship Commission. The main point for the articulation specialist is to make firm contact and remain in communication with such agencies. As particular articulation problems arise, personal contacts will pay off handsomely in the student's behalf.

The nature of local private or volunteer efforts can be illustrated by three programs in the Chicago area. The Ada McKinley Community Services, financed by philanthropic and community welfare funds, serves a variety of needs in a severely deprived black ghetto area of Chicago. The McKinley director of educational services, working on a very limited budget, has had an effect on minority group college attendance and academic success disproportionate to his resources because of the force of his personality, his ability to get directly to the sources of power at higher education institutions, and his ability to identify and express, with maximum publicity, the inconsistencies and gaps between intention and practice regarding service to disadvantaged students at institutions. He maintains a nationwide network of contacts with key persons in admissions and financial aid, officials of professional associations concerned with college admission, and others with important roles in the school-to-college process. More often than not, his contacts bear the expense involved in the relationship.

The Chicago Area College Assistance Program, a voluntary association of colleges and universities in Illinois and neighboring states, exists for the purpose of sponsoring semiannual college information and inspiration programs for seventh and eighth graders in Chicago's inner city elementary schools. The program usually starts with a two-part school assembly. Illustrated with slides, a lecture about residential life at a typical college campus is followed by an interview of a minority first-year college student from the neighborhood conducted by one of the college representatives. After the assembly, college representatives go to classrooms to answer the individual questions that were stimulated by the assembly program. Generally, about twelve schools participate in half-day programs each year. The Chicago Area College Assistance Program has no budget, so each representative pays his own expenses; program coordination is handled by volunteers assigned to the coordinating committee on a rotating basis.

The Council for College Attendance, the third example, is notable for encouraging minority group college attendance through informal articulation. The membership includes counselors at inner city high schools and community colleges, college admissions officers, members of agencies concerned with minority group college attendance, representatives of the College Board or ACT, members of Upward Bound and Talent Search programs, and just about anyone else who has something to contribute and is willing to attend the monthly meetings. The Council for College Attendance has lobbied for more state financial aid for disadvantaged college students, exerted public opinion pressure on particular colleges to change admission policies, initiated and conducted pilot programs supported by federal or foundation funds, and persuaded local, state, and national professional associations to make greater commitments to the disadvantaged. All of the council's efforts are conducted without any direct, steady source of funds by volunteers.

Public, private, voluntary, state, national, and local agencies can be of varying degrees of help in the school-to-college progress of disadvantaged students. The problem for the organizations—a well as for high school, community college, and four-year institutions—is coordination, so that efforts are complete but not duplicated unnecessarily. There is bewildering variety here, and the school or college professional often finds it difficult to sort out the best services for his clients and keep up with the activities of the counseling groups. There is also the problem of separating the good from the mediocre, for some activities are little more than window dressing or misdirected efforts, albeit with good intentions.

The best approach for most high school and college personnel is to become involved with those few activities that seem most worthwhile for their clientele and with which they are most comfortable. At the high school level, responsibilities might be parceled out in such a way that one counselor becomes the NSSFNS and NASP contact while another relates to the organizations similar to the Council for College Attendance. Nor is it incumbent on any one person to be involved in or even aware of every one of the myriad programs in operation. Articulation specialists will have to evaluate each special program as it becomes known and use their experience in making proper selections for involvement.

Admission criteria

A comprehensive survey of literature on the transition of disadvantaged students from school to college concluded that little is known about the best measures to use for predicting the college success of disadvantaged students.[11] High school records or standardized test scores may be better or worse measures for the disadvantaged than for the majority of students. Standardized tests such as the ACT or SAT have been attacked as being culturally biased, and while much research has been focused on the problem, there is still no clear answer to this issue. Research indicates that predictions of scholastic average for black college students, based on their SAT scores, are accurate or higher than actual performance when the equations suitable for majority students are used.[12]

Research on nonintellective correlates of achievement and counselor recommendations have proved no more reliable than the standard variables. If anything, the variables proved less reliable.[13] The best assessment of admission problems of disadvantaged students at selective institutions is stated by S. A. Kendrick and C. L. Thomas:

> Action in the educational system is being taken, as it must be, without any regard for the research schedules of . . . scholars or agencies. . . . Neither the disadvantaged young people who intend to go from school to college nor the school and college officers involved in the process are prepared to wait upon conventional research procedures. It will increasingly be the case that much of

11. S. A. Kendrick and C. L. Thomas, "Transition from School to College," *Review of Educational Research,* February 1970.
12. George Temp, *Test Bias: Validity of the SAT for Blacks and Whites in Thirteen Integrated Institutions* (Princeton, N.J.: Educational Testing Service, 1971).
13. Kendrick and Thomas, "Transition," p. 164.

the research that really affects the transition from school
to college will appear in the literature long after its principal applications have been made.[14]

School and college articulation professionals are left in a particularly critical and important position. School counselors who take the
initiative in advocating the admission of their disadvantaged clients
often find a receptive ear among college admissions officers; indeed,
admissions officers often solicit their advice about useful admission
regulations. It is essential that the two groups work together closely
and carefully, for out of combined efforts will come the data that will
form the pattern for stable admissions and graduation practices for
disadvantaged college students.

The two groups must first be honest with each other about the
reasons supporting the high school's prediction of success and the
college's appraisal of what was or was not done for the student at the
college. It is well known that intensive counseling, tutoring, financial
support, and peer support are important elements in the success of disadvantaged college students. As hard as such components are to come
by, it is harder to achieve an even more basic element necessary for
successful transition from school to college for the disadvantaged—
adaptations in college curricula.

There is little doubt that the traditional subject matter, teaching
methods, and educational goals of colleges are not entirely suitable
to most disadvantaged students. While the ingrained conservatism
and inertia of higher education stand as formidable obstacles to the
progress of disadvantaged students, school and college articulators can
make inroads to remove college curriculum barriers. By the same
token, articulators can also move secondary school administrators to
make adaptations at the high school level that would better prepare
the disadvantaged for college.

Superior Students

More attention and effort has been devoted to promoting the educational transition of superior students than to any other group of
concern to school and college relations. Consequently, the most ambitious and successful articulation programs have been and still are those
designed to serve superior students. Long before the current interest in

14. Ibid., p. 173.

articulation, study after study documented that duplication in the school curriculum was greater for superior students than for average or below average students.[15]

Institutions and associations, such as the College Entrance Examination Board have translated the studies' recommendations into action programs. Most programs developed in the 1950s, the period when the Soviet Union's Sputnik I shocked America into concern about the "talent waste" in the schools. Crash programs and pilot projects appeared across the educational scene, many backed by federal funds in much the same way as programs for the disadvantaged were initiated and funded in the 1960s by the War on Poverty and civil rights concerns.

In the 1950s the Portland, Oregon, public schools and Reed College experimented with a combined program to identify gifted students as early as possible and then to provide special seminars at the college level for them. Participants later reported the experience to have been very helpful to their college studies. The Talented Student Program for High School Seniors (TSPHSS) at the University of Illinois at Chicago Circle, initiated in the mid-fifties, is a similar program that allows superior local high school students to take college courses concurrently with their senior year classes and during the summer between their junior and senior high school years. Student performance has been of very high quality. In Atlanta, Georgia, enriched high school curricula, introduced in 1954, have allowed graduates to gain college general education credit in three local cooperating colleges, as well as in other institutions. The much older, comprehensive programs sponsored by the University of Buffalo offer advanced credit through examination. The project gives special attention to bright students and stimulates independent study while simultaneously encouraging high schools to offer enrichment programs. Follow-up studies show that the more credit examinations a student takes, the better his college performance will be. More than 1,700 students had taken over 4,000 examinations under the Buffalo program as early as 1957.[16]

The most influential and successful program of allowing superior students to transcend the arbitrary division between high school and

15. A. C. Eurich and J. J. Scanlon, "Articulation of Educational Units," *Encyclopedia of Educational Research,* ed. Chester W. Harris, 3d ed. (New York: Macmillan Co., 1960), p. 88.
16. Ibid., p. 90.

college study has been the Advanced Placement Program of the College Entrance Examination Board. Begun in 1955, the program enables high school students to take examinations for college credit in thirteen different subject areas after completing a specially designed course in that area.

Another approach to improved transition of superior students has been the early admission of students to college before they have graduated from high school. The University of Chicago, under the presidency of Robert Maynard Hutchins, was an early pioneer in early admissions during the 1930s. Between 1951 and 1955, a total of 1,350 high school students of exceptional ability were admitted to twelve colleges participating in an experimental program to test the effects of the practice. The results of the experiment were reported to be:

> They were about two years younger than the average college freshman, and almost none of them had completed high school. Their performance in college was impressive. Academically, they consistently out-performed not only their classmates as a whole but also a carefully selected group of matching students who were equal in aptitude. They participated actively in extracurricular activities, received more than their share of academic honors, and made a satisfactory social and emotional adjustment to college life.[17]

Early college admission and programs that award college credit for accelerated high school courses form the two major thrusts to minimize obstructions in curricular forward progress for superior students. The most significant program of incentive and financial support for very bright students is the National Merit Scholarship program, which also represents a reaction to the frenzied search in the 1950s for gifted students. Begun in 1955 at the same time as the Advanced Placement Program, the National Merit Scholarship program proposed to search the nation for the most talented high school students and bestow on them the program's recognition and scholarships. An equally important purpose was the identification of able students for other national sources of college financial support, colleges, and the general public.[18] In the initial year of the program, 10,300 schools entered

17. Ibid.
18. *National Merit Scholarship Corporation Annual Report, 1970* (Evanston, Ill.: National Merit Scholarship Corporation, 1970), p. 2.

58,100 students in the competition. In the 1969–70 competition, 17,256 schools entered 734,375 students in the program.[19]

The main criterion for eligibility is a standardized examination— the National Merit Scholarship Qualifying Test, and, for semifinalists, an equivalent second test. The high school record and high school recommendations are also considered in making awards. The awards are made without regard to financial need, which represents an anomaly in the present financial aid climate. In the 1969–70 program, 3,832 scholarships were awarded, bringing the total since the program's inception to 29,378 scholarships worth over $88 million.[20] While most of the winners probably would have attended college anyway, the program has heightened interest in college and academic competition and has broadened the range of college choice for many students, leading them to more satisfying, productive college experiences than would have been possible without the National Merit program.

Colleges and universities do not all sit back and wait for superior students to seek them out. Many efforts to recruit scholarly students are almost, but not quite, comparable to the efforts to recruit athletes. A prime example is found at Michigan State University which contacts all Merit semifinalists and earnestly woos them. Michigan State is able to pursue semifinalists because the college is structured to offer concrete benefits. It supports a number of Merit Scholarships and supplements them with "MSU Alumni Distinguished Scholarships," the "MSU Scholarship Extension Policy," and "MSU Trustee Scholarships." In addition, Michigan State is advertised as the "home of the honors college," as in the following typical letter sent regularly to students of exceptional ability:

> Michigan State is a large institution, but we "beat" out size in many different ways. One way is to have limited-enrollment, self-contained small colleges within the larger university. These have their own curricula, their own faculties, their own residence halls. Their students have the best of both worlds—they are large parts of a small college when that is an advantage, but they use and are a part of the total university, when that is a benefit.
>
> One of these small units now in its second year is our Justin Morrill College. It offers a broad, liberal

19. Ibid., p. 5.
20. Ibid.

education emphasizing the international scene, and it
has a heavy foreign language requirement. It started a
year ago with about 350 freshmen, now has only about
650 students, and will be limited to about 1,000 total
enrollment.

A second small college will open here next fall. It will
emphasize science and it, too, will have a limited enrollment, a special curriculum, a special faculty, and its own
residence hall. It has not yet been named, and its
program is not yet specified, and we can't accept applications for it until at least January. However, those
freshmen who already have been admitted will have the
first opportunity to apply for this "New College Number
Two" whenever the rolls are open. As soon as the faculty
planning committee has more decisions, I'll write you
about them.

* * *

One of our Honors College directors once said: "He who
rests on his laurels . . . wears them in the wrong place."
As you can see, Michigan State University does not rest
on its laurels. We're not perfect, by any means, but we
never stop trying to improve.

The main point in such recruiting—whether the target population be
athletes, blacks, or whatever—is that the college must offer specific
benefits for attendance not easily duplicated at other institutions. Further, the recruiting institution must communicate its message effectively to reach the intended target population. Michigan State assured
the latter point by writing to National Merit semifinalists. The same
could be done on a smaller scale by enlisting the aid of counselors
at selected schools. Usually, if the college can demonstrate the real
value of their offer, counselors will cooperate by identifying students
and making the college's literature available to potential applicants.

As for encouraging talented high school students to take advantage
of opportunities for accelerated forward progress, secondary schools
must recognize student achievements and those of its staff to highlight
available opportunities. A good practice followed at many schools is
the awards assembly. Another is the more specialized, advanced placement recognition breakfast, an annual program that can reinforce even
a small number of advanced placement program participants. Teachers
participating in the program, administrators, and college officers are
included, along with the students and their parents. A college representative and representative students might address the group, and

the breakfast can leave all with the feeling that what the students have done is worthwhile and appreciated.

To summarize, certain programs and procedures maximize forward progress of the brightest students through the educational system. Some, like the Advanced Placement program and the National Merit Scholarship program, have a national scope, while others serve as local or regional prototypes that have proved successful and can be easily adapted to a variety of special circumstances and conditions. Programs that allow secondary students to earn college credit before graduation and the college admission of students who have not graduated from high school are the main procedures.

Veterans

Since the introduction of the historic G.I. Bill at the end of the Second World War, the educational interests of military veterans have been viewed as an obligation of the national government. In turn, the government has found that subsidizing the higher education of veterans is an excellent investment in terms of increased national productivity and additional tax revenues from the greater earning power of educated veterans and the higher level of general citizenship function resulting from the opportunities afforded veterans.

Whereas the earlier concern was whether or not veterans should be paid to go to school as one reward for military service, the present concern is how to communicate most effectively with the large number of returned Vietnam veterans and assist them in meeting their diverse educational needs and interests. While the veteran's prior educational attainment may not be high, his maturity and motivation more than counterbalance past educational deficiencies. A study of the educational progress of World War II veterans suggested several reasons why veterans tend to do better in college than nonveterans: forced delay leads to stronger motivation; G.I. Bill assistance engenders a sense of gratitude and attendant desire to justify the implicit faith in the veterans; greater family responsibilities motivate them to do well in college in order to get good jobs; and veterans are less interested in outside activities so they concentrate more on their studies.[21] A study

21. E. A. Taylor, Jr., "How Well Are Veterans Doing?" *School and Society,* November 1947, pp. 210-12.

that examined the performance of veterans, including Vietnam veterans from the cold war era found that they performed almost three-tenths of a grade point better than a sample of nonveterans matched on year and term of entry, curriculum, ACT composite score, and high school percentile rank.[22]

As a group, then, veterans represent a challenge to articulation. They are potentially good college performers; the government wishes to subsidize their education; and they have given up a good deal for educational opportunity.

But they are outside the mainstream of school and college relations, since their schooling was interrupted by military service. Articulation specialists must tap nontraditional resources and, in much the same fashion as for the disadvantaged, go where the action is. Articulators must also develop materials and techniques that are different from those found useful in standard school and college relations work.

Project Hope was one such program that sought out potential applicants. Jointly sponsored by the Department of Defense and the Department of Health, Education, and Welfare, Project Hope sent admission and financial aid officers to Vietnam to stimulate interest in college and provide whatever assistance they could. The officers interviewed thousands of veterans, answered their many questions about possibilities for higher education, and supplied them with admission and financial aid applications and cards self-addressed to many other colleges and agencies in which the veterans were interested. Project Hope was part of a larger program called More Education More Opportunity (MEMO) which encompassed a variety of services, including identification of servicemen interested in specific institutions. The names of veterans and whatever academic and nonintellective data were available were passed on to the institutions.

Another way to reach veterans when the elaborate arrangements and funding necessary for Project Hope are not available is to find the veterans in the vicinity of the college or university. Veterans hospitals and the many veterans clubs that appear on college campuses can provide many leads. Also, every military base at which servicemen are processed for return to civilian life has an education center. The civilian

---

22. John Paraskevopoulos and L. F. Robinson, "Comparison of College Performance of Cold War Veterans and Nonveterans," *College and University,* Winter 1969.

education officers that staff the centers are generally very eager to develop communication channels with colleges and universities. They and their clients are in continual need of information on such topics as admission to college under all kinds of unusual circumstances and transferability of United States Armed Forces Institute (USAFI) courses and military service school courses to colleges. Periodic visits to nearby base education offices should become part of the standard traveling schedule of the college representative. Similarly, military education personnel should be invited to the campus and to conferences regularly held for admission information purposes.

Even if the percentage of veterans typically served by a college is small, it is incumbent upon the institution to provide specialized literature for returning servicemen. The best type is a brochure that can be handed out or mailed in standard envelopes. In addition to the normal information for prospective students, the brochure should include a description of procedures for early release from military service, optional admission qualifications available to veterans (such as petition procedures and General Educational Development Tests), financial aid information (including the G.I. Bill and state benefits), and institutional policies governing the acceptance of credit earned in USAFI courses and other military schools.

The brochure should be available at the college admission office, at all military separation centers where interested veterans might be, at nearby veterans hospitals, and with groups such as Concerned Veterans of Vietnam, the American Legion, Veterans of Foreign Wars, and similar organizations. The pamphlets should also be routinely mailed to high school and junior college counselors since they, too, have contact with veterans. Finally, it should be mailed to all veterans writing for information even when their questions can be answered without it. Not only might the brochure answer later questions, it might also be passed around to others for whom it could be the initial stimulation to return to school.

Appropriate policies for veterans maximize the serviceman's formal education, including military schools, and take into consideration his greater motivation and performance, compared to the typical undergraduate student. Generally, policies are more flexible for admission and the crediting of on-the-job experience and experience gained in standard or nonstandard classrooms. In this area, communication established between university articulation officers and military and Veterans' Administration educational personnel can really pay off. Information about nonstandard admission policies can be disseminated effectively through military advisors to servicemen who are separating from the military. The military education specialists can also update information about military instructional programs and provide more details about particular programs that can be found in *A Guide to the Evaluation of Educational Experiences in the Armed Services.*[23]

The *Guide* is the authoritative evaluation of military experience for award of collegiate credit, and new editions will appear annually beginning in 1974. Even so, investigation beyond the *Guide's* recommendations is necessary. The credit award decision should be at least partially based on the value of the particular training to the individual veteran-student pursuing a certain course of study at one institution. The thorough analysis needed to meet such singular decisions can only be accomplished through excellent communication between university and military articulation personnel. Enough veterans apply to colleges, defense department training programs, USAFI courses, and so forth to warrant special articulation conferences and other contacts between higher education and military education specialists.

In areas where there is a heavy incidence of returning veterans, colleges, community colleges, and high schools could improve the efficiency of their articulation by forming a consortium. The consortium could be organized either on their own initiative or under the auspices of some central coordinating agency, such as a state board of higher education or state department of education. Under the plan, each institution could contribute to a detailed catalog designed for wide distribution and could supply human or material resources for a veterans college information center housed at one of the participating institutions to represent all consortium members. Such a center would be responsible for disseminating literature and counseling individuals. It would also be a focal point for sponsoring broadly based admission conferences for veterans and professionals working with veterans

23. Cornelius P. Turner, ed., *A Guide to the Evaluation of Educational Experiences in the Armed Services* (Washington: American Council on Education, 1968).

education plans at military bases, veterans hospitals, and Veterans' Administration offices. Also included in such activities would be financial aid personnel at national, state, and institutional levels, and all others who at one time or another could influence the educational plans of veterans. The end of the Vietnam war should not mean the end of higher education's concern for veterans. Tens of thousands of former servicemen and women still have not taken advantage of available educational opportunities, and more continue to enlist in, serve, and be discharged from the military services. They represent a continuing obligation and source of strength to higher education.

Mature Adults

In a society that increasingly emphasizes and demands continuing education, it is not surprising to find that colleges and universities are now faced with large numbers of mature adults from varying educational backgrounds who wish to enter higher education. For example, the extension program at the University of California at Los Angeles took a random sample of students and found 706 over the age of fifty and 11 over the age of seventy. Further, the entire UCLA student body is growing older: 37 percent of graduate students are over thirty, and 41.5 percent of undergraduates are over twenty-one. The percentage of entering freshmen over the age of twenty-one has increased from 1.6 percent in 1969 to 5.5 percent in 1972.[24] Adjustments are needed in articulation practices and academic programs as well as in admission policy if mature people are to be served adequately. Elinor Waters surveyed admission practices and policies for adults at forty-four four-year colleges and universities, primarily in urban areas.[25] Although no discrimination against older undergraduates was found, Waters concluded that these atypical students received little if any special treatment in accordance with their peculiar needs. While better tests of adult academic ability are now available, only 10 percent of the institutions, approximately, even considered differential admission in testing for adults; nor did many bother to take life experiences into account in deciding admission or related matters. Only 25 percent of

24. Pamela Swift, "Never Too Late," *Parade Magazine,* June 4, 1972.
25. Elinor Waters, "The Other Generation Gap: Admissions Procedures for Adults," *Journal of College Student Personnel,* November 1971.

institutions reported using the College-Level Examination Program (CLEP), which has as one of its purposes assistance for college officers in determining admission, placement, and college credit awards for adults. Perhaps most telling was Water's finding that not only do most institutions not designate adult admission as a staff specialty, but that their procedures for adult admission are no different than those used for young people.

The informational role for high school, community college, and university specialists can best be performed by seeking out adults in much the same manner as veterans and the disadvantaged are found. The community college person responsible for adult education will find high school continuing education programs to be fertile fields. The specialists' work, however, could be made considerably more effective if high school programs had counselors who discuss the educational plans of adults. The postsecondary institutions should complement the high school efforts by staffing respected persons who are knowledgeable about adult admission and education problems and who are easily available to adults.

Precise literature should be available that focuses on adult problems and interests, even if limitations restrict the medium to a mimeographed page. The topics for an adult admission information publication should include such items as the policy on "life experience credit," alternative admission criteria, relevant extracurricular activities, the availability of ancillary services (such as day care centers for young children), financial aid, and scheduling changes available for mothers with young children and for working adults. Institutions serious about serving adult needs will recognize the responsibility to develop information systems for adults that approximate systems for the typical college-going student even though the college may not feel any urgency to recruit adults. Adults generally do not attend school or, if they do, their academic pattern deviates from the norm. Therefore, the information flow must also deviate from the norm. Aside from the obvious contact point of the adult education program at any level, there are numerous other channels for information. Excellent distributors are the various adult organizations that attract people interested in education. Such clubs include Parent-Teacher Associations, voter awareness and other civic improvement groups, book reading and review clubs (such as "Great Books" study groups), study groups connected with churches, and many, many similar types of organized activities related to learning and self-improvement.

Literature could be disseminated routinely to groups, and speakers could be sent out in response to requests stimulated by the literature. Both the literature and speakers should encourage visits to the campus, correspondence, and telephone calls. Individualization of communication processes is crucial since most adults do not fall within several convenient categories, as is often the case for new students moving directly from school to college and from junior to senior college.

If information services to adults are to be meaningful, college administrators must recognize the needs of the mature person. If the institution is not going to do anything extra for adults, it need not bother with specialized literature, contacts, and the rest. The institution must, however possible, adapt to adult needs. A personal example may illustrate the point. A 32-year-old, self-supporting graduate student with a wife and two children applied for an NDEA student loan. The form to be completed asked for parents' names and occupations, their bank balance, the amount of their contribution to the student's college support, and other inapplicable and confidential information. It can be extremely frustrating to complete the application in a manner appropriate to such circumstances. In such cases, the help of an understanding financial aid officer can be invaluable for adapting the items to individual situations.

Such examples indicate the way in which institutions of higher education and the attendant ancillary services are biased against adults. More flexibility is needed, not only in supportive services, but in general academic policy as well. A number of institutions and groups are moving ahead to adapt academic policies to adult characteristics. Mundelein College in Chicago has for several years allowed adults to gain graduation credit for life experiences by a careful review of the information and background that mature persons bring to college study. Many other programs exemplify the academic adjustments that institutions of higher education can make for adults and other classes of atypical students whose continued educational forward progress is better served through deviations from the normal program. The University of Oklahoma offers a liberal arts bachelor's degree that can be obtained through a combination of independent study and short-term campus seminars. Syracuse University, the University of South Florida, and Goddard College have similar programs.

Another important program to serve adults began in the fall of 1971. Called the University Without Walls, it has its administrative base at Antioch College, Ohio, and is supported by a $400,000 Ford Foundation grant. Nineteen cooperating institutions offer course work to students between the ages of nineteen and sixty. There is no fixed curriculum and no time limit. Students can study independently or select courses at any of the participating colleges. The emphasis is on educational experiences that are derived from and utilize community resources and job experiences.

Two developments in New York are worthy of mention. One is the New York regent's degree, which is to be an external degree program similar to the British model. No instruction will be offered, but students will be provided with syllabi and other guidance material. Graduation will be determined solely by examination. The other program, called Empire State College, will hold classes and examinations prepared by teachers at regional learning centers throughout the state, although the program will be coordinated from a center at Saratoga Springs. Students who wish to participate will enroll at one of the centers at any time during the year. After an orientation period they will meet with a mentor to design a program of full-time or part-time studies. A learning contract is developed along one of three basic modes. By the discipline mode, the student inquires into a particular body of knowledge, such as economics or history. With the problem mode, learning is concentrated on a major social or physical problem, as ecology or international relations. The experience mode emphasizes on-the-job experiences as the base for increasing knowledge; readings, written work, and observations are used to improve functional capabilities. Students are not restricted to regular classroom attendance and proceed at their own pace primarily through self-starting independent study. Assistance is provided through libraries, extensive audiovisual materials, tutorial sessions and seminars, as well as from regular classes.

The developments only represent the tip of the iceberg in the educational part of the revolution of rising expectations. With the availability of more leisure time and increased demand for higher education from a number of new sources, more improvements are sure to follow.

The Revolution in Nontraditional Study

The foregoing examples of innovations in higher education apply not only to persons beyond the usual college attendance age; they also apply to other atypical students. The changes are part of a powerful new movement directed at broadening the impact of higher education throughout all segments of American society. *Less Time, More Options,* published in 1970 by the Carnegie Commission on Higher Education, marked the starting point for movement by calling for an end to duplication and waste of student time within and between high school and college. The next year the Carnegie Commission funded a joint enterprise of the College Entrance Examination Board and the Educational Testing Service called the Commission on Non-Traditional Study. The purpose of the commission was "to discover and look into all aspects of non-traditional postsecondary education (including the external degree) now in operation or being planned." [26] The commission, chaired by Samuel B. Gould, was not only to identify programs, but to evaluate them and recommend improvements. The importance of articulation was noted by the commission in one of its earliest public papers:

> We find a general lack of communication, and a consequent duplication of effort among those individuals, agencies or institutions engaged in or planning for nontraditional education. Furthermore, opportunities for study that presently exist for the individual are not easily identifiable, nor are there enough systematic ways to communicate such information to him.[27]

Even innovations designed to add a new dimension of flexibility and service for postsecondary education must have an orderly and effective system of communication. Indeed, nontraditional study demands better communication systems than does traditional education, because of the diverse, unusual clientele that unconventional study was created to serve. Nontraditional education must, in particular, combat five barriers that atypical students usually encounter in traditional education:

1. *Classroom access:* Over one hundred million people in primarily rural areas are remote from traditional free-access educational opportunities. Other categories of people without access to the traditional

26. *New Dimensions for the Learner* (New York: Commission on Non-Traditional Study, 1971), p. 7.
27. Ibid., p. 11.

classroom are young mothers, physically handicapped people, and prison inmates.

2. *Credit accumulation:* Mobility handicaps servicemen and the wives of men whose jobs require the family to move frequently.

3. *Scheduling barriers:* Attempts to combine educational activities with other adult responsibilities often create scheduling conflicts for those with jobs and for married women.

4. *Financial barriers:* Part-time, adult students are at a disadvantage when obtaining financial aid at many institutions and suffer additionally from fee schedules that discriminate against the part-time student.

5. *Restricted definitions of education:* Large numbers of highly talented, creative young people do not accept the values and goals of traditional college programs. At the other end of the spectrum are those young people whose common school experience has alienated them from continuing into higher education, even though they may have the ability to succeed in any number of programs.[28]

Encouraged by major foundations, educational associations, and organizations such as the College Board, Educational Testing Service, and others, programs have been initiated to reach identifiable groups of atypical students. The support has made it possible to publicize the programs and to coordinate program impact. For example, the College Board's 1972 *External Study for Post-Secondary Students* contains an annotated bibliography of about 150 different published sources of information on external credit and other forms of nontraditional study.[29] The bibliography includes journal articles, bibliographies, reviews, directories, advertising brochures, philosophical statements, books, guides, and handbooks.

Also in 1972, the Commission on Non-Traditional Study published its first book, *Explorations in Non-Traditional Study.* The work detailed the existence or development of a variety of external degree programs classified according to six basic models that clear the barriers imposed

28. K. Patricia Cross and J. Quentin Jones, "Barriers to Traditional Education," *Explorations in Non-Traditional Study,* ed. S. B. Gould and K. P. Cross (New York: McGraw-Hill Book Co., 1972), pp. 43-49.
29. Office of External Study Programs, *External Study for Postsecondary Students* (New York: College Entrance Examination Board, 1972).

on atypical students by traditional higher education models.[30] The simplest and most common model, administrative-facilitation, explains how a traditional institution adapts to the needs of atypical students while holding to the customary degree pattern. Adaptations include separate evening colleges (or similar administrative structures that provide special counseling and advising), registration by mail, once-a-week class sessions, weekend and evening courses, televised and audio-cassette courses, correspondence courses, and courses held at industrial and other community sites, including prisons.

The modes-of-learning model from the commission's book illustrates how an institution may establish a new degree pattern of teaching and learning to adapt to the needs of new clientele. The degrees generally have names like *independent studies, liberal studies,* or *general studies* and allow for different admission requirements and radically altered degree requirements or methods of accumulating credit. The examination model permits an external degree to be awarded by an authorized agency solely on the basis of examination results. The New York regents degree is a prime example of such a mode. The validation model enables the institution to evaluate the student's total learning experiences, using the broadest definition of learning experiences. An assessment is made as to how much the experience matches the objectives of the degree program, and then a plan is developed by the student to obtain the unmet degree requirements.

Two other models are described in *Explorations in Non-Traditional Study* (complex-systems and credits), neither of which has made much headway in the United States. The credits model allows a non-instructional agency to award credits and degrees, the standards and quality of which are set and vouched for by the agency. The American Council on Education's Commission on Accreditation of Service Experiences (CASE), which makes recommendations on the award of college credit for instruction taken in the military service, is the closest American effort.[31] The final model, complex-systems, is the commission's dream scheme of possible combinations of programs

---

30. John R. Valley, "External Degree Programs," *Explorations in Non-Traditional Study,* ed. S. B. Gould and K. P. Cross (New York: McGraw-Hill Book Co., 1972), pp. 95-128.

31. The Office on Educational Credit, formerly the Commission on Accreditation of Service Experiences, has assumed the CASE functions of administering the GED Testing Program and of evaluating formal military training programs.

uniquely tailored to the needs of atypical clientele. Among the ideas are proposals for a national university to offer external degrees based on the examination, credits, and validation models. Another is the Wisconsin idea for an open education system, which would organize a state-wide network of learning resources. The New York Empire State College plan for nonresidential students who could draw on a variety of traditional and nontraditional resources is another prototype for the commission's complex-systems model.

The extensive thinking and publicity given to nontraditional opportunities for atypical students have already made quite an impact and promise even broader variety; more important, atypical programs now are well established and serve significant numbers of nontraditional students. It is encouraging to note that New York Regents College Proficiency Examination (CPE) program, which allows for credit in the regents external degree program, accounted for the award of over 40,000 college credits through 1972.[32] In the same publication of the Commission on Non-Traditional Study, it was also reported that in an evaluation of its external degree program, California State University, Chico, found no "statistically significant differences" between the academic performance of its external degree students and regular students.[33] These are the harbingers of a revolution in nontraditional study that promise to meet the growing expectations and educational awareness that has caught the American consciousness.

32. "CPE in New York State," *Educational Recaps,* Spring 1973, p. 18.
33. *Ibid.,* p. 18.

five

Internal Communications

Counselors, whether at high schools, two-year or four-year institutions, have little influence on curriculum and instructional methods. Secondary school academic policy is primarily formulated by administrators, and college academic policy falls in the purview of the faculty. As a result, teachers at all three levels tend to remain relatively unaware of the effects they have on the future performance of their students. Job descriptions that emphasize instruction are partly to blame; but teachers generally lack access to information about the performance of their former students. Instructors are left in an articulation vacuum, ignorant of the implications their methods have for instruction at the next level. Nor have teachers been prepared to meet the instructional needs of new students and to avoid duplications or gaps in the curriculum.

Administrators make many academic policy decisions in an articulation vacuum, unaware of the ramifications that their decisions have for school and college relations. Administrators show concern for good articulation, but they are usually too busy for more than pro forma participation in the process and leave most activity to counselors or admissions officers. The quality and regularity of articulation thought affecting the administrator's academic policy decisions thus depends on the communication patterns existing between administrators and articulators.

It is true that teachers are becoming increasingly more involved with school and college relations through subject articulation conferences sponsored by colleges and annual meetings of professional associations that include teachers of the same subject at more than one academic level. However, annual meetings are necessarily short, infrequent, and generalized. A similar situation applies to the increased school and college relations activity of administrators. The articulation specialist thus faces a formidable problem. The responsibility for initiating institutional change to improve coordination is an important part of his job. Yet, he finds it extremely difficult to participate in the decision-making and finds those who make decisions affecting articulation to be only vaguely informed. The specialist can best discharge his responsibility by channeling the energy used to influence decision-makers or obtain a share of decision-making power into the more productive avenue of accepted articulation practice. Many of the excellent techniques and programs presently employed in interlevel and interinstitutional articulation can be adapted for intrainstitutional use. The skills are available. The target populations would be teachers, administrators, and others who affect articulation or otherwise influence transition. If such authorities are well supplied with current, accurate articulation information that is geared to their interests and needs, the probabilities are good that decisions benefiting articulation will be made. In a sense, the articulation specialist will have entered the decision-making councils by way of internal use of the tools of his trade.

At the University

Academic policy is decided by the faculty in cooperation with the administration and is subject to review by the board of control at most universities. In the increasingly complex milieu of the contemporary multiversity, particularly, the practice has come under criticism. Boyd R. Keenan has pointed out that the increased specialization of professors comes at a time when the issues of university policy are ever more complex, and today's "community of scholars" contains "relatively few individuals who can speak with authority on each policy issue."[1] Keenan advocates a new reliance for policy making on broader specialists who emphasize cooperation rather than the traditional reliance on independent, free-thinking professors. In rebuttal, Allan Carlsson asserts that only faculty are competent to formulate general educational policy, although he allows that several groups (faculty, administration, students, alumni, general public, and board of control)

1. Boyd R. Keenan, "A Qualified Yes" in "Academic Round Table," *Journal of Higher Education,* November 1962, pp. 446-47.

should be involved in decision-making.[2] Carlsson cites John Ciardi in support of his position: "If our colleges are to be colleges and not social clubs or employment offices, only the faculty can be trusted to decide curriculum and degree requirements . . . and the academic goals of the colleges."[3]

It is particularly interesting that both positions fail to include lower units of the educational system from participation in decisions of academic policy that will affect the progress and curricular continuity of students. Decisions are reached without any direct input from other levels. Many of the powerful faculty—department heads and full professors with distinguished research and publication records who have little time left to broaden their interests—are the least likely to communicate and interact with high school and community college teachers. These are the persons who give credence to the isolation of academicians, immersed in their academic field, moving frequently from one campus to another, more familiar with colleagues and events nationally that relate to their professional interests than they are with the high schools and community colleges from which their students come. Some have only the vaguest idea of what a community college is all about, and a few have never heard the term even at colleges that enroll significant numbers of transfer students. Some of the senior academics who are more familiar with community colleges tend to lump all two-year colleges into the same category, that of a substandard academic community that must be tolerated for political and economic reasons. As a result, transfer credit is carefully scrutinized and applied only grudgingly to a major field by department heads and their representatives.

High schools are also regarded with suspicion by some of the most illustrious members of the college and university community. Through ignorance or prejudice some faculty see their role in school and college relations as that of guardians of high school academic standards. Patterns of high school subjects are imposed as a freshman admission requirement to ensure that high school "life adjustment" advocates will not drop foreign languages; minimum test scores are required even for freshman applicants with superior high school records. Such attitudes develop partly from the college or department folklore and partly from

2. Allan Carlsson, "An Affirmative Answer" in "Academic Round Table," *Journal of Higher Education,* November 1962, p. 448.
3. John Ciardi, "Manner of Speaking," *Saturday Review,* May 19, 1962, p. 16.

a negatively biased selective perception of students. The best way to modify the attitudes is to provide professors and administrators with data that clearly demonstrate the incorrectness of their views. Professors are certainly amenable to changing their views on the basis of factual evidence, so the time and effort of providing it would be well spent. It would seem reasonable to conclude that:

> Most college teachers are more interested in their subject than in their students. This is not to say that professors have no concern for their students, but rather that in the competition for the energies of professors, circumstances dictate that a careful inquiry into the backgrounds and aspirations of the students they teach takes second place to proficiency in research, publication and related activities. Yet, teachers are concerned with the effect they have on the minds and careers of their students. Therefore, it would seem appropriate that professors be given as much support in understanding the academic and non-intellective characteristics of their students as can be provided. . . .[4]

Schultz saw two major impediments for transfer students at the senior institution: "senior college faculty members and counselors— and administrators also for that matter—lack information about policy agreements that exist between their institution and junior colleges. Worse, too many hold a deep-seated conviction that junior college transfer students are inherently less competent and have had a distinctly inferior education to students who take their freshman and sophomore years at *their* senior college."[5]

Intrainstitutional articulation programs are needed for informing and influencing the university decision-making councils on matters that may affect student transition. Given the milieu in which academic decisions are made at universities, a simple presentation of complete and pertinent information to the decision-makers is most effective. Also, it is necessary to provide factual data about student backgrounds to university teachers in order to sensitize them to student needs.

Because of their interest in external articulation, many universities have already established procedures and equipment for good internal

4. Julius Menacker, "Internal Use of Articulation Materials," *Improving College and University Teaching*, Autumn 1971, p. 301.
5. Raymond E. Schultz, "Articulation in Undergraduate Higher Education," *Virginia Journal of Education*, September 1969, p. 17.

articulation. Techniques of interschool articulation can be adapted for the additional dimension of internal articulation with a minimum of time, effort, and expense. An excellent example is provided by current practices regarding freshman profiles and feedback reports on academic progress that are routinely prepared by several colleges and universities as an informational guidance service to feeder high schools and community colleges. The range of information falls into five categories.

1. Preadmission academic characteristics, such as high school class rank and admission test scores for new students as a group and for students entering particular colleges within the university.
2. Preadmission nonintellective characteristics, such as student educational and vocational goals, part-time work, extracurricular plans while in college, and distributions by sex, age, family income.
3. Summaries of new student performance for the university as a whole and for its colleges by academic term and for the academic year.
4. Data on student performance by subject grouping such as English, physical sciences, or foreign language.
5. Data on the performance of students categorized by the high schools and junior colleges from which these students matriculated.[6]

The profiles and progress reports are usually prepared by articulation or research offices for prospective students and their counselors to provide information that will facilitate the best possible college choices and help college faculties improve academic service to students. The reports are widely disseminated among feeder high schools and community colleges, sometimes resulting in high school and community college counselors being far better informed about the university's freshman class than are some of the university's professors and administrators. If one wants to ensure the effectiveness of the material, simple distribution must be followed by a number of specific efforts.

One useful technique is to make a presentation to a particular department or college within a university at one of their regular meetings. The smaller group is preferable to a general meeting or the university faculty, where the tendency for invidious comparisons of

6. Ibid.

student quality or performance from college to college and department to department would detract from the purposes of creating more awareness and sensitivity to student needs. Further, large meetings with an audience of diverse backgrounds reduce the general tone of participation and interest of the group. A meeting with one particular college or department can focus on issues unique to them, as the mediocre high school records of students electing that department or the uniformly poor performance of students in one of the required subject areas. At such meetings, the basic documents, distributed prior to the meeting, should be supplemented by such visual aids as slides and transparencies with overlays, which allow for data to be presented and discussed with a concerted group focus.

To complete the job, the initial meeting might be followed by another, in which representative freshmen or transfer students informally discuss the implications of the data. If interest has been sustained, a third meeting might be held in which representative teachers and student personnel administrators from feeder institutions meet with the faculty on specific items of interest generated by the first two meetings. School and college relations officers should. not only provide the data and administrative support for meetings, but should also be able to provide the administrative follow-through for additional data and services needed to clarify or resolve issues.

Documents specifically designed for initial articulation are another avenue of good college relations. While it would seem most expeditious and economical to prepare general material applicable to both internal and external purposes, literature prepared with one or the other in mind will be substantially more relevant and useful. The costs and man-hours necessary for production are minimal, because almost all universities possess the basic equipment to accumulate necessary data for such documents. Annually, *A Profile of Ohio State University Students* is prepared by The Ohio State University Office of University Evaluation and Testing.[7] The 1970–71 edition contains over one hundred pages divided into three sections dealing with future higher education enrollments nationally and in Ohio; a status report on the characteristics of the 1970 class based on their entrance to OSU; and

7. R. B. Thompson and E. T. Mahr, *A Profile of Ohio State University Students, 1970-71* (Columbus: Ohio State University, Office of University Evaluation and Testing, 1971).

a study of the rates of persistence and attrition achieved by students, primarily at OSU.

The profile is distributed to faculty and administration, providing them with a wealth of data about new students and a comparison of the new class with national norms. For academic departments and various administrative offices, the document is supplemented with the names and addresses of students categorized according to interests and needs expressed approximately three months before enrollment. Information about special academic interests, abilities and needs, athletics, sororities, music activities, social groups, financial need are sent to the appropriate university personnel in time for the staff to react to the data. Many of those served by the *Profile* feel that the supplement represents the most valuable service of the Office of Evaluation and Testing.

The supplement is not—as are so many other documents and data lists—hastily reviewed and discarded. University officers and faculty receiving the lists see in them a relevant resource for improving transitional services in an objective, specific way, and the information is the supplement acted upon. The entire *Profile* should meet the same enthusiasm, but the data are not adapted to particular colleges and departments. In the present format, attrition data are categorized only by total undergraduates, and no performance data are provided for specific subject areas. Faculty and administrators who had not noticed the implications of the data would have to be informed at meetings dealing with the pertinent concerns of one university group or another. Due to the diversity of interests and allegiances within the typical multiversity, perhaps such an internal profile would be best prepared with a short general section and additional sections specific to the various colleges and departments.

A profile prepared for internal use exclusively has one distinct advantage over those used for both internal and external purposes, in that the material can be constructed to improve horizontal articulation within the university. When faculty and deans examine data on inter-college transfers, the patterns of elective course choices both within and between college units, and similar data, they can then improve the complementary nature of interchangeable units.

Research studies to resolve doubts or disputes should be part of a continuing program of internal communication. A study entitled *Com-*

parative Performance of Beginning Freshmen and Junior College Transfers was produced at a university facing the problem of faculty acceptance of community college transfer students. For years, some faculty had complained about the burden they were forced to assume because of the increasing number of community college transfers to be taught. Believing that students from community colleges were inferior to native students, the teachers continually lobbied to restrict the number of community college transfers and to raise admission standards. The articulation staff investigated the matter and found that while the attrition rate was greater for community college students than for freshmen, transfer students faced stiffer academic regulations. The injustice of dual academic standards was exposed by hard data, which showed that community college students performed better than freshmen in every subject except mathematics.[8] The report caused some professors to take a second look at their negative attitudes toward community college transfers and stimulated some adjustments in academic policy.

Categorical academic performance data can also serve a very useful horizontal coordination function. However, great care must be exercised in the presentation and discussion of these data so that traditional college rivalries are not exacerbated and the focus stays on student service. The important concern here is one of interpersonal relations or organizational climate. Before launching into a discussion of comparative performance in specific disciplines, school and college relations personnel are obliged to establish a friendly mood. It is simply a matter of making university personnel aware of the need for cooperation and an attitude toward their work that is centered on students rather than territory.

If the proper climate is obtained, a number of useful professional interactions can take place. The business professor can discuss with the mathematics professor the causes and cures for the poor performance of business students in required mathematics courses. The engineering school could ponder the reasons for the underachievement of their students as compared to physics and chemistry majors whose entering characteristics (high school record and college aptitude test

8. Julius Menacker, *Comparative Performance of Beginning Freshmen and Junior College Transfers: Fall and Winter Quarters, 1968-69* (Chicago: University of Illinois at Chicago Circle, Office of Admissions and Records, 1970).

scores) were generally superior to those who chose physics and chemistry. Similarly, a particular department would be prompted to examine critically the causes and remedies for the low quality of its students as compared to another department or think about what special experiences the department ought to provide majoring students who are clearly of a higher calibre than those entering other departments.

Ideas could be exchanged on related subjects with the possible result that each department and college would adopt the best rationales and methodologies that rise from these discussions. Faculty insularity could be broken down, and a new collegial relationship—developed to supplement the traditional one based on academic discipline—would be formed on the basis of academic instruction and student service. The possibility exists of transforming the traditional interdisciplinary faculty rivalry over the quality of students and the rigorousness of curriculum into healthy competition serving students.

At the Community College

Intrainstitutional articulation at the community college is more complex than at other levels due to the great range of student ability, interests, and educational background and to the diversity of its programs. Pecking orders and rivalries are far more distinct than at colleges because of academic division between the transfer program and the career program. Further complicating the matter is the need to focus attention on articulation in two directions—upward to the university and downward to the high school. The main strength for internal articulation at the community college is a widespread concern for student needs that makes teachers and administrators more receptive to articulation.

One issue that should be attacked is the attitudinal distinctions between transfer and career programs and the resulting problems for curricular integration and academic policy. Community college articulation specialists should stimulate the same kinds of communication and discussion of issues among their own faculty as they do between the transfer program faculty and high school or university counterparts. A good place to start is with the presentation of basic data about community college students. Community college teachers would probably be surprised to learn, for example, that some studies have found that females in career programs have higher academic characteristics than males.[9] More often than not, faculty would also be surprised that graduates of career programs eventually enroll at four-year institutions or that many students continually switch between transfer and career programs.[10] The faculty would also be greatly interested in student performance after transfer.

Such knowledge should lead to easier integration of transfer and career programs at the community college, based on a commonality of student academic characteristics and interests. While articulators may help stimulate changes, they should recognize that the decisions and implementation must be left to the faculty and administration.

Those responsible for internal communication must have dependable sources of information. Preenrollment data can be controlled by requiring high school records and test scores. The best way to secure posttransfer data is to ask the four-year institutions to supply it. Intrainstitutional program changes and comparative performance data can be secured from cooperative community college administrators who are responsible for the collection of institutional data. Almost all community colleges gather such information. The formats for summarization and presentation should be left to the articulation specialists.

A comparison of pretransfer and posttransfer performance by subject area and by total class would be useful internally. The posttransfer institution could supply data, which could be integrated with community college records. Additional categorizations could show the relationship between community college and university majors, and associate the extent of extracurricular participation at both levels.

The students themselves are excellent advisors for apprising community college personnel of client needs. Questionnaires completed periodically by community college students can be the best way to keep programs, procedures, and policies up-to-date and effective. Information on a variety of internal issues should be tapped in such a poll. Students could enlighten faculty members about the usefulness of self-evaluation or program selection guidance; student beliefs, hopes, and fears about education beyond the community college level; and attitudes concerning career courses and programs. It would also be in the

9. K. Patricia Cross, *The Junior College Student: A Research Description* (Princeton, N.J.: Educational Testing Service, 1968).

10. Dorothy M. Knoell and Leland L. Medsker, *From Junior to Senior College: A National Study of the Transfer Student* (Washington: American Council on Education, 1965), p. 55.

spirit of community college student personnel philosophy to allow students to query the faculty and administration about pertinent academic and social issues and to present their unsolicited views on subjects affecting their well-being.

Present students, transfers, potential students still in high school, as well as high school and senior college faculty and student personnel specialists should be brought in to supplement impersonal data with human perspectives. Unanticipated issues can often be uncovered as in the case of one meeting with an internal focus sponsored by a community college. Former students who had transferred and university personnel were included in the meeting. A loosely structured discussion led into the unanticipated topic of reverse transfer, the transfer from four-year institutions to community colleges. The community college professors were chagrined to learn that their college would not credit D grades earned at the university toward the associate degree. At the time, the same professors had been complaining to the university about the discrimination of counting D's earned at the university but not D's earned elsewhere toward degrees. Additional discussion between community college faculty members and administration quickly led the community college to abolish the unfair distinction.

The example illustrates two important concerns of intrainstitutional articulation: One is the need for faculty and administration to be thoroughly conversant with the policies and procedures applied in each other's areas, and the other is the need for constant internal evaluation of policies to ensure the most current and beneficial approaches to student transition.

At the High School

Professional expectations for high school teachers make internal articulation both imperative for the school system and an acceptable responsibility for classroom teachers. At the secondary school level, it is an article of faith that each teacher be involved in the whole child—concerned with the task of instruction, the future ramifications of that instruction, and the student's mental health and future academic and social adjustment. In order to fulfill his role successfully, the teacher must have systematic support from the administration and the counseling staff. Conversely, teachers must be in regular contact with guidance personnel, supplying them with information about individual students and performance characteristics in particular subject fields.

The obvious person on whom the leadership responsibility for such communication should devolve is the college consultant. He is the one professional in the high school whose major responsibility is student transition into higher education. It is unfortunate that many high school systems disperse the function of college consultant among a number of counselors with other responsibilities. In other systems that have college consultants, the status of internal articulation may be no better than in systems without college consultants, since the role may be narrowly defined to exclude faculty and administration.

Every high school should employ a college consultant who assists students in making the best possible postsecondary educational choices. But the college consultant should also improve the total high school environment as a facilitating force for smooth transition to further educational experiences. Since in-service training for high school faculty is firmly established, an excellent avenue is open to the college consultant to improve intrainstitutional awareness of transitional issues.

Interest among faculty and administration in articulation in-service training can be developed—and the need for such training demonstrated—by asking the staff to respond anonymously to a questionnaire surveying the extent of their awareness and information about transitional issues. The questions might include the following:

> What percentage of our graduates go on to college?
> What percentage of the above graduate from college?
> In what subject area do you think they perform best?
> How do our graduates compare with national norms on college aptitude tests?
> In what respects is our curriculum out-of-date in relation to college preparatory needs?
> Is class rank more important than test scores for admission to the colleges to which our students usually apply?
> Are our course requirements (tests, homework, papers) similar to the requirements our students will encounter in their first courses in college?

If the results demonstrate a need to add student transition to the range of in-service topics, the college consultant should take charge of the arrangements. He might well start by assembling a panel of former students who are freshmen at a variety of colleges, universities, industrial training programs, and technical institutes. By adroit questioning, the college consultant can highlight the major transitional problems and further stimulate faculty and administration concern. A similarly effective introductory session would be to bring in a representative group of college admission officers and teachers to discuss student transition from their perspective.

The introductory informational sessions should lead the faculty to identify weaknesses that need strengthening. The college consultant can best stimulate discussion and problem identification by furnishing feedback on admission such as rejection of college applications and freshman performance.

The task of the college consultant is more difficult if statistics are withheld by colleges, but a persistent and flexible consultant can obtain some useful information even if he must contact the students directly. National normative data, available from the American College Testing Program, the College Entrance Examination Board, the American Council on Education, and similar sources should accompany institutional data to make the latter more meaningful.

Useful internal coordination can improve student transition by focusing staff attention on one particular subject area, such as mathematics. When poor student performance in college mathematics has been corroborated by lower-than-average scores on the Scholastic Aptitude Test quantitative section and the American College Test mathematics subtest, the mathematics faculty has a clear challenge. Changes in teaching methods and course organization and further academic preparation for mathematics teachers may be necessary, particularly if performance levels are higher in most other academic areas.

The investigation might reveal that student performance and aptitude compare well with the amount of high school preparation received although the curriculum is obsolete for college admission and performance. The same might be the case for the school offering only advanced algebra and solid geometry due to constraints on staff and finances and competition from other areas of study. It may become evident that curricula changes at many colleges make trigonometry a necessity for adequate freshman performance in engineering, architecture, or business administration. The faculty may well be stimulated to revise offerings and adjust staffing so that trigonometry is added in place of a less important aspect of mathematics.

Similarly, foreign language departments and administration might be surprised to learn that many colleges no longer require foreign language credit for admission or college foreign language study for graduation. The school might have been proceeding for years on the assumption that everyone in a college-preparatory program had to take at least two years of the same foreign language. Accepting language requirements as an unalterable condition of college entrance may have kept many students from taking more useful and interesting courses. While students might still enroll in foreign language courses for a number of excellent reasons, language study as a desirable option rather than an absolute requirement would probably represent an improvement in school academic policy. The college consultant would have satisfied his obligation simply by making the facts known. Whether or not to change the requirement would be a matter for faculty and administration to decide.

Meaningful internal articulation can lead the administration to include the college consultant and his guidance colleagues in all deliberations on curriculum and academic policy that might have ramifications for student transition. Pass-fail options or modular scheduling programs would be viewed not only on the basis of immediate usefulness for students, but also in terms of implications for college admission and transition from school to college. The college consultant that had made clear the importance of high school policy for student transition would be consulted about such changes and would be able to assess the inferences. He could suggest flexible bookkeeping procedures that would allow for great individuality yet meet the college admission criteria for class ranking and academic units. At the least, the college consultant could reasonably assess whether or not planned innovations were likely to create admission or transitional problems.

As the school takes more external factors into consideration, the faculty may be stimulated to offer further observations to the college consultant and the guidance and counseling staff. It should be a routine matter for teachers returning from conferences on their specialty to inform guidance personnel of developments that might affect potential college students. A good intrainstitutional articulation program would also enable teachers to influence college counseling programs and techniques just as counselors contribute to the teaching program and academic policy. The college consultant should be a model of a professional staff member who willingly exposes his expertise and activities to his colleagues and solicits their advice and help to refine his ability to accomplish his mission.

six

Curricular Integration

As the diversity and number of postsecondary students and institutions continue to increase, accompanied by more innovation in high school and community college programs, the task of integrating the academic experiences among levels becomes increasingly difficult. Yet, schools and colleges accept the necessity to have good, clear curricular integration within disciplines as students pass from one level to another. According to Jack N. Arbolino, "the integration should be coordinated and continuous, the passage as smooth and efficient as we can make it. The stages of study should mesh and each student should move at his own best pace."[1] He sees the solution as proper subject placement in educational levels through more and better testing. However, such approaches are minimally successful if they are not efficiently coordinated with a cooperative communications system. As Arbolino says, "articulation, like art, does not advance under compulsion."[2] Even so, it is often necessary to prod recalcitrant individuals and institutions with external examinations, politically imposed settlements, or statewide voluntary interinstitutional compacts arrived at independently or under the coaxing of some state educational agency. In such cases it is hoped that a horse led to water will eventually decide to drink.

Methodology becomes an important element in the success of articulation procedures even where positive, willing attitudes already exist. It is a way to order techniques and programs that maximize the results of articulation efforts and to counter lethargy born of intangible results and seemingly endless combat to achieve an apparently simple goal.

1. Jack N. Arbolino, "Proper Placement—Key to Articulation," *Chicago Board Review,* Spring 1971, p. 11.
2. Ibid., p. 12.

A first principle in articulation, contrary to the familiar axiom, is that familiarity breeds respect. Therefore, the first order of business is to bring teachers at different levels together in one way or another. Through the years, some of the best formal methods have been faculty exchange programs, summer institutes sponsored by the university for high school students and teachers, junior college teachers, and in-service training programs. While such activities do not aim to improve school and college relations, mutual understanding usually occurs as a by-product.

The faculty exchange idea, in particular, breeds respect and even empathy, leading to improved coordination. One professor who left Carnegie Tech for a year of high school teaching on a faculty exchange program was not so much impressed by the excellence of high school instruction as he was by the fortitude of the teachers:

> The sharpest contrasts between high school and college teaching were in the physical environment and pace. There was no quiet space . . . nothing was leisurely . . . too little time to see students individually. . . . To expect high school teachers to plan . . . with such a work load and without help . . . is to expect the impossible. . . . Nor were teachers in high school accorded the consideration as professional people which we know in universities; they were required to be clerks, truant officers and policemen.[3]

The professor also developed a new appreciation for the frightened and confused freshmen who came to the university. He was concerned about the university's initial effect on freshmen whom he had known to be "fun to teach" and "hungry for intellectual stimulation." After his high school teaching experiences, the professor's attitudes changed about the school to college process and the professional responsibility of professors to facilitate transition.

High school and junior college teachers who enroll in in-service training institutes sponsored by universities not only update their academic knowledge, but also gain insight into the college curriculum. Students making the transition in that subject cannot help but benefit from the teacher's program. Conversely, college teachers could benefit equally should such institutes be conducted by their counterparts at

3. Edwin Fenton, "Working with High Schools: A Professor's Testimony," *School Review,* Summer 1961, pp. 159-62.

lower levels. Motivational techniques, providing for individual differences, and the like could be substantially improved. At the very least, the idea of year-long or semester exchanges could be approximated by regular programs of visits between teachers at different levels. Even if each high school and college teacher made no more than four or five visits a year, the empathy, understanding, and communication that would result would improve the climate of curricular articulation.

School and college relations methods are best analyzed by dividing them into formal and informal methods. Because formal methods are distinctive, high school-college programs are treated separately from those of the junior-senior colleges. Methods of informal articulation are similar at both levels and therefore are discussed without distinction to level. The arrangement does not suggest that the goals of curricular articulation are any different between formal or informal methods. In both cases the objective is the same—smooth, efficient, intellectual transition from one academic level to another.

Formal Methods for High Schools and Colleges

In its most amorphous form, subject articulation dysfunction is represented by differences in teacher styles and relationships to pupils. The high school teacher will prod students to turn in assignments, laboriously review material he senses that the class has not completely grasped, and either deliberately or unconsciously establish a style of two-way communication with the class. These factors hold true through all the variations in class organization and teaching philosophy presently found in secondary schools.

At the college level, teacher style is often much more impersonal. Some classes are scheduled with one professor lecturing from a platform to a hundred or more students. The effect can only depersonalize and inhibit exchanges. Classes taught by the lecture method to a large audience are supplemented by regular small group discussion sessions, generally led by a graduate student. Although the sessions do reduce class size to that of a typical high school class, the presence of a teaching assistant, acting as a surrogate for the teacher responsible for the material and grading, detracts from the relationship.[4]

4. Julius Menacker, "Subject Articulation between High School and College," *Clearing House,* December 1969, p. 221.

The first step in approaching the area of subject articulation is to obtain information from a variety of sources that provide as complete, comprehensive, and objective an overview of the state of curricular integration or inarticulation as possible. Programs and attitudes related to subject articulation can then be based on fact rather than, as is often the case, on conflicting folklore believed by high school and college faculties.

Of several useful methods for assessing curricular inarticulation, the two most productive are asking new college students and analyzing student performance in subject areas common to high school and college. The simple expedient of asking students to evaluate subject transition is overlooked to an astounding degree; it should always be part of the assessment of curricular articulation. Two inventories of student judgments of curricular articulation conducted by university articulating offices in different parts of the country showed some interesting similarities.

One questionnaire asked students to identify subject areas as "extremely difficult," "about right," or "easy and repetitious." While the majority chose "about right" for every subject area, "extremely difficult" led "easy and repetitious" in every area except English. The greatest percentage choice of difficult over easy was for science, followed by foreign language.[5] The other survey asked students to evaluate high school preparation for similar college courses as either "strong" or weak." The greatest percentage of responses reported subject preparation as "strong" for mathematics. The weakest preparation was in chemistry, followed by foreign languages.[6]

The data, compiled from the answers of more than 2,500 students from the northwest and the midwest, pointed to science and foreign language as the subject areas needing attention for school-to-college curricular articulation. The first questionnaire allowed students to make unstructured comments about the causes of inarticulation. The most numerous responses for chemistry were as follows:

1. High school chemistry was poor or insufficient as a
   background.

5. J. Robert Long, *Curricular Continuity from High School to the University* (Seattle: University of Washington, Office of High School Relations, 1971).
6. Julius Menacker, "Chicago Circle Students Evaluation of Their Transition from High School to College," mimeographed (Chicago: University of Illinois at Chicago Circle, Office of Admissions and Records, 1968).

2. The university has poor instructors.
3. Chemistry is too difficult and too fast.
4. High school chemistry needs more theory or better continuity with university courses.

The leading responses for foreign language were:

1. Placement tests are accurate (usually too high).
2. High schools need more grammar and vocabulary.
3. High schools provide poor teaching and preparation.
4. High schools need more speaking.
5. High schools and the university do not emphasize the same approach.

While the second questionnaire did not permit unstructured responses to specific subjects, students were able to choose among a variety of responses to the questions. Specific items asked students to identify the major problems of university adjustment, major impediments to good grades, and how the university could have been of more help. The two leading adjustment problems were judged to be "handling the work load" and "unfamiliar techniques of instruction"; these were far more popular than the other choices of assuming greater independence, commuting, competition, finances, friends. The leading impediment to good grades was "poor self-discipline," closely followed by "poor time-budgeting." Both were marked far more frequently than all other choices—poor instruction, competition, extracurricular distractions. "Better course placement advising" clearly led all other options in the category of how the university could have been of more help.

Although the two surveys are not directly comparable, it does seem clear that the physical sciences, with chemistry as the example, and foreign language are important problem areas for subject articulation. Further, the evidence clarifies the need for better course placement policies and coordination of both content *and* instructional techniques between high school and university teachers of the same subject.

Information elicited from students should be balanced by teacher input. B. E. Blanchard surveyed a national sample of high school and college teachers on the amount of curricular duplication between the last two years of high school and the first two years of college. Totals for all subjects combined showed that the 665 teachers from 520 high schools estimated a 30 percent overlap, while the 400 faculty members from 269 colleges put the amount of duplication at 23 percent. Of the four areas studied (English, social science, science, mathematics) there was general agreement that English had the greatest overlap and mathematics the least. The study's implications were that "colleges have not kept up with changes and improvements in secondary education" and that there was "poor coordination and articulation between colleges of liberal arts and secondary schools." [7] A similar survey conducted at one college and its main feeder high school would be an excellent method for stimulating interest about school and college relations in both faculties and obtaining baseline data for a subject articulation program.

Curricular articulation needs can also be interpreted from objective data on student performance generally and from particular subjects or subject areas. Both the College Board and the American College Testing Program provide high school grades by subjects, self-reported by students, and almost every college collects the high school transcript. Depending on the organization and the resources of the particular college, a variety of useful formats can be developed. There should be little difference between the comprehensiveness and quality of such evidence produced by multiversities and small four-year or community colleges. While the small institution may not have the sophisticated computing hardware or programming expertise of large universities, it does not have to deal with the great numbers typical to the large institution. Two representative types of detailed progress reports used at various institutions appear as hypothetical examples in figures 1 and 2. Reports that are less informative can also play a useful role.

Institutions armed with facts such as standardized college aptitude test score comparisons, high school rank or scholastic average comparisons, performance in subject areas, and retention and attrition percentages can develop meaningful programs of improvement. Either high schools or colleges should feel free to initiate programs. Due mainly to its greater resources, the college would be the most natural instigator and the professional articulation specialist the main catalyst for action.

To be productive, formal programs of subject articulation must involve the teachers and administrators of a specific subject in the planning, implementation, conclusions, and follow-up. The articula-

7. "Teachers Find Much Duplication in High School, College Courses," *Chronicle of Higher Education,* May 3, 1971, p. 5.

```
From:      College X

To:        Union High School

Re:        Union graduates attending College X compared to
           all X freshmen, fall semester 1973
```

Statistical Performance in Mean Scores:

	Union Alumni	All Freshmen
High school percentile rank	73	76
Verbal SAT	495	550
Math SAT	520	535

Course Performance in Mean Scores:

	Union Alumni			All Freshmen		
	Number	College G.P.A.	School G.P.A.	Number	College G.P.A.	School G.P.A.
Biology	15	1.96	2.49	2,860	2.24	2.52
Chemistry	12	1.84	2.15	1,695	2.07	2.30
English	26	2.30	2.75	3,180	2.60	2.75
French	10	2.50	2.60	1,247	2.65	2.80
German	13	2.06	2.80	1,320	2.72	2.73
History	23	2.74	2.54	2,706	2.40	2.95
Composite	28	2.46	2.66	3,243	2.47	2.83

Academic Status of All Freshmen:

	Number	Percent
Clear	2,706	23
Probation	342	4
Withdrawn	158	1
Dismissed	37	0

Fig. 1. Sample progress report on Union High School
alumni at College *X*.

tor's role is restricted to developing initial interest, administrative
support, and the identification of some of the more general issues,
goals, and procedures. The articulation specialist can represent a dis-
passionate force with no vested interests or hidden agenda. He can

concentrate on the best interests of students and direct the momentum toward articulation objectives and away from divisive side issues.

The most powerful tool at the specialist's disposal for promoting curricular integration is the data collected from high school and college records, for test results, and the guidance information from the College Entrance Examination Board and the American College Testing Program. In the hypothetical case of Union High School, factual reports demonstrate that freshmen are performing below expectations in a number of areas—biology, chemistry, and German (see figure 1). Other areas do not have real problems, because performance is adequate. The differences between high school and college averages are not extreme except in the case of German language study. The great variation in grading practice among educational institutions could explain low correlations, but there should not be such an extreme variation as the .74 drop in German, particularly when the average in German for all freshmen is relatively constant from high school to college. Biology seems to be a problem of school evaluation or poor preparation to meet university expectations and grading practice; chemistry appears to represent a case of improper instruction or grading at the university, as the entire freshman class is earning low grades.

It would seem most appropriate that Union High contact the university upon receiving the report. Ideally, the principal would pass the report to the guidance staff and concerned departments for review and discussion. In all too many cases busy principals simply file such data and forget it; but colleges are still well advised to send such reports to the chief officer of the school. To do otherwise would not only antagonize the administration and threaten formal cooperation, it would diminish the possibilities for solving the problems indicated by the report. About the best approach to use with principals unconcerned with school and college relations is to send a cover letter highlighting the major items in the report and summarizing possible implications. For important feeder schools or ones with serious problems, the college staff might follow up the letter with a phone call or visit to discuss the report and its possible internal uses.

While the high school may conduct useful in-service training based on the report, the university's school relations office should make it known to the school's administration that the representatives are available to discuss the report with the school faculty. If one discipline is

To: Union High School

From: University Y

Re: REPORT ON ALUMNI PERFORMANCE

Freshmen from Union at the University:

	College	School per-centile rank	ACT:C*
Adams, Frank	Engineering	82	29
Brown, Susan	Education	78	22
Collins, Jane	Liberal Arts	75	23
Drucker, Steven	Business Admin.	72	23

Performance in Fall & Winter Quarters 1971-72:
(compared with all University freshmen)

	Union Freshmen		University Freshmen	
	Number	Mean	Number	Mean
School Per-centile Rank	10	70	3,500	72
ACT:C*	10	22	3,200	23
Grade Point Average				
Cumulative	10	3.16	3,400	3.25
English	6	3.01	2,800	3.42
Natural sciences	4	3.75	2,100	3.09
Social sciences	8	3.08	2,600	3.68
Foreign lang.	3	3.50	1,900	3.56
Humanities	5	3.07	2,700	3.42
Mathematics	6	3.62	1,750	3.02

Academic Status:

	Union Freshmen		University Freshmen	
	Number	Percent	Number	Percent
Clear	6	60	2,700	77
Probation	3	30	600	17
Dismissed	1	10	100	3
Withdrawn	0	0	100	3

*ACT:C, American College Test Composite Score

Fig. 2. Sample progress report on Union High School alumni at University Y.

138

noticeably weak, a professor from that field might accompany the articulation specialists.

Such a meeting should be attended by concerned faculty and representatives from the guidance staff and administration. The only structure necessary is the data in the feedback report, which participants should have read beforehand. The articulation specialist's main concern during the meeting should be to keep discussion focused on student transition in a particular subject. High school faculty may become aware of the need to cover additional topics in junior and senior courses, or the university staff might discover teaching techniques to complement the high school methods in order to avoid shocking freshmen with entirely different instructional modes. But even without specific outcomes, the meeting may be judged a success if greater sensitivity and awareness are developed for curricular problems. Such progress can heighten activity between subject specialists, generating more letters between them and more informed counseling of students at both ends of the continuum.

The subject articulation conference

Economy of time and resources dictates that conferences serve a number of feeder schools. Geographic areas containing significant numbers of feeder schools are delineated, and a site is selected where university representatives can hold an area workshop on articulation. Other conferences should be held on the college campus for school representatives who can attend. The first step should always be to plan the meeting jointly by meetings, phone, or correspondence.

At one university, a conference on German was arranged when the academic feedback reports of two successive years signaled poor freshman performance in that subject. While comparable high school grades were not available, mean and median scholastic averages hovered precariously below the *C* level, convincing the university German department of the need to meet with their high school counterparts.

Contacts with representative high school teachers were made mainly by the university articulation officer, working through his associates in school guidance departments. Because the university primarily served commuters, a luncheon meeting was easily arranged for the articulation officer, three high school German teachers, and two members of the university German department. A conference format and date were decided upon, and responsibility for arrangements was left with the articulator. Presentations were made by both high school and university teachers, and ample time was set aside for discussion.

First the professors explained the university German program, its requirements, and typical methodologies. Then school participants described the salient features of their programs. Participants toured the university language laboratory and discussed university placement policies for German and methods for improving student academic transition. The most significant finding was that almost without exception the high schools made extensive use of the audio-lingual method (ALM) of instruction while the university taught classes in the traditional manner. Used only for supplementary instruction, the university's laboratory was far more sophisticated and better equipped than anything at any of the schools. The situation was an obvious case of poor methodological integration and poor utilization of resources for the student's benefit. The high schools emphasized audio-lingual instruction but had only minimally satisfactory laboratory equipment. On the other hand, the college had very elaborate ALM equipment but did not place major emphasis on that mode of instruction.

Another important topic was university placement policies. The placement test, an entirely written examination, stressed grammar, reading comprehension, and vocabulary. Students with the greatest number of high school units in German achieved the highest scores. Those with only two units often placed so low that a new language was recommended, while those with four units were usually considered ready for advanced work in the language. The clearest performance distinctions on the placement tests were between those who had taken German in their freshman and sophomore high school years and those who had German during their junior and senior years. Students with more recent instruction performed far better.

The recommendations made at the conclusion of the conference were on two levels—highly specific "technical" items and broad ideas related to improving student transition. On the first level were the following recommendations:

- Teachers at all levels should demand improved elementary German textbooks.

- Students completing two units of high school German should have a passive reading vocabulary of about two hundred words.
- Courses on both levels should be more eclectic in methodology, that is, there should be a balance between emphasis on reading and on speaking.
- Neither level should emphasize grammar courses. The objective of grammar is as an aid to the *use* of language, not as an end in itself.
- Neither level should emphasize translation courses. The objective of reading is comprehension and appreciation of content, not the development of translators, which is a specific skill unto itself.
- Both courses should be as active as possible for the student.

The more general recommendations are far more instructive as examples of the broad improvements in school and college relations that can result from structured interaction between academic personnel from both levels:

1. The facilities of the university language laboratory should be made available to high school German students on a selective basis. Such a program could be done with ease and convenience, since the lab had equipment that allowed students to dial particular numbers from home telephones and be connected with specific instructional tapes. Selectivity would be necessary to insure that circuits were not overloaded and that university students would receive priority.

2. High school counselors should recognize that programming students for two years of German in the freshman and sophomore years is poor educational practice. The nature of foreign language study is such that the two-year break between German in high school and German in college destroys the necessary continuity. Prospective college students wishing only two years of high school foreign language should be encouraged to take it in the last two years.

3. Information about instructional materials (syllabi, texts, examinations) should be exchanged on a regular basis. Also, high school instructors should be sent the results of placement examinations. Communication and the exchange of information are to be generally encouraged.

4. High school teachers do not have enough information about the skills and outcomes expected of students by professors of German. Agreement should be reached

about the skills to be acquired in each high school and college German course.

5. There is considerable evidence that calls into question the assumption that one year of high school foreign language is equivalent to one semester of college study. The assumption should be subjected to verification.[8]

The conference both increased mutual understanding and brought cooperation to a higher level. Specific transitional improvements were identified that could be made quickly and easily, such as the use of the university language laboratory and the placement of foreign language in the last two years of high school. Probably the longest range improvement in curricular transition was the mutual recognition of the difficulties caused students by different instructional modes. The agreement led to a balanced approach between the two methods that was best for all concerned, particularly the students. Finally, the questioning of the high school-college course equivalency held possibilities for basic changes in placement and even admission requirements.

The German conference was limited to less than thirty persons—two-thirds from the schools and one-third from the college—because it was important to keep the meetings small enough to promote maximum interaction among the participants. Size restrictions leave the problem of disseminating the conference information to the much larger number of concerned parties. The simplest method is to mail a summary of the conference to the appropriate department at all feeder high schools. The mailing should include forms for requesting additional copies and an offer to send a representative to those schools that are sufficiently stimulated by the report to want to discuss the findings.

The most common complaint heard about subject articulation conferences is that the meetings do not produce results commensurate with the time, effort, and expense that go into them. Objective evidence for evaluating findings is hard to obtain, and the search can be discouraging. The only defense for subject conferences is that interlevel meetings and the resulting exchange of ideas and information cannot help but benefit teachers and students alike. The very existence of such efforts testifies to the importance of curricular integration to both faculties who keep concern for articulation in the academic consciousness.

8. Julius Menacker, "Subject Matter Articulation Report Topics: The Teaching of German," mimeographed (Chicago: University of Illinois at Chicago Circle, Office of Admissions and Records, 1968).

The Advanced Placement Program

The formal subject articulation program that has had the widest impact and deepest effect is, without question, the CEEB Advanced Placement Program. Here is an example of an extraschool organization, the College Entrance Examination Board, organizing and maintaining a national program of curricular integration. The most obvious inadequacy of the program is that it is structured only to serve a small segment of the college-bound population—superior students. Even so, its impact on improving school and college relations has gone far beyond the program's participants. An atmosphere permeates participating schools, affecting many nonparticipating students and faculty through contact with participants.

The communicators, primarily the high school and college teachers, play the critical role of circulating to the other level updated information about teaching methods, course content, grading philosophies, instructional materials, and similar topics. The teachers learn such information by attending joint advanced placement conferences in the subject matter that they teach, by taking part in joint reading sessions on grading examinations, and from simply receiving information connected with teaching the course. Such activities not only improve school-college academic intelligences but are instrumental in developing positive attitudes about school and college relations. One history professor who was typically skeptical before attending his first advanced placement meeting, said afterwards, "Some of the college men on the program were poorly prepared and came off second best, while instructors from public and private high schools described existing history courses more demanding than many of the college survey courses I know about." [9] This is the very common reaction of professors who interact with schoolteachers within the formal structure of the Advanced Placement Program. Similarly, high school teachers gain new respect for the professionalism and concern for students exhibited by professors.

The interaction and information dissemination that results from the Advanced Placement Program is only one aspect of its importance to school and college relations. The general acceptance of the concept of advanced placement by both high schools and colleges is an equal con-

9. Fenton, "Working with High Schools," p. 158.

tribution. Best exemplified by a regularized system of external communication and internal procedures, the program ensures course parity. Some procedural and attitudinal problems and solutions were detailed in the last decade by Clyde Vroman, and they are as valid today as they were then.[10] Vroman's enumeration of problems and solutions was based on a survey of the fifty largest high school Advanced Placement English Programs and the hundred largest collegiate receivers of Advanced Placement English examinations. Vroman concluded that both schools and colleges shared a number of common deficiencies related to the program. Among these were the lack of clear policies and published statements of advanced placement policies, poor understanding of the program and participating students, a paucity of follow-up studies and summary data, wide variation in college acceptance policies, poor administrative provisions in support of the program, and a lack of organized school-college cooperation to maintain and improve it. Most damning from the articulation view was the finding that "many colleges demand higher standards of advanced placement students in granting credit and placement than they apply to their regular freshmen." [11]

Vroman recommended local and regional school-college advanced placement conferences, more efficient procedures for informing colleges about high school advanced placement courses, follow-up studies, more precise college policies that are explained better to schools, and greater awareness and better communication of the Advanced Placement Program. A recent critical examination found that even though the program represents the largest national effort to improve the transition of superior students, gains in program participation have been declining in comparison with earlier years. Some of the reasons advanced for the declining rate of expansion are a growing reaction against elitism in education; wide dissatisfaction with formal examinations, particularly of the objective, quantified variety; growing concern for individualized teaching and learning; the national trend to diminish to irrelevance the significance of grades and grading; the development of programs of independent, individually guided instruction; and the

10. Clyde Vroman, "Let's Get Together on Advanced Placement," *College Board Review*, Spring 1963, pp. 18-19.
11. Ibid., p. 18.

rising participation of students in educational policy and decision-making, including the shaping of courses and programs of study.[12]

Still, each year more and more students enroll in advanced placement courses and submit more examinations to more participating colleges. To illustrate the extent of the program, in the spring of 1969 more than 53,000 students took more than 69,000 advanced placement examinations and sent scores to more than 1,200 colleges. Program improvements and an accelerated expansion rate will come only when there are articulation specialists or staff members who are oriented to articulation and are willing to push for changes. As fine as it may be on its intrinsic merits, the program's success and benefits for students at any school or college will be in proportion to the amount of attention and effort expended by professionals.

Formal Programs for Junior and Senior Colleges

Junior-senior college curricular integration involves all of the formal techniques and issues of subject articulation discussed in the preceding section as well as additional ones unique to the college level. The greater scope of junior-senior college curricular integration can be attributed to the overriding concern at this level for the transferability of credit from the community college program to the senior college degree. A very concrete and specific matter, transferability contrasts with the ambiguities surrounding matters of adequate preparation, placement, teaching methodology, and the like. Transfer credit issues become better defined, battle lines are drawn more firmly, and solutions are more clearly structured and implemented.

Subject articulation conferences

Since professors from each level assume that they know what college teaching is all about, they are reluctant to admit the wisdom of a different point of view. John W. Gardner captured the essence of this problem in the following words:

> I must report that even excellent institutions run by excellent human beings are inherently sluggish, *not* hungry for innovation, *not* quick to respond to human need, *not*

12. William R. Hochman, "Advanced Placement: Can It Change with the Times?" *College Board Review,* Fall 1970, p. 17.

eager to reshape themselves to meet the challenge of the times.

I am not suggesting a polarity between men and their institutions—men eager for change, institutions blocking it. The institutions are run by men. And often those who appear most eager for change oppose it most stubbornly when their own institutions are involved. *I give you the university professor, a great friend of change provided it doesn't affect the patterns of academic life. His motto is, "Innovate away from home."* (emphasis added to final two sentences)[13]

It is therefore crucial that the subject articulation conference be a joint venture that carefully observes the prerogatives of each group and, whenever possible, imposes mutual obligations for change or compromise. Two excellent guidelines worth following in junior-senior college curricular articulation conferences are suggested by G. Robert Darnes:

1. An articulation conference must be cooperatively planned. What do I mean by cooperatively planned? It must be planned by representatives of both two- and four-year institutions. Both groups must have mutual respect for each other, recognize the roles of each other, and everyone must be motivated to work for the welfare of the student. I never serve on a planning committee for an articulation conference unless there is *equal* representation from both two- and four-year colleges. One of the most important roles that a . . . coordinating agency or its representatives . . . can do is to be the spark plug—to call this group together and then to serve as the secretary for the group. This first planning conference should only identify articulation problems and develop an agenda. . . . I can tell you that the first time you try this procedure it will take two or three hours of hard, fast talking, soul searching, as both groups begin to develop their positions and understand each other.

2. This planning group should then plan the program and select the participants making sure that both two- and four-year institutions are equally represented. Before this articulation conference is completed the senior people may wish to meet as a group and try to arrive at a meeting of minds on their point of view, while the junior college people should do the same. They should then

13. John W. Gardner, *No Easy Victories* (New York: Harper & Row, 1968), p. 32.

come back together and see if these differences can be resolved. Eventually this step can be omitted.[14]

Some extracts from the minutes of two junior-senior college subject articulation conferences organized according to the principles illustrate the kinds of outcome that can be expected.

Engineering:

1. There are a few university engineering classes that may have as many as 200 students, while junior college engineering classes rarely exceed 40 students. These size differences make for necessary differences in teaching and assignments.

2. There is much variation in the types and amounts of junior college engineering, mathematics, chemistry, and physics courses. The junior college faculty participants pointed out that it is neither desirable nor possible for all junior colleges to parallel the lower division curriculum of any particular university, since there is great variation among senior institutions and junior college transfers attending many different senior colleges. Therefore, senior institutions must be flexible in the evaluation and acceptance of junior college courses toward engineering degrees.

3. Junior college representatives raised the problem of the junior college student who may have enrolled in a terminal electronics program or related career field and later decided to pursue a university engineering degree. The issue is that most of the terminal courses would not transfer, even though they are, in many respects, relevant to baccalaureate engineering degrees.

4. It was agreed that students should be given every opportunity to establish useful transfer credit in doubtful cases. This should include proficiency examinations, a careful review of the course syllabus and text, student interviews and anything else that might be useful.

Mathematics:

1. Junior college classes involved much more homework and feedback to students on the homework than university classes demanded. The same was true for tests.

2. Junior college classes were much smaller and encouraged discussion. University classes were larger, and students had to initiate questions.

14. G. Robert Darnes, "Articulation in Illinois" (Paper delivered to the National Council of State Directors of Junior Colleges at the annual convention of the American Association of Junior Colleges, Dallas, Tex., Feb. 28, 1972).

3. It was decided that the most useful post-calculus courses for junior colleges to offer were: sets and real numbers, multivariate calculus, number theory, ordinary differential equations, probability, and statistics.

4. It was agreed that transfer credit should be decided on a qualitative basis rather than a quantitative one; that is, the *course content* rather than the course number or year in which it is normally taken should determine the manner in which credit should be used.

5. It was noted that there was much more university and junior college teachers could do to improve transition in mathematics. A proposal was advanced to seek National Science Foundation funds to support a jointly sponsored and directed mathematics institute.

6. Junior college professors indicated they and their students needed concrete information about the kinds of courses that would transfer usefully for a mathematics major.[15]

Both conferences identified important issues of academic transition. In some cases, not much was done to resolve problems, but at least both groups returned to their respective campuses with additional perspectives and information, which generally improved transition for students in countless small ways. In other cases, concrete general solutions were developed.

Concurrent enrollment

One of the problems of curricular transition from junior to senior college is that it is not always possible to parallel a university lower division program at a community college. This is particularly true in highly specialized and technical fields such as architecture, but the problem also exists in many other fields of study. Often, when requirements are not known, part of the student's program may not be counted toward the degree; even when the curriculum is known, additional credit may still be demanded for the degree. Students may still have to leave the community college earlier than either institution would like or follow a disjointed program that does not offer much in the way of academic continuity.

15. Julius Menacker, "Subject Matter Articulation Report Topics: The Teaching of Engineering," mimeographed (Chicago: University of Illinois at Chicago Circle, Office of Admissions and Records, 1969); Julius Menacker, "Subject Matter Articulation Report Topics: The Teaching of Mathematics," mimeographed (Chicago: University of Illinois at Chicago Circle, Office of Admissions and Records, 1969).

Meetings of representatives of both levels have brought forth another, more preferable alternative—concurrent enrollment. Enrollment in both colleges is feasible for junior-senior college articulation, since the overwhelming majority of community college students tend to complete their education at nearby colleges. It has the advantage of allowing students to make maximum progress toward a degree while remaining primarily attached to the community college, a tie which is usually beneficial from a developmental viewpoint. The potential disadvantages include a reduced enrollment for particular junior college departments, threatening the strength of the department or making an inordinate demand for particular university courses that might cause native university students to lose their space to a concurrently enrolled community college student.

Before a cooperative program can be planned, student and institutional need must be well documented. How many students would find concurrent enrollment profitable? What time and days should the courses be offered? Would it be better for the courses to be taught at the junior or senior college? All such questions must be carefully answered before procedures are set in motion.

Mutually approved guidelines can smooth the way to a functional enrollment program. The first guideline should state that participation is not related to admission requirements, as the emphasis is on program integration. Since class size will usually be limited, there must be instructions for enrollment priorities. One such rule should be that concurrent enrollment spaces are available only in required or recommended degree courses that are not available at the parent campus. Another rule is that native students have priority in classes with limited space. This is essential to forestall discontent among native students and to keep responsibilities in their proper perspective. After all, the first responsibility of an educational institution is to provide instruction to its own students. Students presenting themselves for the program should have been previously screened by counselors at both levels who considered the need for concurrent enrollment, the course availability, and the personal educational value to the student of concurrent enrollment at that time.

Before the program becomes operational, feedback and evaluation components must be built into it. Performance should be carefully monitored, as should data about concurrent enrollees' preferences for the times and days at which courses should be offered. Such facts should form the substance for periodic review of the program. Finally, it is of paramount importance that the joint group of program facilitators consider the question of advertising the program and recruiting students for it. Students do not automatically hear of such innovations, nor do they take much interest in notices posted on bulletin boards or in flyers distributed at random.

In order to make the program as successful as the planners envision, community college student personnel specialists must personally contact students and teachers about it and be available to handle administrative matters. Specialists can make presentations to faculty meetings, student group guidance meetings, and personal student interviews, activities that are especially necessary at the earliest stages of the program's development and still required once the program is well established and generally publicized.

Feedback services

Enough has been said about the needs and methods of feedback on academic performance, but a few comments are warranted about the unique elements of feedback between the receiving and sending college. Facts about time and credit needed for senior college graduation should augment information on scholastic performance by subject area and academic status. An inclusive ideal data feedback report would follow the general lines of figure 3.

The data can be put to several uses for improving academic transition. Figures under *Students in Attendance* show that there is very poor program integration between the community college and university education programs. The statistics indicate that students leave the community college education program early and that those who complete the program are not able fully to utilize their transfer credit. Here is a curriculum articulation problem that deserves attention. Inarticulation seems to be the result of an inadequate community college transfer program in education coupled with a restrictive credit acceptance policy at the university. The solution would necessarily require communication and cooperation between the levels.

The grade average data identify other disorders. The university should be interested in why most community college transfers perform so poorly in German in contrast to the excellent performance of LL

From: University Y

To: Community College LL

Re: Feedback Report on Student Status

TRANSFER STUDENTS

Entered Fall 1971:

	College	Entering Credit Hrs.	Current Credit Hrs.	Level
Abrahams, S.	Liberal Arts	60	115	Jr.
Brown, J. L.	Education	60	120	Sr.
Kowalski, S.	Bus. Admin.	60	110	Jr.

Entered Spring, 1972:

	College	Entering Credit Hrs.	Current Credit Hrs.	Level
Jones, P. A.	Liberal Arts	55	170	Sr.
Malone, J.	Education	50	60	Jr.
Morris, S.	Arch./Art	40	60	Jr.
Wayne, R. F.	Liberal Arts	60	60	Sr.

===

STUDENT PERFORMANCE
1972-73 Academic Year

	LL Transfers		All Community College Transfers		
Subject	Number	Transfer G.P.A.	Present G.P.A.	Number	Transfer G.P.A.	Present G.P.A.
English Comp.	6	2.95	2.80	338	2.65	2.20
Biology	3	2.50	2.30	315	2.30	2.14
History	5	2.60	2.20	340	2.50	2.45
German	4	2.32	2.50	215	2.20	1.98
Education	5	2.80	1.95	105	2.70	2.70
Mathematics	3	2.10	2.10	200	2.15	2.05
Composite	6	2.60	2.42	340	2.50	2.35

Academic Status of LL Students:

Clear	4
Probation	1
Withdrawn	1
Dismissed	0

Fig. 3. Sample university feedback report on community college alumni and transfers.

Community College transfers. Transfers from LL do better in university German courses than in their community college courses, reversing the usual trend. Certainly, the question deserves attention. Perhaps the methods used at LL Community College should be adopted by other community colleges and by the university. The important point to note is that the value of the data is not intrinsic, but rather lies in the uses to which the knowledge is put.

Parallel programs and curriculum guides

The rapidity with which universities change their degree requirements and course offerings is rivaled by the rate of community college alterations, all of which leaves students attempting to transfer in the middle of an academic juggling act. Even if course offerings and degree requirements were stable, there would still be students who would consult misinformed or uninformed counselors. Therefore, curriculum articulation devices are sorely needed in this important area of student transition.

The parallel program or curriculum guide is one approach to the problem and has proved useful in a number of variations. The basic idea is to prepare documents for each transfer program specifying possible applications of each community college course upon transfer. The best pretransfer course of study in any particular area is described completely. The parallel program approach requires great exactness because it is concerned only with one program between one community college and one senior institution. The individualistic method includes documentation by title and number of pertinent courses in the university program juxtaposed with the same information for each community college course considered as an equivalent.

The main advantage of such an approach is that the document's precision makes misunderstanding almost impossible. Also, a small community college can take the initiative as easily as the university can. The disadvantages are that parallel programs must be constantly updated to reflect changes in courses and even course numbers, and the very specificity of the document excludes and even discourages a number of options and alternatives that might be possible. Figure 4 is an abbreviated sample of a typical parallel program.

The curriculum guide is a document prepared by a senior institution to serve as a basic pretransfer course selection guide in a particular major for all feeder junior colleges. As such, course labels and numbers are avoided in favor of descriptive information about course

```
┌─────────────────────────────────────────────────────────────────┐
│                        Parallel Program                          │
│                             in                                   │
│                        ENGINEERING                               │
│                                                                   │
│  Community College      Qtr.     University lower        Sem.    │
│       course            hrs.     ·division course        hrs.    │
│  ===============================================================  │
│  FIRST YEAR:                                                      │
│  English 101, 102        8     Composition 101, 102        6     │
│  Math 123, 132          10     Math 130, 131               8     │
│  Chemistry 112, 114            Chemistry 102, 104          8     │
│     and 116             13                                       │
│  Three electives        11     Three electives             8     │
│        Total hours      42           Total hours          30     │
│                                                                   │
│  SECOND YEAR:                                                     │
│  Math 220, 221, 222     12     Math 150, 201               6     │
│  Physics 107, 108, 109  12     Physics 112, 113            8     │
│  Engineering 152, 211    8     Engineering 101, 102        8     │
│  Three electives        13     Three electives            10     │
│        Total hours      45           Total hours          32     │
│  ===============================================================  │
│                                                                   │
│  Courses required of University lower division engineering       │
│  students which have no equivalent at Community College:         │
│      Systems Engineering 160 (Introduction to                    │
│          Engineering Design III)              3 sem. hrs.        │
│      Materials Engineering 103 (Engineering                      │
│          Mechanics III)                       3 sem. hrs.        │
│      Materials Engineering 142 (Properties of                    │
│          Materials I)                         4 sem. hrs.        │
│      Materials Engineering 230 (Properties of                    │
│          Materials II)                        3 sem. hrs.        │
│      Information Engineering 219 (Introduction                   │
│          to Electromagnetic Fields)           4 sem. hrs.        │
│                                                                   │
│  Approved                  Total hours       17 sem. hrs.        │
│  September 1, 1973                                                │
│                                                                   │
│                            _____           │
│                            Dean of Transfer Programs             │
│                                Community College                 │
│                                                                   │
│                                                                   │
│                            _____           │
│                            Dean, College of Engineering          │
│                                  University                      │
└─────────────────────────────────────────────────────────────────┘
```

Fig. 4. Sample recommended parallel program in engineering.

Curriculum Guide for Transfer
to University Business Administration Degree Programs

General University Requirements
Freshman Rhetoric and Composition   8 qtr. hrs.(6 sem. hrs.)
   Courses in English, composition, or communication. May
not include any remedial courses in reading or writing,
courses below the college level, or courses directed at
specific vocations, such as Business Writing.
Physical Education   6 qtr. hrs.(4 sem. hrs.)
   May be met with the equivalent or by taking any activity
course at the two-year college.
   EXCEPTIONS: Veterans; students transferring with 90 or
more quarter hours (60 or more sem. hrs.) of baccalaureate
courses; students with medical waivers from the University
Health Service.

General Education Requirements
Natural Science   12 qtr. hrs.(8-9 sem. hrs.)
   In sequence. Any of the natural sciences, including
biology, chemistry, physical geography, geology, physical
science, or physics. Two 4-semester-hour laboratory courses
usually will satisfy the requirements.
Humanities   12 qtr. hrs.(8-9 sem. hrs.)
   In sequence. Classics in translation, Greek or Latin ·
literature in the original. English in one of two sequences:
Introduction to poetry, drama, and fiction; or survey of
English literature. French or Spanish literature in translation. Speech and theatre excluding public speaking.
History of architecture or art. Humanities survey sequence
plus one additional course.
   IN ADDITION: Elementary logic (4 qtr. hrs. or 3 sem.
hrs.) and fine arts (3 qtr. hrs. or 2 sem. hrs.) must be
taken. Fine arts may include music, theatre, or art appreciation but not methodology courses.
Social Science   All are required
   ECONOMICS: (8 qtr. hrs. or 6 sem. hrs.) Including one
course in microeconomics and one in macroeconomics.
   BEHAVIORAL SCIENCES: (8 qtr. hrs. or 6 sem. hrs.) In
any combination of anthropology, psychology, or sociology.
   HISTORY or POLITICAL SCIENCE: (8 qtr. hrs. or 6 sem.
hrs.) In any combination of courses in the area.

Elective Requirement
A total of 19 quarter hours (12-13 sem. hrs.) may be offered.
Must be in the general education areas. Students should

Fig. 5. Sample curriculum guide for transfer to a university college of business administration.

154

avoid technical or occupational business courses, such as typing, salesmanship, business machines, which will not be counted as credit toward the degree.

~   Mathematics Requirement
Although not counted toward the degree, high school mathematics through college algebra should be completed as preparation for the finite mathematics-calculus sequence required of all students in the College of Business Administration. The community college student is also encouraged to complete one course each in analytic geometry and calculus, or two courses in calculus, as the equivalent of two mathematics courses that beginning freshmen in Business Administration normally take during their first year at the University.

Accounting   9 qtr. hrs.(6 sem. hrs.)
    Introductory Accounting will be credited for Accounting 100 and 101 (6 qtr. hrs.), and 3 semester hours of Introduction to Cost Accounting or Cost Accounting will be credited as Accounting 102. These three courses satisfy the core accounting sequence required of all students in the College of Business Administration.
Other Business Courses
    Since most university business courses are at the 300 level, junior college courses with similar titles are not usually transferable. Credit will be granted on the basis of a proficiency examination or a petition to the dean of the college, who will consider each case individually.

Approved
September 1, 1973   _____
                           Chairman, University Community
                           College Advisory Council in
                           Business Programs

                           _____
                           Dean, University College of
                           Business Administration

Fig. 5. *Continued.*

155

areas. The disadvantage of the approach is that the generalization allows for misinterpretation that could occasionally lead students to take an improper course. Junior college personnel would claim that the university reneged on the agreement, when the real cause of the dispute was ignorance. The guide, however, does not require revision as frequently as the parallel program and can list all possible variations. Samples of a curriculum guide in business administration, traditionally a restrictive area, are presented in figure 5.

The type of curricular guidance document that is most appropriate in any junior-senior college set of relationships depends on the resources of the institutions involved and the attitudes of academic decision-makers, particularly at the senior level. If those with authority over credit acceptance take a restrictive attitude, the parallel program would be best because of its precision. Where acceptance policies are broad and flexible and curriculum guide is preferable. There is also no sense in opting for parallel programs if the requisite staff is not available for the necessary continual monitoring and updating.

Regardless of which method is used, the documents must be developed on a cooperative basis. More than an agreement to drop or keep a guide, a decision to cooperate means joint development and negotiation about which courses to include, when to update the material, who should be responsible for producing the documents, how the information should be disseminated, and similar matters.

It may take a long time from the decision to create a parallel program or curriculum guide until the material is completed. Especially with parallel programs, complicated negotiations will be needed both within the university and with each community college; for this reason, the curriculum guide is recommended. An articulation specialist should coordinate the project and supply clerical and administrative support. He should bring the necessary parties together, working to establish a permanent consortium or committee. As someone neutral to the subject field under discussion, the specialist should keep teachers and administrators moving forward by suggesting compromises and alternatives and by continually focusing on the need for the document.

The best system of production is ditto or mimeograph, so that very large quantities can be cheaply produced for wide distribution to both students and counselors. The material should be available in quantity at community colleges and for visitors to the university. Everyone involved in the document's production, as well as everyone concerned with the transition process, should have copies. If money is available, a loose-leaf notebook labeled with the recipient's name would be a good binding so that future prepunched materials could be added to supplement the notebook. It is advisable for each document to carry the signature of the chief academic decision-makers who approved it, the date on which it was approved, and the duration of the policy. Finally, the articulation documents should have a preface in which the university agrees that the curriculum guide protects the transfer student from changes in university requirements during the period that the guide is in force.

The College-Level Examination Program

The last two decades have seen a steadily rising level of college aspiration among all classes and varieties of Americans. The community college and an increasingly more complex society have both been the cause and result. As part of the movement, colleges have been pressured to respond better to American aspirations. Just as the College Entrance Examination Board responded to an earlier demand for more opportunity for academically talented high school students with the Advanced Placement Program, so the CEEB now has developed the College-Level Examination Program (CLEP).

The College-Level Examination Program has as its main purpose the establishment of college credit and certification of academic achievement for those who have gained knowledge through nontraditional means. According to the College Board, it is based on the following assumptions:

1. People can and do acquire learning at the college level in nontraditional ways.

2. Institutions of higher education must be concerned primarily with what an individual knows, not how many hours he has sat in class or the number of credits he has amassed.

3. Nontraditional learning can be measured and compared with the learning acquired by traditional students.[16]

16. *College Credit by Examination Through the College-Level Examination Program* (New York: College Entrance Examination Board, 1970), pp. 7-8.

The premises have led the College Board to establish the following goals for CLEP:

1. To provide a national program of examinations that can be used to evaluate nontraditional education at the college level.
2. To stimulate colleges and universities to become more aware of the need for and the possibility of credit by examination.
3. To allow colleges and universities to develop appropriate procedures for the placement, accreditation, and admission of transfer students.
4. To provide colleges and universities a means by which to evaluate their programs and their students' achievements.
5. To assist adults who wish to continue their education in order to meet licensing and certification requirements or to qualify for higher positions.[17]

The main interest for junior-senior college curricular articulation is with the third goal. Both the college level general examinations and the college level subject examinations are useful for subject articulation. The general examinations allow for an evaluation of the level of general education, usually understood among colleges to be learning in English composition, mathematics, natural sciences, humanities, and social sciences-history. The subject examinations are designed to measure achievement in specific subjects that range from American government to college algebra, computers and data processing, educational psychology, geology, money and banking, statistics, and a score of other subjects.

Both types of examinations, while not based on the curriculum of any particular college, are designed to approximate the general expectations of American higher education for a level of general information and competence in certain subjects. In order to make such evaluations, both tests are developed by committees of two- and four-year college teachers and normed on representative samples of college students who have completed the pertinent courses or programs.[18]

The CLEP started in 1965, and by 1970 about one thousand colleges were participating. Presumably, CLEP is here to stay and must be reckoned with. The question to consider here is the methodology

17. Ibid., p. 8.
18. *Tests and Services: College-Level Examination Program* (New York: College Entrance Examination Board, 1970), p. 5.

through which colleges and universities can best use CLEP "to develop appropriate procedures for the placement, accreditation, and adminission of transfer students."

The CLEP general examinations can be useful in resolving one of the thorniest problems of credit transfer—satisfaction of lower division general education requirements. In less advanced articulation, students often suffer from the scrutiny put to each course offered for general education requirements. In strict analyses, a science course that did not include enough laboratory work is counted as elective credit, but not as a general education requirement. Similarly, general education requirements will vary from one community college to another and among senior colleges. Thus, a student following his community college's pattern of six hours each of English, social science, natural science, and humanities may find himself lacking lower division general education hours after transfer because the senior institution required three hours in social science and nine hours in humanities.

The CLEP could be used as an impartial arbiter to resolve quibbling about aspects of one course or general education areas that are needed to satisfy requirements. Standardized on large, representative populations and embodying a broad spectrum of academic thinking, CLEP would seem an ideal neutral force to settle disputes of general education transfer policy. Even where articulation is more advanced, periodic use of CLEP general examinations can be an extremely useful tool for monitoring the viability of general education compacts. The test could also qualify a new community college, as yet not accredited regionally, for inclusion in a consortium of institutions in which completion of the associate degree automatically satisfies the senior institutions' general education requirements.

The CLEP subject examination would be useful in settling such junior-senior college issues as were raised in the engineering conference, where it was agreed that "students should be given every opportunity to establish useful transfer credit in doubtful cases." CLEP can avoid some of the community college objections to the institutionally biased proficiency test, usually some professor's final examination, and can be an excellent compromise where such testing ambiguities exist. CLEP subject examinations can also answer the point made at the mathematics conference that "transfer credit should be decided on a qualitative basis rather than a quantitative one, that is, it is the *course content* . . . that should determine the manner in which credit should be used." What better way is there to assess actual course content than to use an independently validated test on the subject?

In all uses of CLEP to improve credit transferability, it should be· recognized that such an external device cannot replace the mutual understanding and communication between junior and senior college personnel that must form the basic fabric for subject articulation relationships. Too much reliance on external tests is dangerous for student transition. The values of CLEP lies in its usefulness as a tool to promote understanding and communication and to serve as one of the many devices for facilitating student forward progress—in this case, through credit transfer—from junior to senior colleges. The danger inherent in CLEP lies in possible misuse as, for example, an admission rejection device. As Joseph P. Cosand, then president of the Junior College District of St. Louis, said:

> The CLEP test, developed by the College Entrance Examination Board, is to me one of the greatest vehicles as a screen-in device. However, I am deeply concerned the CLEP test is being prostituted and is being used to screen out students. This must not be! The need for and importance of advanced placement, not only from high schools, but also for transfers from community colleges is becoming increasingly important. The maturity of many of these students demands this, the cynicism of students demands this; the cynicism of students is indicative that the rigidity of credit demands by specific subjects is outmoded.[19]

Initiatives

The overwhelming majority of two-year colleges are public institutions that have been developed over the past decade as part of state master plans for public higher education. The success of the comprehensive plans depends on the ability of junior colleges, four-year colleges, and capstone senior institutions to cooperate on the integration of programs and the transfer of credits. This has led to great interest in curricular articulation by state educational coordinating agencies. It is to the credit of most state boards or agencies that they have not

19. Joseph P. Cosand, "An Equal Opportunity to the Transfer Student," *The Transfer of Credits from Junior College to Senior College,* ed. Roy E. McAuley (Warrensburg: Central Missouri State College, 1971), p. 13.

legislated articulation agreements or ordered compliance with curriculum agreements that were developed without the approval of affected institutions.

The junior-senior college curriculum coordination achieved in Florida serves as a good model of appropriate methodology. Conditions were good because the state board of education had constitutional and statutory authority and responsibility to coordinate all levels of education. The University Regents, the State Junior College Board, the county boards of education which control the general school programs, and all other public educational agencies were responsible to the state board of education. Shortly after the community college movement got under way in Florida, the state board appointed a special committee for articulation activities composed of representatives from each educational level and the state board.

In 1965, the committee promulgated a "Policy Regarding General Education in Florida Public Higher Education." The policy encouraged state universities and community colleges, while retaining their own character, to develop mutually agreeable programs of general education for students with a baccalaureate goal. Once an institution developed and published its general education program (thirty-six semester hours were recommended for all), its integrity was to be recognized by all other public institutions. Further, students certified to have completed such a program were not to be held to any further lower division general education requirements by the public institution to which they might transfer.[20]

The policy, developed cooperatively by representatives of all levels of education and the state board, did not set forth the general education program for all institutions of higher education in Florida. Rather, the committee used its prestige and that of the state board of education to stimulate the interinstitutional dialogue necessary to win unquestioned acceptance of a junior college program of general education to satisfy the university requirements. This represents quite a step forward in thinking from the traditional course-by-course evaluation approach.

A five-year period of communication and debate within Florida public higher education followed the policy statement. The committee,

20. G. Robert Darnes, *The Articulation of Curricula Between Two- and Four-Year Colleges and Universities* (Gainesville: University of Florida, Institute of Higher Education, 1970), p. 10.

the state board, and other state agencies kept up the pressure for junior and senior colleges to work out mutually acceptable procedures for implementing the policy. The compact was ignored or deviated from in several instances, but the committee and the board moved in to resolve differences and encourage continued efforts. The state resisted the temptation to produce articulation by fiat and to exact penalties for noncompliance. The result was a longer, more detailed statement issued in 1970, that included the 1965 statement and the following statements affecting curricular articulation:

> Florida's universities and community colleges are, therefore, adopting this Agreement to (1) recommend specific areas of agreement between community colleges and state universities; (2) set forth criteria for the awarding of the Associate of Arts degree; (3) define the Associate of Arts degree as a component of a baccalaureate degree; (4) provide for a review of policies and procedures affecting the transfer of students; and (5) recommend such revisions as are needed to promote the success and general well-being of the transfer student. . . .
>
> (1) At the core of any agreement between the community colleges and the state university system designed to establish an efficient, orderly transfer process for community college students is the mutual acceptance of the nature and purpose of the Associate of Arts degree. This degree reflects the completion of an integrated two-year program of studies beyond secondary school, and serves as an efficient basis for the admission of its recipients to upper division study in the state university system. As such, the following principles should be incorporated in the formulation of an associate degree program:
>
> a. The requirements of the successful completion of sixty semester hours (ninety quarter hours) of academic work appropriate to the student's occupational choice and choice of upper-division concentration;
>
> b. A general education program consisting of thirty-six or more semester hours;
>
> c. Achievement of a grade point average of not less than 2.0 in all courses counted toward the accumulation of the associate degree requirements. . . .
>
> (2) The baccalaureate degree in all state universities shall be awarded in recognition of lower division (freshman-sophomore) combined with upper division (junior and senior) work. The lower division general education requirement of the baccalaureate degree shall be the responsibility of the associate degree institution. Upper

division general education requirements of the baccalaureate degree institution should not be of such volume as to extend the total program beyond the usual time requirements. . . .

(3) Lower division programs in all state institutions enrolling freshmen and sophomores may offer introductory courses which permit the student to explore the principal professional specializations that can be pursued at the baccalaureate level. These introductory courses shall be adequate in content to be fully counted toward the baccalaureate degree for students continuing in such a professional field of specialization. The determination of the major course requirements for a baccalaureate degree, including courses in the major taken in the lower division, shall be the responsibility of the state university awarding the degree. . . .

(4) Other associate degrees and certificates may be awarded by a junior college for programs which have requirements different from the Associate of Arts, or a primary objective other than transfer. Acceptance of course credits for transfers from such degree or certificate programs (and for students who have not completed a degree or certificate program) will be evaluated by the upper division institution on the basis of applicability of the courses to the baccalaureate program in the major field of the student. . . .

Credit generally should be given for courses in which the grade of D or better is received, and no penalty other than loss of credit should be attached to other courses attempted. . . .

(5) Each university department shall list the requirements for each program leading to the baccalaureate degree and shall publicize these requirements for all other institutions in the state. . . .

(6) Each state university shall include in its official catalog of undergraduate courses a section stating all lower division prerequisite requirements for each upper division specialization or major program. The sections of the catalog may also list additional recommended courses, but there shall be no ambiguity between what is required of all students for admission to upper division work and major programs, nor in any other stated requirements. The catalog in effect at the time of the student's initial enrollment in college shall govern lower division prerequisites. . . .

(7) A review committee shall be established to review individual cases or appeals from students who have encountered difficulties in transferring between a Florida

> public community junior college and a Florida univer-
> sity. Decisions reached by the review committee will be
> advisory to the institutions concerned. The review com-
> mittee shall be composed of seven members, three of
> whom shall be appointed by the Director of the Division
> of Community Colleges, and one by the Commissioner
> of Education. [21]

This policy statement represents what is probably the most thorough curricular articulation agreement ever concluded on a statewide basis. The strength of the statement lies not only in its state government backing, but also in the mutual participation in its development by the junior and senior colleges affected by the policy. Problems still remain. Florida officials point to changes in personnel as the most important current problem. Kintzer claims that conflicts still exist between universities and community colleges involving especially teacher education and the level at which particular courses should be taught.[22] At issue still are a synchronized calendar, an acceptable definition of *general education,* and the status of vocational or occupational courses. In the words of the commission, "Since articulation involves many decisions by many different people, it is difficult to keep agreements among institutions well understood and regularly implemented in the same measure, especially when such procedures are unlike more traditional decisions." [23] To cope with personnel changes and the variety of individuals at many intra- and interinstitutional levels, the review committee was created to monitor articulation activities and to work with institutions to see that the compact is followed.

Consistent with all of Florida's statewide articulation efforts, the review committee follows the premise that articulation cannot be coerced. The review committee's decisions are advisory for the institutions. However, "advice" from a prominent statewide committee of colleagues and state educational officials is bound to carry a great deal of weight with public educational institutions.

21. "Articulation and Transfer Agreements between Florida Universities and Community Junior Colleges," mimeographed (Document supplied to the author by Clifford R. LeBlanc, Santa Fe Junior College, Gainesville, Fla., April 28, 1971).

22. Frederick C. Kintzer, *Middleman in Higher Education* (San Francisco: Jossey-Bass, 1973), p. 40.

23. Frederick C. Kintzer, *Nationwide Pilot Study on Articulation* (Los Angeles: University of California, ERIC Clearinghouse for Junior Colleges, 1970), pp. 30-31.

In California, which serves more students in higher education than any other state, legislation and governmental interest have stimulated but not dominated statewide articulation. The major mechanisms for articulation is the California Articulation Conference, a voluntary, informal association of all segments of California higher education (the University of California system, state universities and colleges, the ninety-six community colleges, and private higher education). Policy agreements reached by the articulation conference generally are expressed through the Coordinating Council for Higher Education. Two of the most significant accomplishments of this plan of voluntary coordination are the present movement to have senior institutions accept completion of the community college transfer program as the certified equivalent of the senior institution's lower division general education graduation requirements and the commitment of senior institutions to give California community college graduates priority in admission.

Most praiseworthy is the promise of all segments of higher education to coordinate their programs and policies so that students can move through the various components of the system with maximum economy and education benefits. Problems still exist, as, for example, generally acceptable definitions must be worked out for terms such as *transferable* or *acceptable* courses, the maximum number of transfer hours that should be transferable, the transfer of vocational courses (particularly to the University of California), and the unqualified acceptance of *D* grades in transfer to the university.[24]

Governmental involvement in the articulation conference guards against backsliding and suggests that the level of curricular articulation will continue to improve. Further supporting the movement, curriculum specialists from all segments of higher education continue to meet in groups of varying size to consider improvements, feeding their contributions to the larger statewide apparatus.

State agencies are uniquely qualified to convene and follow up statewide subject articulation conferences. A summons to a subject articulation conference sponsored by a state agency will generally stir more interest and attendance than meetings sponsored by a single educational institution. Involving a broad spectrum of the educational community as well as state officials, the conference has great potential

24. Kintzer, *Middleman*, pp. 96-102.

for widespread and lasting results due to the magnitude of statewide resources and publicity.

Some state educational boards, particularly junior college boards, have taken the lead in promoting subject articulation conferences. The first step is to identify problem areas, a reasonably straightforward task for the staff that has developed familiarity with people and issues through regular board-sponsored meetings with junior-senior college articulation coordinators. The next step is to call together, at board expense, representative junior and senior college teachers for a planning conference to identify common, significant articulation problems in one subject and to develop an agenda. Representatives from all concerned institutions should be invited, and the program for each conference should be suited to the nature of the articulation problems. One meeting might last for a day, another for two days; some might have general speakers outside the subject field, while others might concentrate almost exclusively on teacher-to-teacher dialogue. The most unusual advantage of conferences sponsored by the state educational board is that they can generally marshall all the important state agencies and institutions to attack the problems at hand.

A number of clear threads run through the various efforts at statewide coordination. Most prominent is the recognition on the part of states and responsible educational officers that an orderly system of credit transfer must replace the haphazard method of earlier days when community college transfers were only a small part of the flow of students in higher education. With literally millions of students enrolled in community colleges, senior institutions no longer can apply individual philosophies of acceptance to students and credits and differentiate among equally accredited community colleges without immobilizing the new two-plus-two system of undergraduate higher education.

All of the state governments taking a leadership role in coordinated articulation have invested heavily in the new system and cannot afford to see it go down the drain. This has provided the impetus for governmentally sponsored conferences and commissions that propose comprehensive, orderly systems of credit transfer and ensure that proposed guidelines are followed. One of the leading suggestions for standardization has been the acceptance of the associate degree in place of lower division general education requirements, thereby giving de jure junior standing to junior college transfers. Carrying the concept of course substitution a step further, lower and upper division programs could articulate. All institutions involved in the credit transfer process are demanding clearly stated information about subject transferability, stability, and a common logic. The development of formal methods of articulation has been guaranteed by the growing acceptance of the idea of peer supervision under the aegis of general state educational authority. The committee of peer supervisors usually has only an advisory relationship to the colleges, but it can exert a good deal of influence through connections with sponsoring state educational authorities.

Informal Methods

Formal methods of subject articulation represent the visible part of the iceberg; a more important dimension is not as apparent to the casual observer. Informal curricular articulation relationships often grow out of formal programs, but sometimes individual professionals take the initiative in making contacts in order better to serve students.

The junior-college counselor who makes it his business to contact the academic decision-makers on transfer credit in universities is using an excellent kind of informal subject articulation. When he becomes acquainted with the department heads, deans, and professors who decide which credits will apply to degrees and which will not, they find it much more difficult to continue illogical, discriminatory policies. Where problems exist, the junior college counselor is well advised to involve junior college professors of the subject in question, just as junior college professors engaged in such matters ought to consult their school's transfer counselor. Similarly the university professor who becomes engrossed in transfer credit controversies ought to confer with his school's articulation specialist and colleagues at his institution or at similar institutions.

The university articulation specialist or his opposite member at the community college is remiss in his responsibilities if he does not take the initiative to develop a strong informal articulation mechanism. The system can become an excellent means of informal institutional policing that not only provides the feedback necessary to monitor curricular transition, but also immediately assists students whose transfers are obstructed. The specialist needs organizational skills and knowledge of human relations techniques and methods of having up-to-date, accurate information.

An example from the business field illustrates how informal junior-senior college subject articulation can work. The theoretical framework comes from the theory of public policy formation developed by the political scientist, Elmer Schattschneider.[25] Schattschneider interpreted policy formation through the *scope of conflict,* in which the special interest group losing a public conflict can regain the advantage by widening the scope of the conflict. New persons or groups are brought into the controversy, or the conflict moves from the limitations of the private to the public arena. As the conflict widens, policy can be modified according to the new variables. Schattschneider's theory implies that the interest group that can best manipulate the scope of conflict, restricting it or enlarging it according to its interests, will determine policy. Applied to informal articulation, Schattschneider's theory explains much of the conflict over curricula. A hypothetical example of the transfer of business credits in the state of Franklin illustrates the maneuvers.

Manipulating the Scope of Conflict

It had been traditional practice for most university business departments in Franklin to give equivalent credit for transfer business courses only grudgingly and after dissecting each course thoroughly with an eye to disqualifying it. One or two introductory accounting courses and an introductory economics course would generally be accepted, plus a general business course when such a course was part of the university business program. More specialized courses, such as finance, management, advertising, marketing, and advanced courses in economics or accounting, would usually be denied. Such was the case at Douglas University. While each department in the business college had its own guidelines, a decision-maker in one of the departments might be more charitable in a specific case for any number of reasons.

From time to time a community college professor might pursue a student's report of credit loss and force a lengthy explanation or even a reversal of the decision. Students would protest sporadically, but they were neither numerous nor organized enough to concern the business faculty or administration. The business school chose to view its

25. Elmer E. Schattschneider, *The Semisovereign People: A Realist's View of Democracy in America* (New York: Henry Holt & Co., 1960).

courses as uniquely appropriate and necessary for persons who would be awarded its degree. Academic restrictiveness was not viewed as selfish or narrow-minded, but as serving the best interests of the university and the transfer students. The attitude generally was formed without much information about junior colleges and possibly reflected a desire to have more students and courses to teach, which would require more staff and more salary for the college or department and further influence transfer credit decisions.

The rapid growth of community colleges and, consequently, the number of transfers, changed the situation. State administrators and legislators began to take an interest in how well the junior-senior college system was serving the citizenry. In turn, a good deal of similar interest matured among university general administrators who had to seek annual appropriations from the state government. The community college administration and faculty also developed a sharper interest in subject articulation, as local boards, state agencies, and the legislature examined the benefits accruing to students from the substantial public investments and the continuing financial obligations for the community college.

The community colleges, led by their counseling departments, began to agitate for liberalized credit transfer. The university people sensed that the political climate demanded a willingness on their part to explain and justify policies, if not to change them. University articulation personnel quickly took the lead at their end of the process. The initial response of university business professors was to cooperate with articulation specialists in sponsoring subject articulation conferences. The aim of the business professors was to invite community college people to campus, entertain them, and convince them of the wisdom of the business college position, which the guests would respect as friends and colleagues.

The community college personnel reacted with stronger determination to force change, regardless of the level of conflict required. The conferences had informed the two-year college staffs about all aspects of the university's business college transfer credit policy, and they found it to be much worse than had been assumed. Community college personnel first responded with threats of directing students to other colleges and with verbal and written criticisms, triggered usually by knowledge of the credit lost by one or two students. The scattered attacks had little general or permanent effect on university business credit acceptance policies, but they did raise doubts and uneasiness among university faculty and administration.

The scope of conflict clearly favored the university at this point. Isolated attempts at dissuading students from transferring to Douglas had not significantly affected transfer enrollment, and few junior colleges seriously pursued strategies for managing students. It is problematic whether or not counselors would have been successful even had they deliberately tried to shut off transfers to Douglas.

Agitation against restrictive policies at Douglas and other colleges and universities with business programs gradually crept into the agenda of a variety of meetings—student personnel groups, junior college groups, and business education organizations—and a new organization was formed called the State College Business Education Association (SCBEA). While more general concerns were included in the association's activities, the main focus was on loosening the restrictions on business transfer credit. The group sponsored conferences, inviting university representatives who were in a minority and defensive position. University people were perceptibly conciliatory as the larger, more organized assault against university credit acceptance policy took its toll.

The small, gradual concessions merely whetted the appetite of junior college people. Group and individual dialogues with university personnel convinced two-year college personnel that no major breakthrough would be forthcoming within the present scope of conflict. The junior colleges moved to expand the arena by writing to the executive director of the state board of higher education, a man who could be counted on to exert pressure where there was evidence of wasted tax dollars or inadequate use of public higher education facilities. The basic elements of the letter were the following points:

- The SCBEA, through its conferences and other activities, had contact with most business teachers in community colleges throughout the state; the position of the SCBEA, therefore, represented the majority opinion.

- After much interaction with senior college business professors, which resulted in some compromise and some progress, it became clear that certain irreconcilable differences existed regarding transferability of business courses. Specifically, community college personnel support and senior college people oppose transferability of intermediate accounting, finance, marketing, management, and money and banking.

- The senior institutions were accused of promoting an arbitrary, self-fulfilling process, in which the standards of the American Association of Collegiate Schools of Business (AACSB) were being used to rationalize a negative position on articulation.

- It was pointed out that students were forced to take courses that were substantially the same as those taken at the community college. Repetitive course work was held to be particularly indefensible from public policy viewpoint, since taxpayers, as well as students, were required to pay twice for the same thing.

- The assistance of the state board was solicited to help rectify the situation, since the board was interested in reducing duplication, waste, and obstructions to student transitions.

Shortly after receiving the letter, which had been circulated among senior institutions, the higher education board's executive director responded with a letter that also received wide circulation. The director's critical point was that waste and inarticulation—if such existed—would not be tolerated. The SCBEA was assured that the matter would be investigated by the board's articulation committee.

The balance had been successfully shifted in favor of the community colleges. Not only was the state board's staff involved in favor of the community college position, but a statewide board committee composed of a broad sampling of two- and four-year colleges had been brought into the matter. None of the committee's four-year members was from the business field. As the pressure increased against the senior college position, the four-year schools moved to redress the balance by calling on their professional accrediting association, the American Association of Collegiate Schools of Business (AACSB). The four-year institutions focused attention on the following item of the association's regulations:

> In general the accredited degree school shall limit transfer credit for business courses which it applies toward its degree requirements, taken at a lower division level, to such courses as it offers at that level. . . . Examples of the level of courses which might be offered at the lower division are: principles of accounting, principles of

economics, business law, statistics and introduction to business.[26]

The statement brought a national organization into the scope of conflict to balance the state forces attacking the senior college. The senior institutions could fall back on the AACSB refusal to count lower division courses as equivalent in transfer to courses taught in the university's upper division. Since all two-year college courses were lower level by definition, the course that senior institutions must follow was clear.

The scope of conflict became relatively static at this point. Forces that could have expanded the conflict, chiefly organized student agitation, failed to materialize. Activities related to the dispute turned to individual contacts and dialogues, leading to numerous unique arrangements between two- and four-year colleges. Some institutions reached agreements whereby students with junior college credit in disputed courses could take university proficiency examinations. Credit in disputed courses would be withheld until students had succeeded in similar business courses in the upper division, whereupon the disputed credit would be counted toward the degree. No conclusive settlement had been reached, but enough accomodations had been made to bring the problem under a reasonable degree of control.

Case study analysis

When interlevel communication on a particular transitional discipline is almost totally absent, problems often appear nonexistent. Persons at one or another level are often ignorant of the obstacles they create for transferring students. When communication lines are reopened, as in the case of the business school, it is not unusual for a great deal of controversy, and even hostility, to result. Often shocking and discouraging to the attacked party, the peer criticism is seen as the negative reward for developing communication. Preparing senior college academicians for an initially negative experience, therefore, becomes one of the major tasks of the articulation specialist. Professors, rather than internalizing the critisms, should recognize the attacks as part of the beginning stages of the articulation process.

Once specific items of inarticulation are discerned, the offended parties seek relief with great vigor, simulating countermanding activi-

26. *Constitution, By-Laws, Accreditation Standards and Interpretations* (St. Louis, Mo.: American Association of Collegiate Schools of Business, 1969).

ties. Usually the side that gathers the most support from individuals and groups outside the immediate arena of conflict will prevail. Because professors are generally influenced by logic and truth, regardless of their vested interests, university faculties gradually have made concessions to the community colleges even when relative parity in the scope of conflict has been achieved. The main observation is that contact first must be established between the opponents. Thereafter, a variety of informal interest groups will coalesce around the issues and resolve the dispute.

Not only must the articulation specialist be aware of the dynamics of conflict, he must also be able to manage informal articulation processes that surround these academic battles. If he is adept at manipulating the scope of conflict, he will generally be an influential factor in settling arguments in the best interests of students. Such skill, however, requires a skill to identify individuals and organized groups who have a vested interest in the controversy, even if their concern may at the time be dormant.

seven

Admission Information

The theory underlying programs to assist students with college selection is relatively simple. Students should receive quantities of concise, well-organized information that will help them make the best choice among alternatives. College admission representatives should consider their first obligation to be helping students to make the right choice and their second objective to be recruiting the proper type and number of students for their institution. All tools of communication should be utilized, and feedback mechanisms should be built in to evaluate the effectiveness of different media and counseling.

Personal approaches should range from one-to-one meetings between a prospective college student and a college representative to coordinate statewide information exchanges between large numbers of counselors and admission representatives. Documentary methods should reach from personal correspondence between a student and an admission office to widely disseminated reports about the admission opportunities and performance of enrolled students at one college or groups of colleges. The uses of television could extend from closed circuit institutional programs shown at one high school or junior college to regionally or nationally televised general information programs about a type of college or consortium of colleges. There is a role for all media and its different adaptations to meet a variety of objectives.

The high school, junior college, and senior college should share responsibilities equally in guiding students from one level to another. All levels must see to it that the student is protected against what could be a very unequal confrontation between the individual, with his limited store of information and resources, and the typical college's vast

array of data and procedures. James Coleman addressed the problem in
a College Board brief titled *Principle of Symmetry in College Choice:*

> The size asymmetry between the individual applicant
> and the college manifests itself principally in an asym-
> metry of information available to the applicant and the
> college, information upon which each makes its choice.
> The college demands and gets specific comparable infor-
> mation from and about applicants: high school grades,
> the information it requests in its admissions application
> form, and often most important of all, scores on the
> College Board's Scholastic Aptitude Test and Achieve-
> ment Tests, or comparable tests from another agency.
> The applicant has only hearsay, rumors, and whatever
> information the college chooses to exhibit in its catalog
> as the basis for his selection of college and program of
> study. If he is fortunate, he has a friend attending a
> college, or he may visit the college and talk to a few
> students there and thus feel that he knows something of
> the atmosphere. The high frequency of college choices
> made on the basis of such unsubstantial and unrepre-
> sentative experiences, as shown in the few studies made
> on college choice, is evidence of the absence of syste-
> matic means by which applicants can assess a college.[1]

While an increasing number of college guidance methods and services are helping to adjust the balance, it is essential that all levels of
education work together to protect the individual applicant against the
powerful, impersonal forces of the typical large educational institution.
Techniques of interinstitutional cooperation offer the best hope for
achieving equilibrium. Many of the philosophical views and practical
applications that support equalized interest groups have already been
discussed in preceding chapters, therefore, this chapter will be limited
to a few particularly useful or exemplary methods of admission guidance that involve cooperative efforts on the parts of high schools,
junior colleges, and senior institutions.

The College Information Day

Interestingly, the cooperative admission guidance method that is the
most widely used is also the most extensively criticized. The college day
is one of the oldest methods of organized communication between col-

1. David V. Tiedman, "Righting the Balance: A Second Look by the Chairman at the Report of Commission on Tests, College Entrance Examination
Board," *IRCD Bulletin,* November 1970, p. 2.

leges and prospective students. In the most popular form, a sponsoring high school invites a number of colleges to send admission representatives to the host school for a day or evening program of a few hours. Each college represented is provided with a classroom or a table in some large open area, and students interested in the institution are directed to that classroom or area. The format may be strictly cafeteria style where students wander about, stopping off at one table for a moment to pick up a brochure and at another for a half-hour to ask questions. Another arrangement provides three or four half-hour time periods, one period for general instructions from the school and the others for meetings with different college representatives. The college representative has synchronized time periods in which he can give a prepared talk to an orderly group and answer questions informally. A compromise between the two formats that is quite popular consists of only a brief introduction, followed by visiting periods with a particular college and ending with a browsing period similar to cafeteria style programs.

One innovation made during the last decade or so has been moving the college day to the evening hours. The new schedule recognizes the importance of involving parents in the college guidance process and does not interrupt the regular school program. Another relatively recent modification is a panel discussion, moderated by the school's college consultant, for an audience of parents and students. The panel generally consists of three or four experts in admission to particular types of institutions. For example, a panel might be composed of representatives of the junior college, private liberal arts colleges, state universities, and technical institutes. Another panel might have representatives from an Ivy League college, a commuter institution, and a state residential university. Still another may be organized by levels of institutional accessibility, as in the Willingham model cited in chapter two: this would call for representation of an inexpensive, open door institution, one with easy admission but moderate to high cost, and so on along the spectrum.

There are many possible combinations and formats for college day programs. Regardless of the approach, certain principles should be followed. Foremost should always be an assessment of the particular needs of the clientele and the information styles to which the clients are most receptive. There should also be cooperative advance planning, in which at least some of the college representatives are involved with the host school and students. Finally, an evaluation mechanism should always be built into the program so that parents, students, and the professional participants can suggest successive improvements and, in the final analysis, decide whether that particular type of endeavor is worth continuing.

Some schools and community colleges invite institutional representatives one at a time, usually during the day. The visit is advertised in advance, and a schedule is arranged for the admissions officer to see students individually or in small groups. Again, the relative merits of such a program depend on the needs of the students and assessments of the best style of conveying admission guidance to particular clients. In the individualized format, parent involvement presumably is less important than the personalized interaction between admissions counselor and students.

Comparing the large-scale college day program and the procedure of inviting a few representatives at a time to meet with small groups of prospective students, a high school official offered this opinion:

> I am not in favor of "college days" as such, and I have found few admissions officers who are. . . . We have replaced elaborate college day programs with a modified program giving more emphasis to individual meetings. I am convinced that having the representatives of colleges meet our students in small, informal groups is a more successful way than any other of acquainting students with the colleges.[2]

The main objections to the college day program are the lack of opportunity for student or parent to engage in any meaningful dialogue or to get sufficient information. By the end of the program, the clients have gotten a little information from so many representatives and so much literature that they leave more confused and discouraged than informed and motivated. While the experience may be the case for many, the college day may open clients' eyes to the broad range of college choice, resulting in positive motivation or decision-making. It depends on the nature of the clientele and the quality of planning and organization that goes into the program.

2. Frank S. Foley, "Communication, the Second Viewpoint," *College Admissions: The Interaction of School and College* (Princeton, N.J.: College Entrance Examination Board, 1956), p. 95.

One excellent cooperative enterprise for preadmission guidance is the reverse of a traditional college day or college night. Instead of bringing college admissions representatives to the high school, high school students are taken to the colleges. The program should present very few problems in urban areas, where community colleges and a variety of four-year institutions are close to high schools. Representatives of both institutions can personally arrange each visit with a minimum of logistics problems. Programs at more distant residential colleges are best planned through committees or organizations whose membership includes representatives of many residential colleges. A one-day or weekend trip can be scheduled to visit one or several colleges within a radius of several hundred miles. The essentials are simply a school bus and thorough preparation.

Before touring colleges, either local or distant, students should be shown how to derive maximum benefit from the visit. Literature about the colleges and general discussion between counselor and students are the most effective teaching tools. The counselors should be careful to include only those students who stand a reasonable chance for admission to the college to be visited or another college in that general category.

The main strength of a college day at college is the availability of a wide variety of resources. The students can talk directly with a financial aid officer, college deans, professors from different disciplines, admissions and registration officers, student affairs personnel, and—most important—members of the student body. It may even be possible to meet with college students who are alumni of the visiting high school, a feature that is always a strong asset to such a program.

The college tour affords an opportunity for personal relationships to develop between college and school professionals as well as between college personnel and students. The college people can be used as general resource persons apart from their role in matters concerning their institution. For example, an acquaintance with the financial aid officer could pave the way for future requests for general information about need analysis, new federal student aid, and related programs.

Similar benefits can develop from the traditional visits to high schools or junior colleges by college representatives. Often, individual faculty members at the school or college are more influential with students than is the counselor. Putting authoritative teachers in contact with college representatives will update the teachers' knowledge about college admissions and college life. Certainly, the high school's college consultant or the junior college's transfer counselor should see to it that the school principal or junior college dean is involved, for this can have important effects on the school's administrative structure that will facilitate or impede precollege guidance and student preparation for college.

The variety of college information programs almost matches the wide range of guidance initiated by high schools. As a rule, the best programs join high school and college efforts, as may be seen in the case of the Wyoming *Post-High School Planning Days* program. Jointly sponsored by Wyoming higher and secondary educational institutions, planning days familiarize high school juniors and seniors with the range of postsecondary educational opportunities available statewide. The University of Wyoming Office of Admissions coordinates planning and arrangements, beginning months before the planning days are held.

Since population is scattered over a large geographic area, the state is divided into quadrants. Planning days are held for one week in each area, generally in October. The program, consisting of three 40-minute sessions scheduled at two schools per day, is presented to students who register in advance for the sessions in which they are interested. Participating colleges present the coordinated program in each host school, which invites students and counselors from other local schools. While the format is standardized, the high school principals and guidance counselors in each area are responsible for the details of their programs. School personnel select the participating institutions and establish regulations for participation and general mechanics. Schools must apply for participation in the program each year.

Four guidance booklets, one for each geographic area, are published by the colleges and secondary schools. The booklets supply information from participating institutions and are available to students prior to their scheduled planning day. In September, the University of Wyoming coordinator sends a packet to all representatives that includes a schedule, suggested motel accommodations, itineraries, high school data, and other information. Each representative is expected to make his own travel arrangements.

The program insists on serious, cooperative commitments on the part of participating schools. The joint financing confirms the commitment and underscores the importance of the enterprise. Preplanning, in the form of the regional booklets, contributes to the excellence of the program. The Wyoming example demonstrates how college information programs for students can be tailored to the advantages found in any particular environment.

To their credit, many professional college guidance organizations have attempted to evaluate and to establish guidelines for college information programs. For example, the Illinois Association of College Admissions Counselors (IACAC) published a document entitled *College Day/Night Guidelines,* which examined the success of current programs. The purpose of the college day programs was described as follows:

> To permit a student and his parents to examine carefully a number of well chosen colleges selected with respect to whatever prior limitations the family must impose. . . . [The college day] should be more than a means of simply introducing students to college. . . . [The program] will be most valuable only if it is considered as part of the school's total counseling for college.[3]

An important point made here is that high schools or community colleges should resist the temptation to use a college night program as a community public relations extravaganza, inviting the maximum number of colleges and prestigious institutions. Too many colleges only add confusion and diminish the returns of the program. The program should complement, not duplicate, other college guidance services and should be concerned with experiences for students that could not be provided as efficiently in any other way.

According to IACAC, topics that the high school should be sure to have representatives discuss are college characteristics, college expenses, college guides and handbooks, assessment of individual admission potential, admission testing, procedures for subsequent campus visits, and application procedures. *Guidelines* also recommends that students be prepared for the college day by meeting with their school counselors beforehand to learn objective criteria useful in evaluating colleges. Such criteria include characteristics of the student body, required courses, faculty characterstics, library facilities,

3. Research Committee, "College Day/Night Guidelines," mimeographed (Chicago: Illinois Association of College Admissions Counselors, 1970).

prominent campus issues over the past year, and the social and extra-curricular options afforded students by the college.

IACAC suggests that neighboring schools consolidate college days and list programs with the IACAC college day/night schedule coordinator by May preceding the academic year in which programs will be held. *Guidelines* recommends that invitations and room arrangements be made on the basis of a survey of student preferences, so that the most popular colleges have the largest and most accessible rooms. Use of a common room for all representatives is discouraged, except for colleges asking to attend even when no student interest has been evidenced.

Arrangements should begin by sending invitations to colleges four to six weeks in advance of the program. Representatives accepting the invitation should receive directions, parking instructions, and specifics on the program two weeks before it is scheduled. A prospectus indicating colleges in attendance, the names of their representatives, and their location in the building should be distributed to students and parents a few days before the program, so that parents and students can prepare properly. For a format, either two 45-minute informational sessions are followed by a 45-minute browsing session, or three 30-minute individual sessions are followed by a 30-minute browsing session.

IACAC urges that students and parents evaluate the program, so future programs may be improved. The evaluation of college representatives would also be helpful.

Use of Students

In the search for new tools and methodologies of admission guidance, articulation personnel often neglect their most obvious resource—students. Feedback from students who recently made the transition from school to college and junior to senior college confirms the value of student perceptions of admission guidance for articulation.[4] That students with minimal training can serve effectively as paraprofessional

4. J. Robert Long, "Summary of Admission Questionnaire," mimeographed (Seattle: University of Washington, Office of High School Relations, 1971); Julius Menacker, "Improving the Admission Information Efforts of Institutions of Higher Education," *National ACAC Journal,* May 1972; R. F. Stahmann, G. R. Hanson, and R. R. Whittlesey, "Parent and Student Perceptions of Influence on College Choice," *National ACAC Journal,* July 1971.

counselors has also been substantiated by counselors and research studies.[5]

Available evidence indicates that transitional students trust peers who have recently made the transition; students can interact with them on a very free, relaxed basis. Students about to transfer can have more of their personal questions answered by peers and feel more confident about taking action on the basis of that information. Articulation based on the advice of siblings produces more assertive and self-directed action than transition stemming from reading guidance literature or talks with counselors.

The main problem in using students in articulation work is ensuring that students are well informed and do not exaggerate conditions of admission, financial aid, and related matters. It is most important that students be carefully supervised with respect to the scope of their mission and the information that they disseminate. Conversely, the peer articulators should be free to use whatever methods they consider most effective. Such a division of responsibility should be observed regardless of whether the students are paid or volunteers, temporary or long-term.

The specific delineation between the responsibilities and goals of student aides and professional staff in articulation can be stated in general terms. The professionals should impart the specific, objective criteria of costs, admission, financial aid, academic programs, facilities, and the like. A main goal is accuracy and currentness of information. Students should handle the prospective student's concern about how the demands of college work compare to high school, aspects of the social environment, incidental expenses, and so forth. Students should freely give their subjective opinions (which should be so identified) on such matters as the value of extracurricular activities, the effectiveness of student government, and the willingness of teachers to give individual attention to students. When professional admissions counselors and student aides work together in an integrated pattern, where the strengths of each complement the work of the other, the result will be better service to the student preparing for transition.

An excellent example of the use of student articulators is found at Miami-Dade Community College. Student personnel adminis-

5. Robert R. Pyle and Fred A. Snyder, "Students as Paraprofessional Counselors at Community Colleges," *Journal of College Student Personnel,* July 1971, pp. 259-62.

trators recognized that faculty and staff were not numerous enough to cope with what appeared to be a widening student information gap between high school and college. The junior college hired, part-time, high school counselors and Miami-Dade students to work at high schools to help students. Miami-Dade students were selected on the basis of their college record and assigned to counseling centers at their former high schools. The paid aides in the Miami-Dade program went through a one-night-a-week training program for four weeks, which was similar to the training program given to the high school counselors. The program's administration evaluated the students' articulation performance as follows:

> The peer relationship proved quite satisfactory. Students who came to the centers seeking information about the college received it firsthand from their peers [who explained] . . . various offerings of the college and [answered] innumerable questions. In many instances they were able to prepare the student's program and submit it to the professional counselor for approval.[6]

The beauty of the Miami-Dade program is that it capitalized on the articulation strengths of both college students and high school counselors to bridge the gap between school and college. High school counselors were available to offer professional services, and college students were at the school to give peer level advice and effective reinforcement. A bonus of the program unrelated to student use in articulation was the strengthened understanding and cooperation between Miami-Dade and important feeder high schools.

Evaluation Methods in Admission Guidance

Admission policies and articulation services to function effectively must have feedback mechanisms built into them. Without feedback, the receiving institution will not know if policies are effectual and if articulation services are valuable. It might well turn out that certain policies or expensive services have exactly the opposite effect of what was intended.

One college may send its most distinguished professors to visit target high schools (at considerable expense when compared to the cost of

6. Albert K. Smith, "Bridging the Gap—High School to Community College," *Junior College Journal,* February 1970, pp. 35-36.

sending admissions counselors) to recruit a certain number of quality students. Such students do not apply. In fact, enrollment from the target schools drops off, and the quality of freshmen from the same schools declines. The college responds by increasing the number of visits by top professors. Had the college some form of systematic feedback, it might have discovered that the professors were good scholars but bad counselors and salesmen. The professors gave an inflated impression of the academic rigors and a narrow view of college life which totally ignored social and extracurricular aspects.

At the secondary level, a high school may insist that all graduating seniors with college aspirations file admission applications before December. According to policy, no transcripts will be sent out after December, since colleges worth attending have applications deadlines at that time. Some students are thereby denied an excellent opportunity because of the lack of communication links between the school and less selective colleges with programs suited to lesser academic abilities.

Based on real situations, both examples indicate the need for continuous evaluation of the effects of admissions policies and articulation practices on student transition. Assessments can be most accurate when means of verifying operational truths are incorporated into evaluative procedures and are supplemented by an efficient communications network.

Indiana State University sends a grade distribution graph to high school counselors to use in advising students about admission. The university also forwards the grade reports of matriculating alumni to feeder schools. Prepared at considerable expense, the documents are assessed periodically in light of the value derived from the feedback services. Counselors are asked to evaluate the usefulness of the graph and performance records. A summary of the responses from all feeder schools is circulated to high schools and university faculty members (see figure 6).

With this simple feedback report, Indiana State University is able to evaluate the usefulness to counselors of its information program. The report highlights areas that need improvement and new services at the same time that it reveals obsolescent services. Perhaps such an evaluation feedback mechanism is as important as the services themselves for establishing rapport and communication with feeder schools. The method shows the college's respect for the counselor's competence.

SUMMARY OF RESPONSES EVALUATING
ARTICULATION SERVICES

1. Do you feel the Grade Distribution Graph is beneficial to you in counseling your college-bound students? (Yes, 93; No, 2)

   *Acts as a predictor of academic success by com-
   parison of SAT scores.*
   *Helps in examination of college achievement and
   high school preparation.*

2. In what way do you feel we could improve the grade
   distribution graph?

   *Include the average grade of all University stu-
   dents and not only ours.*
   *Compare the achievements of students by quartile
   ranking.*
   Include midterm report for comparison.

3. Do you use the individual grade reports for purposes
   other than determining an individual's achievement?
   (Yes, 56; No, 31)

   *Not particularly, but we think the graph is im-
   portant for comparison purposes.*

4. In what ways do you feel we could improve the grade
   report of individual studies?

   Make it for all students, regardless of grade level.
   Include drop-out report.
   Keep it brief so it will be less time consuming.

Source: Office of Student Research and Student Administrative Services, Summary of Questionnaire to Indiana High School Counselors (Terre Haute:
Indiana State University, n.d.).

Fig. 6. Report on articulation services assessment.
Sample responses appear in italics.

and a real desire to cooperate in helping students to make a better transition.

An excellent informal method for community colleges and universities to evaluate literature sent to the schools is simply to visit the
school and observe how the material is used. Are the institution's
brochures readily available in quantity in some convenient place? Is
there a current catalog on the shelf for students to use? Have coun-

selors organized the information sent to them? Is the articulation specialist's name, address, or phone number readily available? Is the material sent for posting displayed on the guidance bulletin board? Is outdated material still posted? These and many other evaluation concerns can be answered by an alert college representative who visits a school or community college.

Again, perhaps the most expedient evaluation of articulation services is student opinion. In the case of a university that has recently shifted from years of a highly selective admission policy to modified open admissions, it matters little that the counselors have a high opinion of the university's letters and other informational services if high school seniors and community college sophomores do not apply because of poor academic records. A system of obtaining student evaluations of admission information is essential. The results should not only be used by the college to improve its service, but summarized feedback should also be shared with high school or community college counselors; counselors can also use the information to upgrade services to students and receiving institutions.

No articulation service should be exempt from evaluation. Even those that are extremely difficult to evaluate should not be ignored; the more subjective evaluation problems only require more research creativity. How, for example, can the effects of high school visits by college representatives on enrollment be evaluated? This problem was attacked by the testing and research staff of the University of Illinois Office of School and College Relations. Schools were divided according to the number of visits made by Chicago Circle personnel over a four-year period. Two bases of comparisons were used: first, in terms of percent change in enrollment from the earliest year to the latest year; and second, using each preceding year as the base for the subsequent year. One conclusion of the study was ". . . that more frequent visits do not serve to increase enrollment in any systematic fashion. . . . There was no relationship between the number of visits made to a school and the increases in enrollment [at Chicago Circle]." [7]

Research conclusions like the above are not necessarily discouraging to supporters of school and college relations. The communication that

7. Susan B. Thomas, *The Effects of Articulation Visits to High Schools as Reflected in Subsequent Enrollment at the Chicago Circle Campus* (Urbana: University of Illinois, Office of School and College Relations, 1971), p. 9.

takes place during calls to schools is of clear and obvious importance. Many interviews properly may have discouraged high risk students from applying; however, visits may be a better informational service than a recruiting device. If the main objective of articulation is to enlarge college enrollment, more visits will not achieve the goal. Perhaps increased and improved literature, conferences for counselors or students, open house programs, or other techniques would be more effective.

Finally, admission information conferences for counselors or students should have a built-in procedure of self-evaluation. The methods can range from verbal to written, direct to indirect, formal to informal means. A good, simple approach is to schedule some unstructured time near the end of the conference for summation, review, and evaluation. A great deal can be learned by paying close attention to the dialogue of first impressions. Alternatively, participants can be queried by mail several weeks later on the main points the conference intended to deliver. If the accompanying letter explained that organizers wished to evaluate the conference, not the conferees, the responses (anonymously returned) should be worth the effort. There are any number of variations between immediate and delayed feedback, including the use of outside evaluators who can add objectivity to the evaluation process. Above all, evaluation must focus on the importance, usefulness, completeness, and quality of information. Praise for the hospitality, the meal, or the humor and wit of a keynote speaker are all important for maintaining and improving good personal relations. Such criteria do not judge the value of the information or the quality of the presentation.

Conferences

During the past two decades, many new ways have been found to provide information through articulation conferences oriented to admissions. Senior institutions and statewide organizations made a national survey of articulation conferences. The questionnaire, prepared by the American Association of Collegiate Registrars and Admissions Officers, identified the following seven regional approaches.

> *California:* 1) Representatives of public universities and colleges, junior colleges, and the state superintendent of public instruction meet with representatives of public high schools in regional conferences throughout the

state; 2) Separate conferences are organized for high school and junior college representatives.

Georgia: Selected high school counselors, principals, and college admissions officers meet to review a specific problem (e.g., college day program) and develop recommendations for improvement.

Missouri: Articulation conferences are sponsored by, and include representatives from, the state teachers association, state department of education, school administrator groups, the state guidance association and college admissions groups.

New Mexico: A coordinating council composed of representatives of the state secondary school principals association and the various colleges and universities meet three times each year.

North Carolina and Ohio: High school counselors and college admissions personnel meet in regional conferences to review and interpret current admission information.

Ohio: Two-day workshops on articulation problems are held for high school counselors at different college campuses on both a statewide and regional basis.

Washington: Admissions officers at all collegiate institutions meet with high school counselors and students at regional centers.[8]

Among the different techniques are interviews between high school counselors and their former students, questions submitted in advance of the conference by high school personnel for college representatives, and clinics at which new high school counselors can learn from more experienced colleagues.[9] Such devices can be used within the four main organization modes for admission information conferences: institutional conferences for feeder school or college counselors; conferences cooperatively sponsored by receiving institutions for large numbers of feeder counselors; institutional conferences for prospective students; and conferences for students jointly sponsored by a number of receiving institutions.

Whichever organizational mode is used, techniques should reflect the preferences, common sense, and experience of potential participants. For example, if controversial matters are to be dealt with, a smaller conference size would be better. Similarly, a conference for

8. Liaison Subcommittee of the High School-College Relations Committee, *High School-College Articulation Conference Ideas* (Washington: American Association of Collegiate Registrars and Admissions Officers, 1965), p. 1.
    9. Ibid., p. 2.

students should be informal, scheduling buzz sessions with representatives who have specialized information or rap sessions with peers.

The best approach to the regional or statewide conference, conducted jointly by a number of collegiate institutions, is to provide a flexible structure utilizing the individual workshop technique. Each participating college uses its own format and agrees to only a few essentials—the keynote speaker, perhaps, or the location of the conference. The main ingredient in such a conference is a structure that allows for participant and host flexibility. Counselors should not have to hear representatives from each college, nor should all colleges have to present their messages alike.

One of the guiding principles for conferences for school counselors sponsored by colleges is that the guests should always be provided with data about their former counselees who made the transition to the higher level. Data should include the high school characteristics used to decide admission and the grades earned at the college. A variation that lends some objectivity to the proceedings is the presentation of statistics about students denied admission to one participating college who were admitted to a comparable institution.

Another productive method is to involve students in admission information conferences, as noted in the Washington procedure. When counselors and admissions officers dispute the clarity of information or difficulty of procedure for student admission, what better mediator is there than the student? College freshmen could react to the transitional process they have just experienced and test out the usefulness of new procedures. For example, students could read a new admission information brochure or fill out a new application to see if they understand the instructions. Details of financial aid forms constitute another important area where student evaluations can be helpful.

Literature

If consultants and transfer counselors tried to read and file all the brochures, announcements, statistical reports, and other documents that come across their desks, they would have time to do little else and would have to surrender most of their office space to filing cabinets. The literature must say more in less space and in better ways, and if intended as a reference, the material must be readily identifiable and easily stored. It is equally important that literature for students be designed for them. Above all, the literature must arouse interest and reaction from the intended parties. Improvements in printed matter can best come about with the cooperation of professionals working in school and college relations, who have set a fine example by developing multischool guidance manuals.

Cooperatively developed guidance manuals

One statewide cooperative effort in Illinois led to streamlined admission information that was more easily assimilated by high school counselors. All of the four-year institutions supported by the state agreed to split the cost of a joint publication about admission requirements, financial aid, special programs, degrees offered, advanced placement policies, veterans benefits, special services, housing, and similar matters.[10]

An entirely different approach to the problem of providing coordinated information to high school counselors is found in Utah, where a booklet of multiple regression correlations predicts the grade point average at each of Utah's higher education institutions for high school graduates with particular combinations of high school grades and test scores.[11] The counselor can use the booklet to give any student an idea of his probable performance at any Utah college or university.

A more expansive approach is found in the handbook, *Focus on Your Future*,[12] produced under the auspices of the Colorado Council on High School-College Relations. The publication, as the one in Illinois, results from a voluntary, cooperative effort on the part of the state's colleges and universities. The handbook improves on the Illinois effort by including community colleges and private institutions. *Focus* also provides predictive tables from which counselors or students can derive the probabilities of earning a *C* average at different Colorado colleges, based on high school grade point averages and American College Test scores.

10. Committee on Pre-College Counseling, Illinois Joint Council on Higher Education, *State Universities in Illinois* (Urbana: University of Illinois, Office of School and College Relations, 1972).

11. Frank B. Jex, *Predicting Academic Success Beyond High School* (Salt Lake City: By the author, 1966).

12. Tilman M. Bishop, ed., *Focus on Your Future, 1971-72* (Fort Collins: Colorado Council on High School-College Relations, 1971).

Similar guides are produced under the auspices of public higher education coordinating agencies, as the Oklahoma State Regents for Higher Education [13] and the University System of Georgia.[14] New Mexico's *Guide* [15] is a joint product of the New Mexico Coordinating Council of Secondary Schools and Colleges and the American College Testing Program, while North Dakota's [16] compilation of prediction tables is produced by the state Association of Collegiate Registrars and Admissions Officers and the State American College Test Advisory Board. Idaho's *Guide* [17] is produced entirely by the American College Testing Program with the cooperation of Idaho's institutions of higher education. Idaho's *Guide* combines all the features of the other handbooks in greater detail. The *General Information* section describes the community, faculty characteristics, faculty-student ratios, the number of volumes and periodicals in the library, and other matters of interest in addition to the standard information about admission and financial aid. Further, predictions of college performance at Idaho institutions are set out for each group of freshman courses with a sample course specifically described for each area of study.

All such documents have one basic flaw in that information for prospective transfer students from community colleges is not included. Comparisons of transfer performance could be useful to high school counselors as well as to transfer counselors in junior colleges. This important phase of articulation has not yet caught up with most statewide cooperative publications. One of the most interesting differences among cooperative guides is the degree of confidentiality with which the information is treated. For example, the Idaho publication states:

> Absolutely no public announcements of any of the
> GUIDE's contents can be permitted. When informa-
> tion regarding colleges is communicated to student or

13. Larry K. Hayes, *Counselors' Guide: Oklahoma Higher Education* (Oklahoma City: Oklahoma State Regents for Higher Education, 1971).

14. John R. Mills et al., *Counselors' Guide to Georgia's Colleges* (Athens: University System of Georgia, 1968).

15. John A. Duling, ed., *Counselors' Guide to Selected Colleges in New Mexico* (Los Cruces: New Mexico Coordinating Council of Secondary Schools and Colleges, and American College Testing Program, Southwestern Regional Office, 1970).

16. James E. Brandt, ed., *1971-72 Guide to North Dakota Colleges and Universities* (Bismarck: North Dakota American College Testing Advisory Council, 1971).

17. John L. Phillips, Jr., ed., *Counselor's Guide to Idaho Colleges, 1971-73* (Iowa City: American College Testing Program, 1971).

parents as part of the counselor's professional responsibilities in assisting with college planning, the receivers
of the information should be informed of the necessity
of treating such data as confidential. No useful purpose
is served by publicizing college differences to persons not
directly concerned with college planning; on the contrary, great harm could be done to individual schools
and to the education system as a whole if analyses of
college differences were made in any context other than
that of normal college planning conferences among
parties directly concerned.[18]

The entire cover of the North Dakota *Guide* is devoted to a display
of the word *CONFIDENTIAL,* supplemented internally by detailed
cautions that elaborate on the Idaho statement. On the other hand,
Oklahoma's handbook makes no mention at all of secrecy. Intended
primarily as a tool to be used by the counselor, the handbooks range
from general information about institutions and admission requirements to detailed guidelines on admission and financial aid policies
and procedures and academic prediction data. All of the guides are to
be commended for providing counselors with a standardized summary
of college information which is easily used, stored, and retrieved.

There is a middle ground in college literature that should be sought
between the brevity of the Illinois booklet and the overabundance of
data in the Idaho *Guide.* The Illinois booklet ignores material on predicted performance, which might be the most useful and critical item
in determining a student's college choice. The Idaho document, on the
other hand, gives so much information that students and counselors
can be overly impressed and make decisions on a seemingly irrefutable
mass of data. In reality, the statistics are only general guidelines that
do not account for an enormous range of individual possibilities. Further, the very specificity and quantity of information can become a
source of confusion and discouragement if not used wisely. The right
balance can be achieved by continual evaluation and attention to feedback as various approaches to the counselor's guide are tried. It is critically important that attention to the counselor's guide extend beyond
publication to the problems of dissemination and use. Schools that
need a larger quantity of guides should be identified and supplied, and,
by the same token, a system for identifying school counseling staffs that

18. Ibid., p. 2.

need personal assistance should be established before counselors use such a tool. The necessary assistance for schools and staffs should come from resources of the general college admission guidance program.

Consortia of high school counselors, junior college counselors, or both, could compile the same guides that are produced by groups of senior institutions. There are too many instances of high school and junior college counselors excusing their inadequate information or resources for college guidance by placing the blame on poor senior college articulation efforts. There is no reason why high schools and the two-year colleges cannot band together, parcel out assignments, and produce their own guides. More than likely, the guide produced by two levels working together would be more useful than those produced by senior college personnel who only interpret high school or junior college admission guidance needs. There are any number of local, state, and even national organizations that can provide the structure and impetus for admission articulation documents developed by high school and community college personnel.

Materials from organizations and agencies

The current, unprecedented interest in college admission has stimulated the appearance of a bewildering variety of college admission reference books, computer selection schemes, and other forms of assistance for students selecting colleges. While many of the devices developed by private organizations are helpful, the tools produced by the older, established, professionally based organizations, such as the National Association of College Admissions Counselors (NACAC) and the College Board, are more reliable. The new *NACAC Handbook of Member Colleges and Universities* is a trustworthy reference, but unfortunately it is limited to NACAC membership.

One effort that traditionally has been ignored by counselors is the *National Norms for Entering College Freshmen,* produced annually by by the American Council on Education.[19] Distributed primarily to college administrators, the reports rarely cross the desks of secondary and college counselors. This is unfortunate, because the *National Norms* provides statistics on such characteristics as age, secondary

19. Office of Research, *National Norms for Entering College Freshmen— Fall, 1971* (Washington: American Council on Education, 1971).

school extracurricular and academic achievement, career and education plans, social attitudes, academic attitudes, and a host of other items that could improve perspectives about college freshmen and how best to prepare students for college and to serve them once enrolled. The report could form the basis for excellent dialogue among feeder and receiving institutions and develop internal articulation.

Both the American College Testing Program and the College Entrance Examination Board have services by subscription that are similar to the American Council's norms. Characteristics of students who are leaving or entering the subscribing institution are compared with national norms for high school seniors or college freshmen.[20] The College Board also distributes a wealth of admission guidance information in its biannual *College Handbook*.[21] The entry for each college is written by the participating institution. Some colleges list only curriculum, cost, and admissions requirements, while others add general information on college life, student characteristics, college academic policies, financial aid, and housing. Recent editions of the *College Handbook* organize statistics volunteered by the colleges. Tables cover financial aid awards, ratios of accepted and denied students according to sex and class rank, academic composites (SAT score and rank) of applicants and of enrolled freshmen, SAT scores of enrolled freshmen, probability charts for obtaining various grade averages with particular academic composites, and more.

In one volume, the *Handbook* offers a wealth of evaluative data on individual colleges and universities in a format that enables readers to compare institutions. It is interesting that a freely available handbook allows the evaluations and comparisons that are expressly forbidden or implicitly discouraged by the statewide cooperative guides. However, all such documents are best put to use when students read them with the guidance and interpretation of the professional counselor.

The College Board has recently introduced a new reference for college guidance called *The Source Book for Higher Education*. It represents a departure from standard college guidance books in that it

20. See College Scholarship Service, *A Description of the Institutional Summary Data Service* (Princeton, N.J.: Educational Testing Service, 1971); and *Using ACT on Campus, 1972-73* (Iowa City: American College Testing Program, 1972).
21. Douglas D. Dillenbeck et al., eds., *The College Handbook* (New York: College Entrance Examination Board, 1969).

focuses on access research rather than information summaries about particular institutions. Prepared under the leadership of Warren W. Willingham, whose access strategy of categorizing higher education institutions is described in chapter three, the volume promises to add an important new dimension to higher education guidance.

A counterpart to the *College Handbook* has been developed for the transfer student by Barron's Educational Series, Inc. Barron's transfer handbook [22] is informative on transfer admission policies and procedures in general and for specific senior institutions, methods used to evaluate transfer credit, and related topics. Such a specialized reference work makes a genuine contribution to school and college relations; however, the book would be more useful if it were regionalized. The typical transfer student goes to a community college close to home and then transfers to a senior institution as near as possible. The pattern suggests that transfer handbooks with the national scope of Barron's transfer handbook would not be used as widely as a more complete guide for the local area. The Barron's handbook provides an excellent model to develop such documents.

The NACAC *Ask Us* service deserves special mention, since it is one of the few national information services that match community college transfers with senior institutions. Also, NACAC's widely circulated lists of college candidates and enrollment opportunities are useful, as are such lists from similar professional organizations. Likewise, the Middle States Association of Colleges and Secondary Schools distributes a quarterly survey of freshman and transfer space availability.[23] However, the lists are useful primarily as a starting point for more definitive investigation.

Institutional literature

As applicants narrow their considerations to fewer colleges, institutional literature assumes great importance. Literature for counselors or students can take the form of a chatty and personalized newsletter telling about resignations and new employees, vignettes about students

---

22. N. C. Proia and B. J. Drysdale, *Barron's Handbook of College Transfer Information* (Woodbury, N.Y.: Barron's Educational Series, 1969).

23. Calvin L. Crawford, ed., *Freshman and Transfer Space Availability Survey*, 7th ed. (New York: Middle States Association of Colleges and Secondary Schools, 1971).

and teachers, and basic admission information. At the other extreme are the businesslike brochures that are totally concerned with the specifics of financial aid, cost, and admission policies and procedures. The extremes leave room for a wide variety between the two approaches. The formats vary from printed, multipaged, stapled documents to color-illustrated brochures that may be mailed, uncovered or in number ten envelopes, to individuals or to institutions for display.

Regardless of audience or style, all institutional admission literature should adhere to a few basic considerations. First, the document should be concerned with either freshmen or transfers—not both. Second, potential consumers must be consulted about the format and content of the document to be sure that the material serves consumer needs. Third, feedback mechanisms that allow for continual evaluation must be incorporated into the literature in the form of mail-back cards or questionnaires. Fourth, mailings should be followed to determine whether material is reaching persons who could profit from it. Variations in distribution techniques may be required, such as bulk mailings to schools or hand deliveries to counselors. Quantity deliveries may be suitable for community centers, parent-teacher associations, professional education associations, and similar organizations. Colleges can usually use a moderate supply of handouts to answer requests for information by phone or letter or from visitors.

Information materials must answer certain minimum questions if the document is to be worth the expense and effort of production and distribution. There must be a clear, honest explanation of admission requirements. If admission decisions depend on vague, subjective factors, this should be stated. If a student who falls below a particular class rank or test score stands almost no chance for admission, this, too, must be expressly stated. Clear figures about costs are essential, as is a realistic assessment of financial aid opportunities; explanations of the latter should detail the availability and relationship of specific aspects, such as loans, scholarships, grants, and employment. Application deadlines should be noted, and if the deadlines depend on the number and quality of applicants received by a particular date, this, too, should be made clear. Finally, the document should advise readers on how to secure additional data or contact other knowledgeable people. Admission information literature should be characterized by openness, honesty, and comprehensiveness, as the material is unquestionably intended as a service to students, not as an advertising gimmick designed to lure students.

The class profile

The class profile is a special form of admission information, intended to provide exacting data about student characteristics and academic and test performance. If properly constructed, disseminated, and used, the profile is one of the most efficient tools that can be employed for improving school and college relations. The College Board pioneered in making freshman profiles generally available; they cooperated with higher education institutions in a particular state to produce a manual of freshman class profiles for that state.[24] The manuals summarized data on SAT scores and class ranks of entering freshmen and set up tables that allowed grades at a particular college to be predicted from high school characteristics. Profiles have gradually disappeared since the *College Handbook* collected the same data and predictors on a national basis. The American College Testing Program, however, actively encourages the publication of student profiles. The statewide *Guides* discussed earlier, which contain data on freshman characteristics and performance, are all products of joint efforts by the American College Testing Program and state institutions or agencies.

Organizational approaches to producing class profiles leave much to be desired, when evaluated by the criteria of an ideal class profile. The persistence/attrition data should be stated very clearly and honestly. Preenrollment characteristics should be related to performance in terms of grade point average and academic status. Statements should appear on the percentage of students at each juncture of rank and test scores who performed in a particular way; correlations between preenrollment and postenrollment characteristics should be made.

In the prototype, pre- and postenrollment characteristics are presented in meaningful subdivisions, as by college, department, and new classes. There should be adequate presentation of nonintellective data that describe the social, economic, political, and educational background, goals, and needs of the student body. Some attention is paid to persistent interests and accomplishments or events lasting longer than one academic year.

24. See *Manual of Freshman Class Profiles for Indiana Colleges* (Princeton, N.J.: College Entrance Examination Board, 1966).

The goals of the model profile can best be reached by institutions which apply the data processing resources of the college and self-knowledge to the maintenance and production of profile data. The articulation specialist must play a central role, feeding user needs into the profile format. He should also be a central figure in determining the format, distribution, follow-up, and feedback activities that stem from the class profile. Probably the most persistent internal problem the articulation specialist will face is the reluctance on the part of the central administration to present unfavorable attrition data. College deans or department heads, as well, may be hesitant to see their area compared unfavorably to other academic units in terms of class rank and test score quality of beginning freshmen or its ability to retain students. The best approach for the specialist is to convince an unwilling staff of its responsibility to applicants to be as honest and informative as possible. Academic issues cannot be solved by sweeping the problems under the rug; rather, they can be met effectively in the best traditions of collegiate education—by exposure and examination of the evidence in search of truth and wisdom.

The University of Wisconsin prepares a profile in pamphlet form for mailing in standard envelopes. The number and quality of freshmen are listed by college and in total; grade point averages earned by college and overall are given, and high school rank is related to scholastic average. Persistence data is presented only for the freshman class as a whole. The data are displayed in a table and a pie chart (see figure 7).

The appearance of qualitative academic characteristics by college is commendable as is the clear presentation of academic persistence for the entire freshman class. The absence of nonintellective data is understandable in light of the pamphlet size. However, the lack of attrition data by college, similar to the examples for the entire class, represents a major shortcoming.

The profiles developed at the University of Illinois at Chicago Circle are far more extensive than those published by the University of Wisconsin. As a result, Chicago Circle cannot produce a document small enough to fit a business envelope. Instead, its freshman profiles are bound in 8½-by-11 inch booklets of from thirty to forty pages and divided into three sections on enrollment, high school rank, and test score academic characteristics of beginning freshmen totally, by college, and by sex; nonintellective characteristics for all freshmen, such

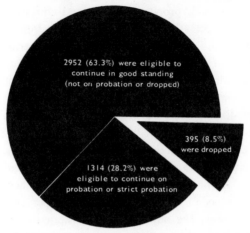

91.5% OF FRESHMEN WERE ELIGIBLE TO CONTINUE INTO SECOND YEAR OF STUDIES

2952 (63.3%) were eligible to continue in good standing (not on probation or dropped)

395 (8.5%) were dropped

1314 (28.2%) were eligible to continue on probation or strict probation

Probation and drop policies differ greatly among the colleges and schools of the University. With the exception of the College of Engineering, generally students are not dropped for academic reasons at the end of the first semester. Generally, students who earn less than a 2.0 (C average) either or both semester are placed on probation or strict probation but are eligible to continue. Students with very poor achievement in both semesters are dropped in June.

ACADEMIC STANDING RELATED TO HIGH SCHOOL RANK
for 4661 freshmen who completed both semesters

HS rank Centile	Total # of students	%eligible to continue	=%in good standing	+ % on probation	% dropped
90-99	1400	98.1	= 86.5	+ 11.6	1.9
80-89	963	94.2	= 67.4	+ 26.8	5.8
70-79	721	90.4	= 50.9	+ 39.5	9.6
60-69	553	86.6	= 42.7	+ 43.9	13.4
50-59	323	78.3	= 39.3	+ 39.0	21.7
Below 50	326	76.1	= 31.3	+ 44.8	23.9
Not Ranked	375				

Source: The University of Wisconsin, Madison Campus, *Our 1965 Freshman Class in Profile.*

Fig. 7. Sample display of information for freshman profile.

as influences on college choice, size of high school classes, percent of students in high school honors courses, self-reported high school grades by subject area, major feeder high schools, leadership achievements in high school, proposed majors and educational and career goals, housing expectations, financial aid expectations, estimates of family income, and student age; and academic performance of the preceding year's freshman class. Sections are related to the rank and test characteristics of students, both totally and by college. Much of the data and summarization is provided by the American College Testing Program. Examples of the two displays for the entire class and for each college are presented in figures 8 and 9, taken from the 1970 edition of the Chicago Circle *Freshman Profile*.

Unfortunately, the attrition displays illustrated in figures 8 and 9 are found only in a confidential version of the profile in accordance with a compromise between the university articulation personnel and the central administration. The administration hesitated to release attrition data to the professional public but agreed to distribute information to the university deans, directors, and heads of academic departments. The central administration found it difficult tó prove that faculty members would not benefit from knowledge of student characteristics and the academic practices of colleagues. The assumption that high school counselors, administrators, and even students cannot profit equally from attrition information is likewise without foundation. The principle of publishing specific attrition data now has been established, and the entire professional community should soon have access to a complete profile. Then the profile's value to student selection will be greatly improved.

High schools and community colleges should contribute to the admission process by publishing profiles. Standardized test results, grades earned by subject areas, class ranking policies, extracurricular activities, honors and advanced placement policies, community characteristics, and other pertinent facts can assist college admissions officers in evaluating candidates from schools that are unfamiliar to them. Finally, the most serious oversight in the current development of class profiles is the failure of senior institutions to characterize transfer students. Instead of test scores and high school class ranks, transfer profiles should compare grade point averages and grades in particular disciplines before and after transfer. General information, similar to

College of Business Administration

There were 290 beginning freshmen enrolled in the fall of 1969; 263 were male and 27 were female. Of these, 290 had ACT scores, HSPR, and GPA-I. The persistence rates for the latter group are described in the table below. Each cell represents the percentage of students with a particular combination of HSPR and ACT:C who were eligible to return for the sophomore year. Cells designated with an asterisk indicate that the total *number* of students in that cell was less than ten.

ACT Composite

HSPR	Below 18	18-20	21-23	24-26	27-29	30-32	Total
90-99	100.00%*	100.00%*	72.73%	100.00%	100.00%	100.00%*	93.62%
80-89	50.00%*	100.00%*	90.00%	85.0%	88.89%*	———	84.21%
70-79	83.33%*	100.00%*	92.85%	80.0%	100.00%*	———	90.00%
60-69	88.88%*	92.31%*	66.67%	77.78%	100.00%*	———	82.35%
50-59	100.00%*	83.33%*	85.71%	85.72%	66.67%*	———	85.29%
Below 50	100.00%*	63.63%*	88.46%	72.73%	100.00%*	———	80.39%
Total	82.76%	86.04%	84.00%	84.21%	95.00%	100.00%*	85.86%

Persistence of the 1969 freshmen summarized in the table above is further described in the figure below.

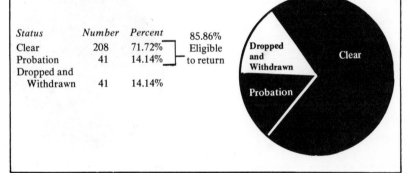

Status	Number	Percent	
Clear	208	71.72%	85.86%
Probation	41	14.14%	Eligible to return
Dropped and Withdrawn	41	14.14%	

Fig. 8. *Freshman Profile* (Chicago: University of Illinois at Chicago Circle, Office of Admissions and Records, 1970). Used by permission.

that used in freshman profiles, and policies on course transferability should also be presented. As more students change postsecondary institutions, the transfer profile should soon become a standard document in the repertoire of admissions information.

All Campus

There were 3286 beginning freshmen enrolled in the Fall of 1969; 1954 were male and 1332 were female. Of these, 3286 had ACT scores, HSPR, and GPA-I. The persistence rates for the latter group are described in the table below. Each cell represents the percentage of students with a particular combination of HSPR and ACT:C who were eligible to return for the sophomore year. Cells designated with an asterisk indicate that the total *number* of students in that cell was less than ten.

ACT Composite

HSPR	Below 18	18-20	21-23	24-26	27-29	30-32	33-36	Total
90-99	86.56%	88.57%	82.14%	91.75%	89.59%	93.59%	100.00%*	88.80%
80-89	71.64%	84.00%	80.23%	86.34%	82.00%	86.95%	———	82.17%
70-79	72.82%	83.33%	75.49%	84.38%	81.92%	66.66%	———	79.54%
60-69	72.47%	78.57%	81.05%	82.83%	78.33%	75.00%*	100.00%	79.32%
50-59	81.97%	79.45%	73.34%	77.03%	68.97%	100.00%*	---	76.68%
Below 50	88.46%	70.53%	82.10%	74.40%	76.67%	80.00%*	---	77.71%
Total	77.49%	80.40%	79.45%	84.19%	83.13%	89.17%	100.00%*	81.50%

Persistence of the 1969 freshmen summarized in the table above is further described in the figure below.

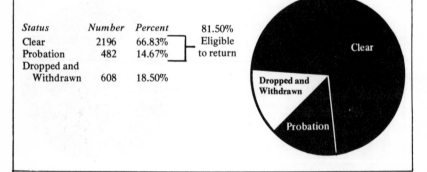

Status	Number	Percent	
Clear	2196	66.83%	81.50%
Probation	482	14.67%	Eligible to return
Dropped and Withdrawn	608	18.50%	

Fig. 9. *Freshman Profile* (Chicago: University of Illinois at Chicago Circle, Office of Admissions and Records, 1970), p. 6. Used by permission.

eight

Organizational Structure and the Future

Students are encountering more demands to make more decisions based on more complex issues and data than ever before. At the same time, a trend toward impersonalized, efficient procedures is noticeable among schools, community colleges, and universities. One natural counterbalance to the negative implications of mechanized processing is to increase the influence of school and college relations programs. However, in order to maximize the principles and practices of good articulation, schools and colleges must each be properly organized for the task. Interinstitutional organizational patterns are also important, as are the priorities given to school and college relations by professional education organizations and statewide coordinating agencies.

The reordering of current priorities for articulation would represent a major step in coping with problems of student transition. Broader, more fundamental concepts and applications of articulation theory could advance to stimulate the long overdue recognition of the importance of school and college relations as a career field and as an academic interest worthy of graduate programs in student personnel services, guidance and counseling, and higher education. Similar consideration should emanate from the U.S. Office of Education, for articulation problems are a national concern that plague most states and a significant proportion of students nationwide.

Once awareness is heightened and manifested in action, the stage will be set for applying the full range of computing hardware and micrographic technology increasingly seen in other areas of higher education administration. Other resources found in education institutions that are not presently utilized to much advantage in articulation programs can also be applied. Most important of all, improved organization and recognition for school and college relations could lead to a climate within institutions, and in the education field generally, that will be conducive to improved student transition in all aspects.

Institutional Organization

While institutional leaders have not supported school and college relations very much in the past, the time now seems ripe to improve on tradition. The current stress on accountability and efficiency and the diminishing supply of students join other pressures leading toward increased respect for interinstitutional relations. The accountability movement has demanded fewer gaps, duplications, and overlaps, and the reduced rate of enrollment puts a premium on efficient communication with prospective students.

An important step in improving the influence of articulation programs is to gain general acceptance of school and college relations as a distinct, independent student personnel service on a par with similar functions. At the high school level, recognition might take the form of expanding the traditional college consultant's role to that of an articulation specialist with the responsibility of relating to all school counselors and providing them with a regular flow of information, special resources, and consultation services. The college consultant or articulation specialist would personally interact with students by showing them how to select a college and by taking on individual student assignments which present particularly difficult college guidance challenges.

The major difference from the traditional job of college consultant would be the external dimensions of the role. The articulation specialist does more than merely seek out, organize, and distribute college admission information. He is actively involved with colleges in the development of admission and articulation policy. He follows his school's college matriculants and is available to individuals who are having difficulty in the first year of college or who wish to reverse an unfortunate first choice of colleges as quickly as possible. Such a professional should be as concerned about downward as upward articulation in recognition of his main responsibility to assist students in transition from one educational level to another. There is important, though often unrecognized, work to be done here. Secondary-elementary articulation, when properly acknowledged, can result in a good deal of activity. In one secondary school, twelve different articulation committees on curriculum structure and content were eventually established between it and feeder elementary districts.[1]

The main task in higher education is to extricate the articulation function from subordination to either the community college counseling and guidance program or the university admissions office.

A growing number of institutions, however, have made the articulation function appropriately distinct by designating transfer coordinators. Community colleges in such states as New Jersey and Massachusetts, where there are few community colleges, have joined colleges in states that more fully recognize the community college movement to establish articulation job slots. Most senior institutions in states with important community college movements are increasingly likely to designate community college coordinators, usually within the admissions office, and senior institutions in states with few community colleges have established offices of high school relations, usually as subsections of admissions or admissions and records. The University of Washington's structure is typical, with an associate director of admissions also carrying the title of director of high school relations.

The institutional organization of articulation efforts in California, Illinois, Kansas, and Wisconsin exemplify the nature of the problem from a management point of view and the varieties of possible resolutions.

Wisconsin

Before their recent merger into the University of Wisconsin system, both the University of Wisconsin and the Wisconsin State University system had recognized the importance of articulation, even though the state had almost no community colleges. At the University of Wisconsin, several years ago, the Office of High School Relations not only was recognized as a distinctive entity, but its director was given parallel standing with the director of admissions, both of whom reported to the dean of students. However, the decision was not accepted by proponents of traditional admissions organizations, and the Office of High School Relations later merged into the admissions office, with the

1. Lloyd S. Michael, "Articulation Problems with Lower Schools and Higher Education," *Bulletin of the National Association of Secondary School Principals,* February 1959, p. 52.

director of admissions as the immediate superior of the director of high school relations.

The campuses of the Wisconsin State University system never developed offices of high school relations, although an assistant or associate director of admissions carried the title and function of director of high school relations depending on the perceived needs of each campus. Where articulation needs were judged minimal, the director of admissions assumed the high school relations title himself. When the two institutional systems merged, the high school relations organization was thrown into a state of confusion, with the articulation specialists operating out of the dean of students' office pending resolution of this organizational issue. Where the importance and definition of articulation services are not clear, such muddles can be expected. It is encouraging that most campuses of the combined state system now have departments of high school and college relations, whose directors report to officers on the campus chancellor's staff.

California

The University of California has achieved what is probably the most independent, powerful, and professionally active institutional articulation organization in the United States. The completely independent office has a raison d'etre derived from articulation and is unrelated to the admissions office. Until July 1972, the Office of Relations with Schools was part of the central coordinating apparatus for intercampus governance. The director was responsible for coordinating articulation activities with high schools and community colleges for all campuses. Each campus had its own articulation specialist carrying the title of associate director, who reported to the central office director. The arrangement produced an excellent articulation newsletter, productive research on student transition, and similar benefits. After July 1972, the central coordinating office concept was abandoned, but the job of campus articulation officer was retained. Each campus has its own director of relations with schools who reports to the campus chancellor. The amount of interaction between each campus' Office of Relations with Schools and the admissions office depends on the views held by the campus chancellor. In no case, however, does the director report to the admissions officer.

The positions of coordinator of school and college relations at some campuses of the California State College system came into being in the past few years by expropriating unfilled faculty vacancies in the personnel budget. The positions are not well defined and vary considerably among campuses where articulation supporters have managed to steal a budget position. In general, the position evolved to answer the need for better communication, to anticipate admission and transition problems, and to improve preadmission advising. At some campuses the coordinator of school and college relations reports to the director of admissions, and at others to the dean of students, thereby allowing for parity between the admission and articulation functions. Articulation is never handled by one person with a dual admission-articulation title. Clearly, the general stability and direction of school and college relations at the California State College system are vague and tenuous, but the very existence of the coordinator position gives cause for optimism.

Illinois

The University of California system has influenced the University of Illinois system. There is a central Office of School and College Relations which provides staff support for the admissions and articulation concerns of both the central university administration and the individual campuses. The staff consists of a director, assistant director, coordinator of junior college relations, director and assistant director of testing and research, a half-time articulation generalist, a data processing specialist, and secretarial support. While the director of school and college relations has no authority over campus directors of admissions and records, he is responsible for achieving a measure of coordination among them, particularly regarding policy implementation for the whole university.

The director of admissions and records on each campus has responsibility for the individual campus articulation programs. He assigns authority within the office and determines the extent of staff support and other resources to be allocated for school and college relations. Allotments to each campus change from time to time depending on leadership perceptions of articulation needs and the availability of funds. During years when recruiting and transitional problems were acute, the admissions office at Chicago Circle was administered by an associate director of admissions-coordinator of school and college relations, who was supported by assistant coordinators for high school relations, junior college relations, and special programs plus a pre-admission counselor, an administrative assistant, and three secretaries. Later, when budget concerns became pressing and chief administrators viewed recruitment, transition, and public relations problems to be sufficiently under control, the articulation staff was reduced. It is important to note that the position of associate director for school and college relations was retained permanently. Current enrollment shortages will probably lead to expanded staff size and influence.

Developments in articulation administration at the Urbana-Champaign campus have been similar. Working from the Office of Admissions and Records, a coordinator is presently in charge of school and college relations activities and is supported by one full-time professional and a half-time secretary. One important difference between the two campus programs is the staffing for college day/night visits. Urbana-Champaign, serving the entire state, receives far more requests from schools for college representatives than does Chicago Circle. Chicago Circle relates to the Chicago metropolitan area, where most of its requests for college representatives originate. Visits to schools and community colleges can be staffed fairly well by Chicago Circle's professional articulation staff, while Urbana-Champaign must rely on volunteer faculty for the bulk of its representation. High school and community college counselors leave no doubt that they prefer the professional representative, who is better informed about the total range of prospective concerns.

Kansas

Concern for the needs of transfer students was the impetus behind the recent reorganization of student personnel services at the University of Kansas. Ignored for years, transfers had become an increasingly important segment of new students. Soon after assuming the presidency of the University of Kansas, E. L. Chalmers, Jr. established the Office of Junior College Affairs. The new administrative unit had responsibility and authority for coordinating activities of the individual departments and colleges that affect transfer students; it also assumed a variety of central student service administrative functions for transfers that put it on a par with such offices as admissions and financial aid.

In a speech, Chalmers described the functions of the new Office of Junior College Affairs and listed those duties most directly related to school and college relations:

1. Identification and advising of prospective transfers. This would involve planned trips to junior colleges and visits of prospective transfers to KU, planned programs in the community, one-to-one pairing of alumnus and transfer, transmittal of informational literature, and direct personalized correspondence.
2. Academic advising that provides advocacy for the best use of the transfer's previously earned credit and integration between that and upper division study at KU. In this area, Junior College Affairs personnel would be particularly concerned with exposing the fact that native students are encouraged to develop programs with extensive diversity from one another to meet individual needs; while junior college transfers are penalized for the very same thing. They would also be concerned with educating departments out of the "my course is better than your course" and "my grade is better than your grade" syndromes.
3. Development of adequate sources of financial support for transfers that gives them financial aid parity in competition for funds with beginning freshmen.
4. Coordination and communication both within the University and between divisions at the University and feeder junior colleges. This includes coordination of visits in both directions and written communication to and from the various areas of the University and community colleges.
5. Recommendations to the University decision-making bodies about policies for junior college transfers.
6. Assistance in the admissions process and in the evaluation of transcripts.
7. Development of course equivalency guides and counseling manuals for prospective transfer students.
8. Special orientation programs for transfer students.[2]

The Goal

Institutions of higher education that equate articulation with other general tasks of counseling or admission have had unfavorable histories in school and college relations, because the attention and re-

2. E. L. Chalmers, Jr., "The 'Other' Campus" (Paper delivered at the University of Illinois Junior College Conference, Urbana, Ill., 1971).

sources provided for articulation have ebbed and flowed according to impressions of immediate situational demands. When an enrollment or public relations crisis occurs, interest in articulation rises only to subside when the immediate problem passes. Such waivering support makes it very difficult to mount and sustain a comprehensive, consistent, long-range program of school and college relations. Consequently, fundamental problems remain, while separate aspects of the overall situation surface as brushfires to be treated independently.

An effective program of school and college relations requires an independent administrative entity on a par with student personnel offices for admissions, registration and records, and counseling. The traditional placement of articulation within admissions—even when an admissions officer carries a second title indicating articulation as his primary concern—is not satisfactory. When admissions personnel cannot completely cope with application processing, registration, or records, the resources reserved for articulation will almost always be redirected to those areas. From the point of view of the director of admissions and records, the university or college cannot function if admissions or registration processes fail or if student records are not kept; but the institution can limp along for years with inadequate articulation services, since the fundamental sustaining processes of the college or university are usually not affected. In the organizational context, articulation is viewed in much the same way as corporations view advertising. Although the results of expenditures cannot always be related to profits, advertising seems wise, provided funds are available. When profits drop, leading management to reduce staff, the advertising and public relations people are the first employees to be laid off, since they are not directly related to the sustaining process of manufacturing, distribution, and direct sale of the product. The analogy applies to the past fate of the Office of High School Relations at the University of Wisconsin and to past reductions in California and Illinois. Now that most colleges and universities need more students, the trend, with a heavy emphasis on head hunting, has been reversed to meet the current emergency.

The best way continuously to ensure students of good transition is to establish the responsibility and authority in an articulation office. Administrators must be educated to the thinking exemplified by the president of the University of Kansas. The articulation unit, however, should expand on the University of Kansas model, a unit solely devoted to community college concerns, to encompass all levels of articulation. The University of California and the University of Illinois both have such prototypes, which offer a full range of articulation resources and integrated balanced programs.

It is particularly important to guard against the jerry-built answers to articulation needs as found in the California State College system. Such an approach is no different from the assignment of articulation responsibilities to a member of the admissions staff. Urgent demands on admissions are met with the resources of the school and college relations program. While the appropriation of staff positions allocated by a budget may be a wise strategy to initiate an independent articulation specialty, such measures can only be a temporary expedient to the development of an independent unit. Articulation specialists operating under such conditions should be careful to produce the programs, documentation, and research that clarify and demonstrate the need to establish an articulation position in budget guidelines.

The recent reorganization of articulation services at the University of California raises an interesting question for universities with several campuses. Should each location develop independent school and college relations programs responsible only to the head of the individual campus, or should coordination and responsibility rest with a central university agency? Neither alternative is preferable, since the former distorts overall perspectives and resource allocation, while the latter limits reaction to the peculiar articulation needs of the local campus. The concept of a central coordinating office and independent campus directors is an excellent compromise. As employed at the University of Illinois, the staff office conducts research requested by campus directors and ensures that directors are aware of developments at other campuses in the same system or at other institutions. The central staff office should also develop and coordinate recommendations for policy changes affecting the entire university and serve as liaison between various university councils and committees that have an interest in and impact on articulation.

It is also important that the school and college relations unit be supported either by an advisory council of university staff and faculty members and representatives of institutions relating to the campus, or by separate internal and external advisory councils whose work is coordinated by an executive board drawn from each group. The latter arrangement is preferable because each group will concentrate on the problems most germane to its area, under the general enlightenment of the coordinating superstructure. Frequently, recommendations are eventually adopted as university policy. The University of Kansas initially had only an internal advisory committee, but an external advisory group is sure to develop as the Office of Junior College Affairs reaches maturity. Whichever approach is used, the important idea is continuously to supply information and recommendations to the director of articulation services (an excellent descriptive title used at the University of South Florida) to monitor and debate institutional policy.

In summary, articulation services in institutions of higher education should be organized as a freestanding entity equal to other recognized student personnel services. The unit should be held responsible for effectively improving student transition in all forms and be given adequate administrative support in the form of staff, funds, and authority. School and college relations work should possess the same stable career opportunities as admissions, registration, counseling, and financial aid work. The range of professional activities should encompass communication with the constituencies of feeder and receiving institutions as well as with internal college personnel. A more specific description of the articulator's function would be providing research, literature, and preadmission counseling and intervening on the student's behalf with admissions, financial aid, and college deans. As a result, students, faculty, and administrators in all institutions affected by student transitions should turn to the articulation office for direction and help.

Professional and Institutional Organizations

If the purpose is to improve coordination among institutions, it is axiomatic that efficient communication must flow among professionals engaged in the task. While committees and councils may dissipate the worker's time in ineffectual discussions, the main resource of the articulation professional is a variety of channels of information and communication. Time spent at several commissions, committees, boards, and councils cannot be viewed as wasted or as a distraction for the articulation specialist, although the specialist has an obligation to develop the most parsimonious organizational network.

Professional organizations for school and college relations

Concern for educational articulation within professional organizations is mixed. The College Entrance Examination Board, an organization primarily devoted to school and college relations, sets standards for the field of articulation through its annual and regional meetings and publications. The main purpose of the CEEB lies elsewhere, so contributions to strengthening the status of the professional articulation specialist are not continuous. The same is true for the activities of the regional accrediting associations. The National Association of College Admissions Counselors (NACAC) comes closest to being an organization with a primary focus on school and college relations. According to its constitution, NACAC aims "to establish and to maintain high professional standards in college admissions guidance . . .; to develop and to expand the relationships between secondary schools, colleges, graduate schools, and professional schools; to assist in the development of efficient programs of counseling and guidance . . .; [and] to serve the students, the parents, the secondary schools, the colleges, the graduate schools, and the professional schools by considering the whole range of secondary school-college relations."[3]

In support of the purposes, NACAC has established standing committees on admission practices and procedures, subject matter articulation, and research and experimentation. Membership is institutional rather than individual, including high schools, community colleges, four-year colleges, and universities. NACAC has also provided the impetus for the formation of eleven state associations in Illinois, Indiana, Iowa, Michigan, Minnesota, Missouri, New Jersey, New York, Ohio, Pennsylvania, and Wisconsin. Nearly one thousand colleges and about thirteen hundred secondary schools comprise the membership. While it seems like the ideal school and college relations organization, NACAC falls short because of a bias toward counselors and college admissions that precludes broad involvement along the entire range of articulation concerns. While a subject articulation committee exists, little action of real impact or importance comes from it. NACAC focuses on college admission guidance, and its annual meetings and publications (*Ask Us, Handbook of Member Colleges and*

3. *The Constitution, By-Laws and Statement of Good Practice* (Evanston, Ill.: National Association of College Admissions Counselors, 1971), p. 3.

Universities, NACAC Journal, and a newsletter) testify to the organization's direction. Matters such as external and nontraditional credit devices, curricular integration, academic advising, orientation, and other aspects of school and college relations that go beyond college selection matters are of marginal interest to the membership.

There are a number of other organizations which, while not primarily concerned with articulation, maintain standing committees on school and college relations or high school-college relations and junior-senior college relations. Among such organizations are the American College Personnel Association, the American Association of Collegiate Registrars and Admissions Officers, and the National Association of Secondary School Principals. Considering the committees in key organizations and the college guidance focus and school-college membership of the National Association of College Admissions Counselors, some observers might deny the need of articulation specialists for a professional organization. Yet, the current organizational base for school and college relations cannot be viewed as entirely satisfactory for the strengthening of school and college relations as a professional specialty.

The supportive organizational structure is in no way comparable to the level of professional organization achieved in such related fields as counseling, admissions and registration work, and similar educational specialties. However, there has been one attempt to maintain a professional organization that focused primarily on educational articulation. The National Council on School-College Relations (NCSCR) was organized December 8, 1965, in Washington, D.C. The NCSCR was created for collecting, organizing, and disseminating information about articulation; identifying and stimulating research in this field; developing organized programs that would avoid duplication of effort; attracting financial support for school and college relations experiments and programs; and generally strengthening the position of school and college relations.

Membership was by professional association, rather than on the basis of individuals or institutions. The charter members of the council were the American Association of College Admissions Counselors, the American Association of Collegiate Registrars and Admission Officers, the American Association of Junior Colleges, the American College Personnel Association, the American School Counselor's

Association, the National Association of Independent Schools, the National Association of Secondary School Principals, and the National Catholic Educational Association.

At the founding meeting active membership was offered to the National Association of Women Deans and Counselors and affiliate membership to the American College Testing Program, the College Entrance Examination Board, the Educational Testing Service, the Educational Records Bureau, six regional accrediting associations, the National Scholarship Fund for Negro Students, and the National Merit Scholarship Corporation.

Council business was conducted by a board of delegates, consisting of one voting representative from each organization holding active membership. NCSCR activities were financed by annual dues of $100 per member organization, and the first couple of years were reasonably productive. As leadership changed and the novelty wore off, the council gradually stopped functioning. In June of 1970, the uncertainty of continued support from the membership became apparent, and a moratorium on dues went into effect. In addition, a questionnaire assessing the effectiveness and impact of the council was sent to as many state school and college relations committees as could be located. The outcome of the study was reviewed by the executive committee, which decided in June of 1971 to dissolve the council.[4]

Some of the council's last leaders and organizational delegates attributed the council's demise to an absence of paid professional staff to carry forth necessary day-to-day activities and to give continuity to programs. Furthermore, college representatives had no authority to commit their organizations to programs or activities, and the primary interests of the members were too diverse to reach consensus or to hold a high level of interest in articulation programs. As one former member put it, "the parts were greater than the whole."

The experience of the National Council on School-College Relations is of value in planning for the development of a sorely needed national professional school and college relations organization. The organization needs to be broadly concerned with all aspects of school and college relations, supporting standing committees on special subjects and administrative matters and relations. The name might well be something like the National School and College Relations Association or

4. Information supplied by Calvin L. Crawford, the last NCSCR chairman.

the American Association for Educational Articulation. Membership might be drawn from school and college relations personnel in community colleges, universities, and colleges, high school-college consul-, tants, college admissions counselors, financial aid information specialists, orientation specialists, and others with tasks directly related to articulation. Membership should be on an individual basis, as evidence of professional commitment. Further, a paid executive, as in other prominent professional associations, must direct the organization.

A national association would enforce professional standards of articulation practice which are sorely missing at present, and it would lobby for professional recognition by related organizations and by the decision-makers of schools and colleges. Most important, the organization would provide a forum for the exposure, debate, and solution of problems of school-college relations and stimulate a generally higher level of professionalism for all the varied aspects of articulation work.

Articulation of articulators

Effective articulation depends on regular contact among the articulation representatives of institutions that must cooperate. Association can be organized on a local, statewide, or regional basis or according to relationships between schools and colleges or junior and senior colleges. Membership can be limited to articulation specialists or broadened to include representatives of other institutional specialties. Participation may depend on representing an institution or a variety of professional organizations interested in school and college relations. Or an omnibus scheme can be used as a framework that brings representatives of colleges and associations together with articulation and other academic specialists into one organization encompassing all sets of educational relationships.

Decisions on organizational forms should be made on the basis of accordant requirements to improve articulation in the particular local context. While local needs and conditions are paramount, two guidelines can help to establish the best possible structure. First, the organization should have a precise mission and scope that reflect the common focus of its membership. Second, members must be equal and have relatively similar stakes in the proceedings. The guidelines reinforce organization by relationships and institutional membership, although many successful councils violate this prescription.

Examples of good statewide organizational plans must always be characterized by periodic change. Student and institutional needs are dynamic, and articulation arrangements designed to keep pace with needs must be adaptable. Hence, the statewide organizations described below may already have changed in light of recent rapid developments in education. Still, the examples serve to outline the basic thrusts in statewide articulation organization.

Washington. Membership of the state Council on High School-College Relations includes representatives from the state associations of junior high school principals and secondary school principals, the personnel and guidance association, each Washington college, the department of public instruction, and the Washington Pre-College Testing Program. The number of principals' association representatives is equal to the number of college representatives. Even though the council has an omnifarious membership, it is said to function quite well. Perhaps the effectiveness of the council can be attributed to common interests among members in school-college concerns.

The Inter-College Relations Commission links high school-college associations and junior-senior college organizations. The latter interest group has its main power base in the Washington Association of College Presidents (senior college, university, and community college) and the Council of Presidents (senior college and university only). The actual policy development and implementation occur mostly within the intercollege commission, where high schools are involved with community college and four-year institutions and the intercollege articulation committee established by the Council of Presidents.[5]

Missouri. The Missouri School and College Relations Commission is an example of voluntary statewide organization based on representation of professional organizations. The Missouri Association of Collegiate Registrars and Admissions Officers, Missouri Association of Secondary School Principals, counselor and teacher groups, and others form the membership. The organization schedules and publicizes all college day/night programs held in the state, awards certificates of recognition to high school seniors, and annually revises its college guidance handbook. The Missouri commission has proved to be an

5. Frederick C. Kintzer, *Nationwide Pilot Study on Articulation* (Los Angeles: University of California, ERIC Clearinghouse for Junior Colleges, 1970), p. 125.

effective and well-respected group. Continuous monitoring and encouragement from the Missouri Commission on Higher Education assures continued effectiveness.

California. Since California has the greatest number of community colleges and a highly planned and integrated system of higher education linkage, it is not surprising that the state also has an elaborate institutional coordinating structure for junior-senior college articulation. Responsibility for articulation is lodged in the California Coordinating Council for Higher Education, which has governmental backing and legitimized status by virtue of the state master plan for higher education, legislation passed in 1960.

The formal, legal activities of the coordinating conference, which include all segments of higher education, are paralleled by the California Articulation Conference, an informal body representing both public and private higher education institutions. The conference in turn has created an ad hoc committee on school and college relations to recommend and perfect statewide articulation policies.[6] Thus, California has organized both formal and voluntary programs of interinstitutional junior-senior college coordination. The statewide activity indicates the professional desire to agree on policies and procedures governing articulation through "voluntary cooperation" and "negotiation,"[7] rather than state fiat. California prods development through the formal structure of a coordinating council, thereby reminding educators that the state can impose solutions.

Virginia. The articulation structure for junior-senior college relations, here, is also well defined and supported by the state. The state Council of Higher Education coordinates all higher education. It has established an advisory council on two- and four-year college articulation, composed of representatives of public and private junior and senior institutions. The advisory council meets at least semiannually to consider articulation problems, suggest needed studies, and recommend guidelines to the state council.[8]

In all of the foregoing cases, the organizational structure has allowed cooperative study of problems of integrated curricula, the policies and procedures for credit transfer, admission policies and pro-

6. Ibid., pp. 14-15.
7. Ibid., p. 15.
8. Ibid., pp. 119-21.

cedures, cooperative guidance and testing programs, and similar matters. Unfortunately, many excellent statewide interinstitutional organizations for junior-senior articulation do not have parallel structures for high school-college relations coordination, as in the state of Washington. The oversight is risky, for articulation resources concentrated exclusively on junior-senior college relations may permit secondary-higher education problems to develop eventually to crisis proportions. If a parallel organization linking junior-senior college and high school-college articulation seems impractical for a particular state, then some other provision should be made to include secondary level representatives in the college level articulation coordinating agency.

Ideally, a state superstructure would oversee all levels of articulation, and regional or local subdivisions would handle specialized needs. Standing committees would be organized according to levels (an elementary-secondary committee and committees for high school-college and junior-senior college relations) or according to problem orientations. The latter group would study subject articulation, admission policies, credit transfer, cooperative conferences, publications, and so forth. While the importance of good articulation should be recognized by state government, the structure should be arranged so that the major activities, recommendations, and procedures stem from voluntary agreements by representatives of member institutions.

Future Developments

Today's electronic hardware and micrographic techniques represent an opportunity to improve articulation to the point where change will become not a matter of degree, but of kind. Before articulation can progress, the modifications already discussed will have to be generally accepted. Without making the necessary alterations, the mechanical advances of micrographics and computer systems will simply be sources of new error and confusion, dissipating large sums of money for no good cause. The use of automated methods introduces a new risk for misinterpretation and misuse that increases proportionally to the type and amount of information available. Correcting errors and guarding privacy are problems that will replace the worries raised by the cumbersome, time-consuming, manual processing of records.

New technology will facilitate the high school's task of transmitting interim and final transcripts for each freshman applicant. Information for the entire graduating class could be put on microform or magnetic form for ready and easy access, thereby streamlining the document transferal process and resolving that hoary bane of existence for college admissions officers, the differences among high school transcripts. The form in which the actual record is kept would no longer matter, as the needed information would be processed uniformly for electronic or micrographic transmittal.

Admission decisions, once made, could be sent instantly to high school guidance offices through cathode ray tubes. The confidentiality of the information could easily be protected by the counselor, who would give the student an individual code to punch to learn the college's decision. If the decision is unfavorable, the student could punch in a request for consideration at a new institution and receive a fast new decision. The filing of complicated multiple application forms and duplicate transcripts can be eliminated, reducing school and college processing costs and making application to college a faster and more relaxed experience for the prospective student.

The greatest danger from mechanization is the reduction of deliberate human attention to the unique characteristics of borderline or nontraditional students. If the threat to this category of applicant is recognized, the additional time gained by electronic processing can be spent giving more attention to the unusual person. As one far-thinking admissions officers noted:

> In my admissions work I know that there are large numbers of applicants who are quite clearly admissible and who have made value judgments concerning their proposed curriculum and objectives. At the present time it takes about as much time to process one of these students as it does the student who finds himself in what I call the "twilight zone," where everything is marginal and further deliberation is called for. Does it not appear that we should take advantage of whatever mechanical and automated means we can to process the student who is patently admissible and in the right "slot," leaving more time available for our counselors, our admissions officers, or what have you, to work with the marginal students—the student who needs considerably more guidance.[9]

9. Harold E. Temmer, "Secondary School-College Articulation" (Paper delivered at panel discussion, the American Association of Collegiate Registrars and Admissions Officers annual convention, New York, N.Y., April 16, 1963), p. 6.

Not only would advanced technological systems make available additional time, but more data about the individual would be known to help counselors in making the best possible decision.

The present sophistication of electronic computing presents the opportunity to resolve long-standing transfer problems of course guidance and credit applicability. All of the possible course equivalencies between junior and senior colleges could be programmed, and the information, stored in magnetic form, could be updated regularly. Maintained at a central station, the data could be retrieved through cathode ray tubes placed in community college counseling offices.

Microform (microfilm, microfiche, etc.) would accomplish the same end when local conditions might dictate an alternate system. The advantage of microform is that current graphic technology allows a print reduction ratio of about 150:1. Thus, all of the parallel programs or curriculum guides of a large university can be recorded on one nine-by-eleven inch microform that can be updated at nominal cost. The information dissemination of micrographics is staggering in its potential for articulation: It could easily transform the very nature of articulation activities.

High school and community college admission guidance programs could take on a new dimension with the use of closed circuit television. Many high schools already have the necessary equipment, and such programs would stimulate more schools to buy systems. High school students could, with closed circuit television, witness and, with the right equipment, even participate in panel discussions on college admission and transition presented by admissions and articulation officers, deans, professors, and college students. The cameras could be reversed, allowing college officials to view a variety of high school or community college instructional situations, college guidance programs, and the like. The same process applies, of course, between community colleges and four-year institutions.

Elaborate procedures should not obscure the greater advantage of such commonplace telecommunications as the telephone. The hot line with a toll-free 800 area code has caught on with a large number of public and private concerns which see an advantage in encouraging clients to call frequently at the organization's expense. A great volume of incoming calls can be handled by coordinating the toll-free number with an automatic call distributor to ship incoming calls to open extensions; computer applications can further improve the communication process. A variety of information on specific articulation topics could be stored in the memory bank of a computer that is activated by dialing a particular phone number. A student with questions concerning the transferability of a particular course or university enrollment need only dial the appropriate number on his home phone, at any time during the day or night, to get his answer. Counselors could also make extensive use of such a service by dialing for audio-access to computerized answers to more complex questions. The method has already proved quite effective for college language labs, and its application to articulation should be equally effective.

The radio is an overlooked tool available to all schools and colleges and most students. Schools and colleges could broadcast programs to each other, and regularly scheduled articulation talk shows could discuss questions phoned in by students. Dialogues on articulation should be a standard feature on radio stations interested in public service and on the many stations sponsored by universities. The schedule of broadcast topics could be advertised on bulletin boards at all schools and colleges, and students and professional personnel should be able to recommend topics.

Numerous different techniques are available for improving the quality and impact of educational articulation; however, bad use of resources is worse than no use at all. Regardless of the approach, articulation can only be realized by serious institutional commitments, a well-organized system of interinstitutional cooperation, and a well-defined professional role for the articulation specialist.

Important social trends are sure to have far-reaching ramifications in the future of school and college relations. Due to declining birth rates, the rate of growth of the college-age population continues to recede. The end of the military draft, which had stimulated many young men to enter college rather than serve in Vietnam, has further weakened enrollments. The majority of American colleges and universities—grown accustomed to continual expansion during the sixties—now find themselves in serious difficulty because they cannot meet previously projected attendance levels.

At the same time that its growth is leveling off, higher education has been assaulted by unprecedented inflation, which has hit postsecondary education harder than most areas of the U.S. economy. At private institutions, tuition rates have risen beyond the means of the average student, and even public institutions have been forced to increase fees by more than many potential and enrolled students can afford. Although state and national programs are still important sources of economic assistance for students, these resources have not kept pace with increased college costs. General apathy by state and national governments toward higher education's predicament means that the situation probably will not improve.

A significant number of colleges and universities are concerned about how to maintain the stability and prominence they have enjoyed without effort until recently. Invariably, administrators focus on student recruitment and retention, placing articulation in the forefront of institutional interest. Administrators have exhorted articulation specialists to recruit a required number of bodies with the result that articulation programs in such instances resemble consumer marketing and advertising. The main goal is to sell the product, and all else is secondary. A considerable segment of higher education has succumbed to such a business mentality. New York University has placed its "admissions marketing" in the hands of an advertising agency, which developed a campaign to "sell New York" across the country as well as to New Yorkers. Literature for prospective students was filled with alluring, exciting photographs of New York, conveying the message that NYU students become an integral part of the city's sights and activities. Admissions marketing has developed the "bonus plan," whereby every enrolled person who recruits a new student receives a one-hundred dollar reduction in tuition.

Such approaches, relying on hard-sell business tactics, cannot be dismissed as unethical or even as undignified for higher education. They enroll qualified students and serve institutional interest. But when enrollment goals become the only consideration for school and college relations, the procedures threaten articulation by subordinating professional principles to numerical strength. Such pragmatism can be self-defeating for colleges that survive present pressures.

Colleges have a public obligation to serve the national, state, or local interest. Instead of shoving the maximum number of bodies into available space, balanced programs should consider present demand, future needs, and long-term institutional stability. A college can build and maintain integrity and an identifiable character by pursuing mixes of students that reflect institutional priorities and goals, yet—regardless of professional or ethical considerations—many institutions hastily hire anyone glib enough to entice any student onto campus with any form of sales pitch. Such a situation threatens all school and college relations practice.

New techniques developed to counteract the effects of less money and growth offer the field an unparalleled opportunity to expand and achieve greater influence and acceptance within the academic community. The higher councils of colleges and universities are aware as never before of the impact of articulation practice on enrollment, the retention of students, and the public image of the institution. These decision makers are now seeking the advice of and often deferring to the judgment of career articulation specialists. Now is the time for the specialists to point out new directions to resolve the current crisis with persuasive, well-reasoned articulation plans. Good programs have the best chance of recent years to attract the institutional support needed to make them work.

It is most important that developing programs be based on proved principles of articulation that have survived the debate at their inception. Among these practices are: preadmission counseling to improve student self-selection of the best higher education experience; conscious efforts to sensitize parents and faculty to the transitional needs and problems of new students; continuous, frank communication among individuals at all educational levels; and the provision of honest, adequate informational resources to prospective students. At the policy level, changes in admission requirements should reflect academic and societal goals rather than the dictates of yearly financial quotas. Overriding all concerns is the need to adhere to the educational and articulation principle of facilitating the most beneficial transition of students from one educational level to another.

Index

139–42; informal methods of, 167–73; junior–senior college conferences on, 145–48; junior–senior college, mathematics, 147–48; need for, 11
Curriculum guides. *See* Parallel programs

D grade transfer policy, 11, 50, 74–75, 125, 165
Darnes, G. R., 146–47
Disadvantaged students. *See* Minority groups

Eight Year Study, 16–18, 70
Empire State College, 110, 114
Engineering Council for Professional Development, 19

Faculty exchange, 131–32
Federal educational programs, 35
Financial aid: discriminates against transfers, 71; for poor minority students, 92
Florida articulation program, 161–64
Fulbright International Exchange Program, 35

G.I. Bill, 19, 103. *See also* Veterans
Gardner, John, 145
General education concept in transfer process, 81–83
Gleazer, Edmund J., Jr., 60–61
Gould, Samuel B., 111
Guide to the Evaluation of Educational Experiences in the Armed Services, 106

Harvard University Special Committee on College Admission Policy, 47
High school–college transition case study, 27–32
High school consultant on colleges, 126–29
High school counselors, 91–93
High school grading practice, 48–50
High school subject requirements for college admission, 45–47
Higher education scope and variety, 33–37

Idaho statewide college guidance manual, 191–92
Illinois articulation program, 207–8
Illinois Association of College Admission Counselors, 180–81
Indiana State University feedback report, 184–85
Industrial education, 35

Jennings, Frank G., 22
Joliet Junior College, 22
Junior colleges: articulation practice criticized, 61; associate degree, 59, 82–83; curricular integration in, 74–83; general education requirements of, 81–82; guidelines for, 72–74, 77, 80; transfer credit from, 74–83; transition case study involving, 62–69. *See also* Community colleges

Kansas articulation program, 208–9
Keenan, Boyd R., 116
Kendrick, S. A., and Thomas, C. L., 97
Kintzer, Frederick C., 2, 22, 60, 83, 164
Knoell, Dorothy M., and Medsker, Leland L., 70, 75
Kraushaar, Otto F., 50

Medsker, Leland L., 1, 60, 70, 75
Mexican-American college enrollment, 88–89
Miami-Dade Community College, 93–94, 182–83
Michigan State University program for superior students, 101–2
Minority groups: admission criteria for, 97–98; college enrollment of, 88–89; college guidance for, 98; college students as role models for, 91, 93–94; community participation in recruitment of, 92; and financial aid, 92; recruitment conferences for, 93
Missouri articulation program, 217–18
More Education More Opportunity (MEMO), 104
Morse, Wayne, 24
Mundelein College program for mature adults, 109